In the Crossfire of History

War Culture

Edited by Daniel Leonard Bernardi

Books in this series address the myriad ways in which warfare informs diverse cultural practices, as well as the way cultural practices—from cinema to social media—inform the practice of warfare. They illuminate the insights and limitations of critical theories that describe, explain, and politicize the phenomena of war culture. Traversing both national and intellectual borders, authors from a wide range of fields and disciplines collectively examine the articulation of war, its everyday practices, and its impact on individuals and societies throughout modern history.

For a list of all the titles in the series, please see the last page of the book.

In the Crossfire of History

Women's War Resistance Discourse in
the Global South

EDITED BY LAVA ASAAD AND FAYEZA HASANAT

R
Rutgers University Press
New Brunswick, Camden, and Newark, New Jersey, and London

Library of Congress Cataloging-in-Publication Data

Names: Asaad, Lava, editor. | Hasanat, Fayeza S., editor.
Title: In the crossfire of history : women's war resistance discourse in the global South /
edited by Lava Asaad and Fayeza Hasanat.
Description: 1 Edition. | New Brunswick, NJ : Rutgers University Press, [2022] |
Series: War culture | Includes bibliographical references and index.
Identifiers: LCCN 2021056999 | ISBN 9781978830219 (paperback) |
ISBN 9781978830226 (hardback) | ISBN 9781978830233 (epub) | ISBN 9781978830240 (pdf)
Subjects: LCSH: Women and war—Developing countries. | Women—Developing
countries—Social conditions. | Women and war in literature. | Women in art. |
Women—Political activity—Developing countries. | BISAC: POLITICAL SCIENCE /
Peace | SOCIAL SCIENCE / Violence in Society
Classification: LCC HQ1236 .I486 2022 | DDC 305.42—dc23/eng/20220127
LC record available at https://lccn.loc.gov/2021056999

A British Cataloging-in-Publication record for this book is available from the British Library.

To all the women of the Global South

Contents

In the Crossfire of History

Introduction

• •

Portraits of Resistance

LAVA ASAAD

"Paint my portrait so I can be free," says Shaheeka, the ghost of a Yazidi woman visiting the narrator of *Sabāyā Sinjār* (The captives of Sinjar), a magical realist novel written by the Syrian novelist Salim Barakat in 2016.[1] Shaheeka demands an artistic expression of herself that does not necessarily replicate her as a fugitive escaping her captivity from ISIS, only to die during the arduous journey to free herself from her rapists. Shaheeka's spirit seeks to have agency over how the media and artists represent other Yazidi women who have died like her, who are being displaced, and who continue to bring their persecutors to justice. Barakat's novel is just one example of many literary works that express writers' admiration of and sympathies for the myriad struggles of women in the Global South. What Shaheeka represents is the resilience to preserve her own image even after her death, and her spirit continues to find ways to denounce her captors' violation of her rights as a Yazidi woman and primarily as a human being. In an attempt to continue to honor women like Shaheeka and to ensure that their stories remain loud among the cacophony of discourses around women, each chapter in this volume paints a portrait of certain women fighting their own battles in different geographical regions. This edited volume is a step toward saving these dissenting counterdiscourses from being virtually inaudible or clumped within other overarching narratives of resistance.

Recently, one of the most extraordinary examples from the Global South of women surviving and continuing to condemn their perpetrators is Nadia Murad, an Iraqi Yazidi who was held in captivity by ISIS for three months and then managed to escape to Germany as a refugee. The international community, stunned by her valor and humbled by her testimonies, decided to award her the Nobel Peace Prize in 2018. Murad is now a beacon of hope for other women in similar situations, and she has become, unequivocally, one of the most outspoken human rights activists to decry multifarious forms of abuse and human trafficking. In her Nobel Prize speech, Murad emphasized that she "do[es] not seek more sympathy"; instead, she "want[s] to translate those feelings into actions on the ground."[2] The limits of sympathy have long been stretched and deemed insufficient in the face of atrocities committed against women in the name of religion, nation-states, ethnic cleansing, and economic and gender disparity.

To save this volume from slipping into the trope of eliciting sympathy for the various representations of resistance, we are indebted to Lila Abu-Lughod's seminal article "The Romance of Resistance: Tracing Transformations of Power through Bedouin Women," where she poignantly argues and reminds her readers that "there is perhaps a tendency to romanticize resistance, to read all forms of resistance as signs of the ineffectiveness of systems of power and of the resilience and creativity of the human spirit in its refusal to be dominated."[3] Accordingly, this volume should not just comfort our consciousness that these women, in a sentimentalized image, are continuing the fight against multiple umbrellas of power. However, as Abu-Lughod points out, the stories of their resistance can "teach us about the complex interworkings of historically changing structures of power."[4] Our theoretical framework also benefits from *Vulnerability in Resistance*, in which the editors Judith Butler, Zeynep Gambetti, and Leticia Sabsay redefine resistance, taking into account other modes of vulnerability that are not specifically linked to "accelerated precarity, statelessness, and occupation." Instead, they focus on patterns of resilience that "resist the neutralization of practices of social transformation that follows when the discourse of protection becomes hegemonic, undermining and effacing varied forms of popular resistance or political agency."[5] To unsettle the discourse of protecting women, taking them out of darkness or "giving" them agency requires questioning axes of power that these women find themselves oscillating between. Abu-Lughod writes in her "Do Muslim Women Really Need Saving?" that "when you save someone, you imply that you are saving her from something, you are also saving her *to* something."[6] This presumption that there are ready-made and packaged patterns of solutions offered to women resisting structures of power further replicates the colonial binary discourse of "us versus them," where the former has the answers for the problems of the latter. In *Decolonizing Universalism*, Serene Khader echoes this presumption and refers to it as "missionary feminism" and "enlightened liberalism," both of which define resistance as forsaking cultural and traditional values in favor of a conceptual and economic understanding of independence.[7] Khader also deviates from overcelebrating "agency," as it is "an insufficient feminist normative commitment" that devalues women's relationships with and dependence on others as a hindrance to self-emancipation.[8]

Our conceptualization of resistance also stems from the oeuvre of Barbara Harlow's seminal contribution to the field of literature of resistance and women in the Global South. Harlow's major concern is unraveling different types of resistance without othering these forms of defiance; her line of thinking continues to be different from a Western conception that seeks to whet its appetite with the inclusion of some non-Western means of struggle. For Harlow, the Palestinian writer and activist Ghassan Kanafani coined the term *resistance literature* in 1966 that inspired writers to be politically involved in and through their writings.[9] Kanafani, Harlow asserts, sees no duality between activism in the street and activism on paper. To that end, we approach resistance with an equally broad stroke, equivalently validating violent and nonviolent struggle as important trajectories of resistance. This volume thus collapses the high-low dichotomy by exploring the multifarious forms of resistance in literature, film, art, and more.

Fittingly, each chapter introduces an alternative and creative practice of resistance to structural forms of power without creating a romanticized notion of resistance or considering the lack of agency a source of victimization. In this respect, we contextualize this volume within multiple vital publications on transnational feminism, globalization, coloniality, and decoloniality of gender and race. The choice to use the term *women of the Global South* rather than *Third World women* or *"other" women* (see Uma Narayan) stems from this volume's emphasis on local productions of resistance. By grouping these forms of resistance(s) in one volume, by no means do we attempt to homogenize the ways in which women of the Global South choose to defy injustices and survive. Moreover, the selection of multiple scripts of resistance presented in this volume is in no way projected as exhaustive and thorough. Other women-led resistance movements demand further in-depth exploration. Digressing from the discourse of protecting non-Western women does not negate finding ways to relate to Western feminism. If there are common patterns between forms of struggle, it is because, as Uma Narayan points out, "women's inequality and mistreatment are, unfortunately, ubiquitous features of many 'Western' and 'non-Western' cultural contexts."[10]

Another main point of this project lies in emphasizing the myriad ways of preserving human dignity and rights that do not necessarily conform to certain global paradigms of prosperity and individual autonomy. In the same vein, our overarching definition of resistance nods to Saba Mahmood's seminal book *Politics of Piety*, an ethnographic examination of the women's mosque movement in Cairo, where women from different socioeconomic backgrounds conducted religious lessons and taught one another inside mosques. Mahmood is cognizant that this might appear to many feminists as perpetuating male hegemony. However, Mahmood's argument dismantles the assumption that "all human beings have an innate desire for freedom, that we all somehow seek to assert our autonomy when allowed to do so, that human agency primarily consists of acts that challenge social norms and not those that uphold them."[11] These social norms are tied to particular cultural and historical moments. Rooting for economic independence, for instance, is not the goal of many women's movements across the globe. Allison Weir notes that in challenging forms of oppression, one must redefine freedom to encompass forms of resistance that work on "renegotiating connections" and aspire to change the equilibrium of power.[12] As a result, this volume does not prioritize a one-dimensional definition of resistance, freedom, agency, or self-sufficiency; each example is born out of a specific necessity to speak or act against a hegemonic and dogmatic practice without universalizing the said experience.

Redefining resistance in this volume espouses an approach similar to that taken by Jennifer Rycenga and Marguerite R. Waller in their introduction to *Frontline Feminisms: Women, War, and Resistance* (2000), in which they address the gaps in U.S. feminism and reconceptualize women's daily battles on the front line, which can be best defined as "standing in a welfare line or a police line-up, stitching a hemline, or writing a byline. The frontline becomes wherever women know that their lives . . . [are] at risk."[13] Compiling this volume in 2020—twenty years after the publication of *Frontline Feminisms*—the project has become a necessity to document the struggles (old and new) and the journeys of defiance that women of the Global South renegotiate and abolish as they continue to create more just alternatives to the existing imbalance of power. Furthermore, this volume partakes in what Margaret A. McLaren points out in her introduction to *Decolonizing Feminism: Transnational Feminism and Globalization*, where she explains the necessity to reevaluate the woman question during the twenty-first century, when we should be directing our attention to "both micro- and macro-political structures; a sense of historical consciousness and specificity."[14] In reapproaching resistance, the chapters in this volume take into account the continuation and emergence of new challenges—global capitalism, migration, environmental degradation, xenophobia, civil wars, repressive nation-states—that women of the Global South fight against. To broadly illustrate our scope in this volume, our contributors aim to explore the reconceptualization of gender relations in connection to the overarching hegemonic and monolithic narrative of resistance. Women in the Global South do not adhere to accorded gender assignations; instead, they continue to reshape and reclaim their space in the history of struggle, simultaneously scrutinizing and unsettling gendered ideologies deeply ingrained in their nations' resistance movements. The volume adopts and celebrates both violent and nonviolent modes of resistance, avoiding the pitfall of condemning the former by labeling it "aggressive" and classifying the latter as "passive." Thus, by steering away from a Eurocentric and individualistically driven idea of female freedom, the contributors elaborate on why each experience of struggle warrants a different type of resistance that is in accordance with certain circumstances that propel women to rebel.

Overview of the Book

The present volume includes authors who have paid careful attention to how women in the Global South have taken action against glaring inequalities in all sectors. Each chapter takes a closer look at how women in a certain geographical area and time period respond to injustices in a unique way. Since the concept of the Global South does not follow any established border or timeline, the chapters in this volume can easily justify their relevance to any and all the countries of the Global South that we were unable to include in this collection. We justified such relevance by thematically arranging the chapters in three parts. The focus of part 1 is the representation of resistance in art and media. Stefanie Sevcik reads the rippling effect of the Arab Spring in Syria and the role of women in accentuating the struggle against authoritative regimes. Sevcik examines how the Syrian women prisoners used their bodies as canvases and created a poetics of incarceration to generate a public conversation on women's prison experiences in the context of justice, state institutions, and creative resistance across the Global South. She draws attention to the female prisoner's use of their body as a site of creative insurgence and analyzes how the body as a written text challenges the oppressive system and plays a dominant role in the Syrian women prisoners' pursuit of justice. Sevcik situates her argument within Doran Larson's essay "Toward a Prison Poetics" (2011), in which Larson describes the importance of narratives written by inmates in calling attention to particular forms of capital punishment as well as constructing a global discourse on the prison experience. Sevcik's chapter expands this framework to more explicitly account for the incarcerated female body. She considers Marwan M. Kraidy's framework for "creative insurgency," in which Kraidy links the body to the art and activism of the Arab Spring uprisings. By engaging these concepts through the work of Syrian women, Sevcik seeks to connect their experiences with larger conversations on justice, capital punishment, and creative resistance across the Global South. Sevcik explores how the body itself can become an art in resistance, not as a metaphor, but as a living portrait of women's strength.

Farzana Akhter examines the issue of violence and resistance as represented in the war movies of Bangladesh. She argues how war movies generally conserve gender stereotypes and popularize the image of the female body as a victim in a war. Akhter explains how women's agency and active participation in war narratives of Bangladesh have been intentionally kept invisible to uphold a conventional, patriarchal ideology. She continues by arguing that even though a good number of movies are being made on the varied themes of nation building or the violence and trauma of war, the role of women is hardly seen from the perspective of agency and active involvement. She examines the contemporary Bangladeshi movies on the war of 1971 and shows how the recent shift of focus from the traditional representation of the victimized female body to its active participation in war has initiated a discourse on women's agency. Using

Nasiruddin Yousuff's award-winning movie *Guerrilla* as her text, Akhter shows how Yousuff deviates from the typical war narratives as he subverts the general perception of women's role in the Liberation War of Bangladesh as mere objects or as vulnerable subjects and highlights their role as freedom fighters.

Lava Asaad focuses on the long-established Kurdish movement the Partiya Karkerên Kurdistanê (PKK; Kurdistan Workers' Party) and its nascent, all-women militia group in northern Syria as they battle against ISIS. Asaad's chapter on the Kurdish women fighters and their political struggle for an autonomous establishment introduces the discourse of resistance from a totally different dimension by bringing in the women of Jinwar, an independent commune in northeast Syria, which was established by women and for women. With its uniquely feminist and ecological agenda, Jinwar becomes a woman's land, a safe haven for women who survived the violence of the Syrian civil war and ISIS. Asaad demystifies Western media's fascination with Kurdish female militia fighters by examining their personal struggles and political defiance within the context of the ideological and intellectual premise of Jineology. Providing a holistic understating of the "Kurdish question," Asaad examines how these Kurdish women fighters problematize the combat narrative, challenge the gendered discourse of political struggle, and in the process, reshape war theories and global feminism. The West's fascination with these women emanates from the degree to which these women redefine feminism, heroism, and social responsibilities.

The chapters in part 2 catalog representations of resistance in literary texts from the Global South. Lucía García-Santana brings back the topic of women prisoners, focusing on their representation in Argentinian literature. García-Santana writes about the Argentinean regime Proceso de Reorganización National (National Reorganization Process), which overthrew Isabel Martínez de Perón's democratic government in March 1976. This regime built a rhetoric of war to justify the suffocation of the young Peronist militants' opposing voices, who were, they argued, creating chaos in the nation, and a narrative of due order grounded on Catholic reactionary morals that affected all society configurations, from political ideology to gender distribution. Citizens were tortured and murdered, and their bodies were hidden, thus marking "the disappeared" as a new political category. The abuses of the female prisoners' bodies were particularly gruesome—a gender violence standing on the need to control the subversives in their unstoppable reproduction and the unacceptable leftist political positioning that questioned gender roles, among other power mechanisms. García-Santana explores the strategies of resistance of the female body as narrated in the testimonial novels by Alicia Partnoy, *The Little School* (1986), and Alicia Kozameh, *Steps under Water* (1996). Drawing on Silvia Federici's explanation of the systemic control of the female body as a capitalist maneuver, García-Santana examines the dictatorial government of Argentina's anxiety regarding female militants and the interpreted women's fight for emancipation as a contesting force that threatened to destabilize their political system.

Her analysis of Partnoy's and Kozameh's novels represents the female body as a repository for a new reading of Argentina's history.

Doaa Omran's chapter shifts attention to Palestinian women writers and how they document political and historical events in the form of fictive autobiography. Using Radwa Ashour's *The Woman from Tantoura* (2014) as her primary text, Omran examines the issues of diaspora, war, and identity politics and shows how Ashour's novel uses autotheoretical (relying on the theoretical application of works by Stacey Young and Lauren Fournier) elements in order to present itself as a work of resistance. Weaving personal narrative with fictional elements, Omran argues, becomes a necessary strategy for survival for Palestinian women writers who aim to preserve major historical events that are obliterated by the dominant and more hegemonic discourse of the Israeli occupation.

Carolyn Ownbey and Margaret Hageman concentrate on the Partition of India in 1947 and trace ways in which South Asian writers have subtly illumed how the Partition gravely traumatized and silenced women on both sides of the newly drawn border. Ownbey examines the trope of gendered violence in Partition novels. She uses Bapsi Sidhwa's iconic novel *Cracking India* as her primary text to elaborate on the affordances and the limits of gender alliances in the moment of dismantling and re-creating national borders. Hageman furthers the discussion by examining gendered portrayals of abduction, displacement, and violence against women in other Partition novels, such as Amrita Pritam's novella *Pinjar* (1950) and Shobha Rao's short story collection, *An Unrestored Woman* (2016).

Moumin Quazi sheds new light on the discussion of South Asian women's participation in political movements and examines how contemporary Sri Lankan women writers reframe the absurdity of wartime violence and its aftermath. Quazi discusses Nayomi Munaweera's debut novel, *Island of a Thousand Mirrors* (2012), as a diasporic tale of resistance to the war violence that plagued Sri Lanka for decades. Quazi shows how Munaweera uses the trope of inversion along with mirroring, mimicry, and postcolonial hybridity in her portrayal of women both as victims and as perpetrators of horrific war violence.

While part 2 focuses on the representation of violence and resistance in the literature of the Global South, part 3 evaluates women's resistance discourse in relation to activism and advocacy. Nyla Khan returns to the topic of the Partition of India but reexamines it from the perspective of activism and personal memories in the context of Kashmiri women activists in the aftermath of the Partition. Khan redirects our attention to the ongoing yet often overlooked conflict in Kashmir by centralizing the role of the Women's Self-Defense Corps (WSDC), which supported and participated in the armed insurgencies against attacks on Kashmir. Khan provides a historical contextualization of the grassroots insurgencies of Kashmiri women against religious, economic, and political divides. In her interactions with some of the surviving members of the WSDC who set the scene for rebuilding their war-torn communities, Khan epitomizes the role of women like Akbar Jehan, who had an influential role in this organization.

Shafinur Nahar takes up the issue of teaching the literature of war and places texts on sexually violated women of war in a university classroom to observe the reaction of her students. Based on her survey of more than a thousand students in various colleges and universities of Bangladesh, she concurs in her report that students either feel traumatized or are still hesitant to face the horrific aftermath of the Liberation War of 1971. Nahar's survey sheds light on the importance of teaching traumatic autobiographical accounts written by Bengali women who were tortured and raped during the 1971 war despite the general societal inclination toward wiping away these memories.

Matthew Spencer reads women's resistance movements against deforestation in Central America as rebelling against national and international axes of neo-colonial capitalism. Keeping the threat of global climate change at the center of his discussion, Spencer combines literary texts with the ecofeminist movement and examines women's involvement in the new Anthropocene epoch. Spencer's chapter pays attention to the Honduran environmentalist, indigenous rights activist, and Goldman Environmental Prize winner Berta Cáceres, who was murdered in her home by unidentified intruders. He examines how the intertwining of extractive capitalism with oppressive governmental regimes has created a global apparatus that views any form of direct environmental activism and protection as a threat to the bottom line. This phenomenon ranges from direct actions and tree sit-ins in the United States to "martyr squads" opposing dam construction in India to Greta Thunberg and the youth climate strike movement to the work of indigenous groups in the Americas and beyond. In each of these struggles, women take an active or leading role and are, therefore, often those most directly targeted by violence.

Our selection of chapters redirects attention to the micropolitical construction of resistance that sends a transnationally reverberating message of women rising in various areas. Cynthia Enloe espouses a similar theoretical approach in championing all forms of resistance, where

> women's collective resistance to any one of these feminized expectations can realign both local and international systems of power. . . . Even stymied or only partially successful resistance by women can expose both who wields power to sustain the gendered status quo and what those power-wielders fear they will lose if women's resistance succeeds. This is why every suffrage movement in every country—the United States, Britain, Brazil, Mexico, China, Egypt, Kuwait—has raised such intense political alarm. . . . Thus, if one is interested in gaining a reliable sense of national and international politics, one should be curious about all sorts of women's resistance, whether or not that resistance succeeds.[15]

Our contributors reconfigure ways in which they introduce micropolitical insurgencies in different geographical representations of the Global South, highlighting how these microresistances are detrimental to hegemonic frameworks that indubitably oppress women. The contributors herein move beyond the point of curiosity to emphatically implement and reshape the discourse of feminist resistance.

Chandra Talpade Mohanty envisioned and proposed in 2002 an inclusive feminist discourse that decolonizes and allows for "feminist solidarity across borders" that is not built on generalizing women's experiences.[16] This volume aspires to annunciate ways to foreground women in the Global South—despite different geopolitical and cultural backgrounds—and to raise an epistemological awareness within current discourse on resistance, female agency, and women's role in reshaping the status quo across nation-states that continue to fantasize about female subordination and silence. The broad contours behind the selection of chapters undermine the strictly defined image of women resilience that is, by and large, predicated on duplicating a Western idea of women's utopia. Thus, the portraits of resistance in this volume are not intended to bring these women-led resistance movements toward "the center"—always and forever presumed to be in the West. Instead, we aim to pluralize and proliferate local experiences without creating a prototype of women's agency that can be translatable into all and every corner of the globe. Each hierarchy warrants a certain mode of resistance without echoing the prevalent academic discourse that generalizes the idea of resistance. The concluding chapter therefore restates the global rise of women against systematic injustices and the embodied resistance of women. We denounce the romanticization of resistance in art, media, and literature, arguing instead that aesthetic poetics must work alongside, acknowledge, and endorse the painful realities lived by women in the Global South.

Notes

1 Salim Barakat, *Sabāyā Sinjār* [The captives of Sinjar] (Beirut: al-Muassassah al-ʿArabiyyah lil-Dirāsat wa al-Nashr, 2016), 43. All quotes from this text are the author's translation.

2 Nadia Murad, "Nobel Lecture," Nobel Prize, December 10, 2018, https://www.nobelprize.org/prizes/peace/2018/murad/lecture/.

3 Lila Abu-Lughod, "The Romance of Resistance: Tracing Transformations of Power through Bedouin Women," *American Ethnologist* 17, no. 1 (1990): 42, http://www.jstor.org/stable/645251.

4 Abu-Lughod, 53.

5 Judith Butler, Zeynep Gambetti, and Leticia Sabsay, introduction to *Vulnerability in Resistance* (Durham, N.C.: Duke University Press, 2016), 6.

6 Lila Abu-Lughod, "Do Muslim Women Really Need Saving? Anthropological Reflections on Cultural Relativism and Its Others," *American Anthropologist* 104, no. 3 (September 2002): 789, https://anthrosource.onlinelibrary.wiley.com/doi/abs/10.1525/aa.2002.104.3.783.

7 Serene J. Khader, *Decolonizing Universalism: A Transnational Feminist Ethic* (Oxford: Oxford University Press, 2019), 3–4.

8 Khader, 18.

9 Barbara Harlow, *Resistance Literature* (New York: Methuen, 1987), 28.

10 Uma Narayan, *Dislocating Cultures: Identities, Traditions, and Third World Feminism* (New York: Routledge, 1997), 13.
11 Saba Mahmood, *Politics of Piety: The Islamic Revival and the Feminist Subject* (Princeton, N.J.: Princeton University Press, 2011), 5.
12 Allison Weir, "Feminism and the Islamic Revival: Freedom as a Practice of Belonging," *Hypatia* 28, no. 2 (Spring 2013): 336, https://www.jstor.org/stable/24542124.
13 Jennifer Rycenga and Marguerite R. Waller, introduction to *Frontline Feminisms: Women, War, and Resistance* (New York: Routledge, 2000), xix.
14 Margaret A. McLaren, *Decolonizing Feminism: Transnational Feminism and Globalization* (Rowman & Littlefield, 2017), 4.
15 Cynthia Enloe, *Bananas, Beaches and Bases: Making Feminist Sense of International Politics* (Berkeley: University of California Press, 2014), 11–12.
16 Chandra Talpade Mohanty, "'Under Western Eyes' Revisited: Feminist Solidarity through Anticapitalist Struggles," *Signs* 28, no. 2 (2003): 503, https://doi.org/10.1086/342914.

Bibliography

Abu-Lughod, Lila. "Do Muslim Women Really Need Saving? Anthropological Reflections on Cultural Relativism and Its Others." *American Anthropologist* 104, no. 3 (September 2002): 783–790. https://anthrosource.onlinelibrary.wiley.com/doi/abs/10.1525/aa.2002.104.3.783.

———. "The Romance of Resistance: Tracing Transformations of Power through Bedouin Women." *American Ethnologist* 17, no. 1 (1990): 41–55. http://www.jstor.org/stable/645251.

Barakat, Salim. *Sabāyā Sinjār* [The captives of Sinjar]. Beirut: al-Muassassah al-ʿArabiyyah lil-Dirāsat wa al-Nashr, 2016.

Butler, Judith, Zeynep Gambetti, and Leticia Sabsay. Introduction to *Vulnerability in Resistance*, edited by Judith Butler, Zeynep Gambetti, and Leticia Sabsay, 1–11. Durham, N.C.: Duke University Press, 2016.

Enloe, Cynthia. *Bananas, Beaches and Bases: Making Feminist Sense of International Politics.* Berkeley: University of California Press, 2014.

Harlow, Barbara. *Resistance Literature.* New York: Methuen, 1987.

Khader, Serene J. *Decolonizing Universalism: A Transnational Feminist Ethic.* Oxford: Oxford University Press, 2019.

Mahmood, Saba. *Politics of Piety: The Islamic Revival and the Feminist Subject.* Princeton, N.J.: Princeton University Press, 2011.

McLaren, Margaret A. *Decolonizing Feminism: Transnational Feminism and Globalization.* London: Rowman & Littlefield, 2017.

Mohanty, Chandra Talpade. "'Under Western Eyes' Revisited: Feminist Solidarity through Anticapitalist Struggles." *Signs* 28, no. 2 (2003): 499–535. https://doi.org/10.1086/342914.

Murad, Nadia. "Nobel Lecture." Nobel Prize, December 10, 2018. https://www.nobelprize.org/prizes/peace/2018/murad/lecture/.

Narayan, Uma. *Dislocating Cultures: Identities, Traditions, and Third World Feminism.* New York: Routledge, 1997.

Rycenga, Jennifer, and Marguerite R. Waller. Introduction to *Frontline Feminisms: Women, War, and Resistance*, edited by Jennifer Rycenga and Marguerite R. Waller, xiv–xxix. New York: Routledge, 2000.

Weir, Allison. "Feminism and the Islamic Revival: Freedom as a Practice of Belonging." *Hypatia* 28, no. 2 (Spring 2013): 323–340. https://www.jstor.org/stable/24542124.

I

Representations of Resistance in Art and Media

• •

1

Syrian Women's Prison Art

• •

Toward a Poetics of Creative
Insurgency

STEFANIE SEVCIK

Women in Syria are struggling against oblivion, as the journalist Yara Badr notes in a 2014 essay titled "Lifetimes Stolen." Badr describes the persistent fear of incarceration that haunts her life and generations of her people. In 1986, her father was abruptly imprisoned for twelve years by the Hafez al-Assad regime. Over twenty years later, the undercover officers of the Bashar al-Assad regime imprisoned her; her husband, Mazen Darwish; and several of their colleagues at the headquarters of the Syrian Center for Media and Freedom of Expression (SCM)[1] in February 2012 for "obtaining banned documents and publishing them to overthrow the political, social and economic system."[2] Although she was released three months later, her husband remained in prison until 2015—a year after the publication of her essay. In "Lifetimes Stolen," Badr recounts her experiences in prison, calls attention to the legacy of arbitrary imprisonment under which Syrians have lived for over fifty years, and raises awareness of her husband's case. One purpose of both her essays and her work as a journalist is to prevent her memories and the people around her from disappearing: "Although I survived the experience of imprisonment as a daughter, wife, and political prisoner myself, it remains my biggest fear. It represents the ultimate *oblivion*. A human being is taken to an undisclosed place where the world will forget him or her, and it reduces people to mere names without identities."[3]

This fear of "oblivion" refers to the forcible erasure of human lives and their political commitments. In many ways, Badr's personal project mirrors the project of the SCM—to protect the freedom of expression of Syrians and to project these voices for others to hear. Badr and her husband, Mazen Darwish, have received multiple awards for their brave actions as journalists and advocates for their people.[4] Here, she calls attention to the fact that many who disagree with the regime are arrested, and many disappear in the night with no word of their fate.[5] Being arrested by the regime means facing the real danger that a person, a story, or a project will be willfully forgotten. This kind of forced, investigative transparency is crucial to human rights journalism. However, Badr's own essay illustrates the value of a more personal, creative kind of intervention. She describes herself in gendered terms as "a daughter, wife, and political prisoner myself," highlighting the fraught, intersecting identities that many Syrian women inhabit. Her essay gives a personal, reflective account that complements her journalistic work.

In this chapter, I will begin to develop a poetics—beyond journalism—that attends to writing and art that advocates for prisoners. This framework must account for the insurgent female body marked by the prison apparatus as the site and organ of creative production beyond the traditional, phallogocentric written text. Underlying this project is an urgency that stems from the thousands of lives that are at stake in this pursuit. For artists, activists, and critics, calling attention to the hidden elements of the justice system and its marginalized voices helps counteract the forcible erasure of incarceration that Badr fears and experienced firsthand. This inclusive poetics can also provide a useful lens in cases beyond Syria as a foundation for comparative work where artists and critics play powerful complementary roles in the pursuit of justice—joining the voices of Syrian women prisoners with other marginalized perspectives across the globe.

Introduction: Why "Poetics"?

In much of the research on prison art, there is a notable lack of representation when it comes to the experiences of incarcerated women.[6] Likewise, there is a significant body of research on "prison writing" by noteworthy men who were political prisoners including Antonio Gramsci, Nelson Mandela, and Martin Luther King Jr. There are also a number of published studies on the role of art and writing as therapeutic in particular incarcerated populations.[7] Constructing a more inclusive poetics of incarceration can help connect the work and experiences of women with larger conversations on justice, state institutions, and creative resistance across the Global South. My work begins where these bodies of research intersect—analyzing both the *collective, political project* of artists calling attention to injustice in the carceral system and the *individual, subjective effects* of creating art while incarcerated.

Approaching this project through the framework of a poetics provides a rigorous basis for comparative work across diverse contexts. It can also provide a point of entry for disrupting power structures such as the carceral state. Dale Tracy lays out a concise formulation of the disruptive nature of approaching a text through a poetics in "Metonymy, Poetics, Performance: World-Making and the Real" (2018): "Poetics is the study of conventional structures and the specific practices by which individuals or texts might disrupt those structures. Within such structures occurs the performance of everyday life."[8] Articulating these "conventional structures" makes visible a point of comparison where scholars and artists can join together and contribute to a global network working toward justice for marginalized communities. Furthermore, conceptualizing a poetics as fundamentally disruptive makes a space for urgent, socially engaged artistic and scholarly work. Artists use their work to "disrupt those structures," and it is partly the work of scholars to articulate these disruptions, to take note of "the performance of everyday life" affecting these structures, and to connect them to wider networks of scholarship and artist activism.

Some work developing this kind of poetics has been done by Doran Larson. He describes a "prison poetics" to identify injustice underlying the experience of incarceration—in particular, "by turning the tools of literary analysis to a comparative assessment of conditions of injustice, we begin to uncloak the prison, and begin to shed light on the punishment regimes that we hold up as systems of justice."[9] Larson's account attends to political, aesthetic, and subjective aspects of prison writing to lay out a framework to connect diverse communities in the project of disrupting systemic violence and oppression. However, Larson focuses almost exclusively on men and their written accounts of the prison experience. In order to achieve a more inclusive prison poetics, I turn to the experiences of women. My project expands the study of prison writing to include marginalized voices—in this case, Syrian women under the Bashar al-Assad regime. In order to adequately tackle the contextual specificity of this project, it is useful to view Syria in terms of its role in the Arab Spring uprisings. This kind of approach pushes the framework of a poetics beyond written texts to include creative expressions of the body. In particular, I incorporate aspects of Marwan M. Kraidy's concept of creative insurgency to link the body to the art and activism of the Arab Spring uprisings. My project also includes visual arts and crafts that can be done in cases where pen and paper are not available or where the written word or body cannot suffice. I also expand the space of the prison to include prison states like Syria, where many citizens experience daily life as a form of incarceration.

Conceptualizing this work as a kind of "prison poetics" brings out the possibility for drawing rich comparisons across global contexts and endows the project of the critic with urgency and weight. As Larson notes at the end of his essay, voices of the incarcerated "offer up a chorus that we would be wise to heed" as readers, viewers, and witnesses. One of the most urgent stakes of attending to prison art is the underlying imperative to disrupt the injustices committed by the carceral state. The role of the reader of prison literature should not *end* with a passive consumption of the text. This is where the work of the literary scholar can *begin*. A poetics-based approach to making connections across artistic accounts of prison experience is a form of work uniquely suitable for scholars and their audiences.

Syrian Prisoners

In order to sketch out the contours of this prison poetics, it is necessary to identify the space in which the "performance of everyday life" takes place in the context of Syria. As Badr identifies in "Lifetimes Stolen," there is a legacy of imprisoning critics of the regime that extends back to the 1963 State of Emergency Law, which suspended the constitutional rights of citizens to allow for the free detention of terrorist suspects for an unlimited period of time without a trial. Generations of Syrians have lived under this protracted "state of emergency" that enabled, first, the Hafez al-Assad regime (1971–2000) and then the Bashar al-Assad regime (2000–present) to suppress all forms of dissent. It is in this context that the first demonstrations in Syria associated with the Arab Spring uprisings occurred in response to the brutal conditions of imprisonment for young critics of the regime. On March 6, 2011, fifteen young boys (ages ten to fifteen) from prominent families in Dara'a were arrested for allegedly writing graffiti on a school with the slogan "The people want the fall of the regime." When residents learned that the boys were being tortured by government security forces, citizens in the community reached a tipping point and began protesting their incarceration—leading to clashes with the regime that came to a head in the war that continues over ten years later.[10] Even though the State of Emergency Law was lifted in April 2011, by 2020, an estimated 200,000 to 300,000 political prisoners had been incarcerated by the Assad regime in the decade since the 2011 protests. Violence instigated by opposition groups, Islamic State of Iraq and the Levant (ISIL), Russia, and Hezbollah tends to get a lot of the international media attention, but an estimated 90 percent of civilian disappearances from 2011 to 2020 have been orchestrated by the Assad government. In 2020, over 100 Syrian citizens were imprisoned each week. There are an estimated 128,000 people who have not emerged from prisons in Syria, and low estimates suggest that around 14,000 have been tortured to death.[11]

Many describe life in Syria as living in a prison—with the constant threat of indefinite incarceration looming over the heads of all who critique the regime. This was true well before the Arab Spring uprisings. Describing the process of writing her 2007 *Dissident Syria: Making Oppositional Art Official*, Miriam Cooke identifies the persistence of the sense that Syria is a prison under the

Hafez al-Assad regime: "Prison literature and the domination of the cell over the Syrian imagination was huge. People in daily life would talk about their houses as cells."[12] For decades, political dissent has been quashed by the repressive regime, and there is a tradition of writing about imprisonment of various kinds in Syria. However, in the decade since 2011, Syria has become even more prison-like. Over half of the population of twenty-two million have fled from their homes, and most have not been able to return. Around seven million have been displaced within Syria's borders, and another seven million lie outside the country's borders—living in mostly inhospitable conditions in the largest numbers in Turkey, Lebanon, Jordan, and Germany.[13] Those who are inside cannot leave, and those who are outside cannot return. Nations are increasingly reluctant to allow refugees to enter—in part because of the proxy war waged by ISIL, Russia, and a variety of groups condemned as terrorists by the international community. Even within Syria's borders, Assad has cut off most resources to the rebel-controlled Idlib province, effectively imprisoning its inhabitants. This imprisonment has only become more acute in Syria in the face of the COVID-19 pandemic. On August 27, 2020, the International Rescue Committee reported a 1,000 percent rise in infections across northeast Syria. The United Nations Security Council failed to extend the cross-border resolution that would enable humanitarian aid to enter areas outside of the control of the Syrian government.[14] The Syrian nation itself is destined for oblivion if Assad continues to ruthlessly attack dissent, and the international community continues to allow it.

Organizations like SCM raise awareness of the importance of the freedom of speech for all—supporters and critics of the regime—inside and outside of prison. Most recently, in 2020, SCM collaborated with the peace institute Swiss Peace and the Caesar Families Association to publish an international study titled "Family Associations of Disappeared and Missing Persons: Lessons from Latin America and Beyond" to collect insights and strategies for families with disappeared and missing members to empower victims and their relatives "to advocate for themselves." This study takes a comparative, international approach to the needs of victims including multipronged activist, legal, and media strategies.[15] Likewise, an inclusive prison poetics can help accomplish a form of advocacy work from an angle that complements journalism and the work of nongovernmental organizations (NGOs)—to consider the impact of the creative work being done by marginalized people in order to shed light on injustice. In particular, the experiences of women prisoners in Syria remain relatively obscure. Former female detainees are stigmatized by their communities—especially if they have been tortured and raped while imprisoned. A May 29, 2020, report by the Institute for War and Peace Reporting (IWRP) titled "Syria: Female Prisoners Speak Out" describes the difficulty of life inside and outside of prison for incarcerated women. The IWRP project "is addressing the stigma felt by many survivors of torture [to] combat the prejudice they often encounter in their communities" by providing women with a social media platform to document and talk about their experiences.[16] Women inside prisons are frequently subject to similar conditions as their male counterparts, including interrogation, isolation, torture, and death. However, unlike men, they are often subject to harsh treatment after their release as well. In the 2020 report, women like "Reem," "Muna," and "Lula" describe the injustice they experience at the hands of the regime and along with being divorced, excluded, and punished by their communities upon release.

An estimated 13,500 civilian women in Syria have been detained as political prisoners in the decade since the 2011 protests, and around 7,000 likely remain in detention as of 2019. Many of these women have been reduced to mere numbers by the international community—when they have been discussed at all. Their individual names and identities have largely been lost to the violent erasure of arbitrary incarceration by the Assad regime. Yara Badr touches on the subjective, psychological "oblivion" that comes with living through the oppressive conditions of imprisonment: "You are lost, as though drifting in the sea, waiting for the wind to bring you a sail that will take you back to life."[17] To stave off "drifting" into psychological emptiness away from life, she turned to knitting and making crafts with olive stones like bracelets, rosaries, and necklaces. Badr's "prison writing," after her release, describes her experiences in Damascus Central Prison and Adraa Women's Prison from a different perspective. She created art *inside* prison to survive a *personal* feeling of oblivion. She writes *outside* of prison to ensure that *others* survive the oblivion imposed on incarcerated Syrians by the regime.

Sketching a "Prison Poetics"

When considering prison art and scholarship, the focus tends to be on high-profile men and written reflections on their experiences while incarcerated or on the Foucauldian "carceral system" itself.[18] There is very little scholarship connecting these texts to a larger poetics. One important exception is Doran Larson's 2010 "Toward a Prison Poetics," in which he discusses prominent examples, including Martin Luther King Jr., Nigerian Wole Soyinka, and George Jackson.[19] By analyzing the generic traits of these exemplary prison writers, he attempts "to uncloak the prison, and begin to shed light on the punishment regimes that we hold up as systems of justice." In the case of Syria, examining the Foucauldian "carceral system" is essential, since imprisonment and the operation of prisons happens almost entirely outside of the public view and the formal justice system—low estimates indicate that over one hundred thousand people in Syria have disappeared without a trace.[20] My interest in Larson's work lies in the ways that his poetics illuminate these dark corners of the justice system as well as the connections he identifies between individuals—between individual prisoners and between collective groups of prison writers and audiences of prison writing.

The spaces where these connections take place, the marginalized individuals who occupy these spaces, and the sense of urgency demanded by a prison poetics are areas that I will expand upon in my own analysis.

Larson identifies writing by incarcerated people as both inherently individual and collective by virtue of the material conditions of the prison system. These complementary "dissociative" and "associative" gestures arise from their position in a particular but generalizable "punishment apparatus" that is "at once layered in documentation and deracinated from systems of justice": "A dissociative turn of voice . . . allows the 'I' of the prison text—even when not opened into an explicit 'we'—to represent communities larger than the prison author and *other* than those insisted upon by the prison; [there is also a] concomitant associative gesture whereby the prison writer names the contemporary communities among whom s/he numbers him- or herself, and/or names an ancestry in the history of prison writing."[21]

The prison writer always and never speaks for herself. One function of the prison is to separate the incarcerated from their communities, but a consequence of this gesture is the formation of a community of prisoners—locally and globally. Through intensely personal narratives, prison writers like Martin Luther King Jr. represent the collective community of prisoners around them, link their work with larger communities outside of the prison walls, and connect with international networks of prisoners and writers. They *dissociate* from their singular voices and *associate* with other communities simultaneously. This is significant in the case of Syria, where civilians are secretly incarcerated—and often tortured, killed, or never heard from again. Despite (or in spite of) this effort to close off prisoners from their projects and communities, communities and projects are constructed. In part, it is the work of scholars to piece together these communities by identifying common structures such as a prison poetics.

Another significant component of Larson's work lends a sense of urgency to the role of the scholar—the identification of a moral imperative for reading and studying prison literature. At the end of his essay, Larson invokes the work of D. Quentin Miller on prison literature in the United States: "By reading this literature we become witnesses with a moral responsibility."[22] At the heart of this scholarly work engaging with prison poetics lies a call to action. Larson himself leads writing workshops inside Attica Correctional Facility in New York state.[23] Miller became interested in prison writing while teaching writing in Connecticut prisons.[24] These two scholars intended for their work to inspire action in their readers—even among scholars in the academic community. For Larson and Miller, there are no casual consumers of prison writing. Larson ends the essay with a further call to action produced by reading prison literature: "The incarcerated provide the labor that we ask of no other citizens: the labor of bearing the lash that the rest of us hear cracking at a distance, beating out the rhythm of our own regimented lives. In response, prison writers offer up a chorus that we would be wise to heed."[25] Prisoners "bear the lash" of the justice system and are able to describe its contours in ways that other citizens cannot. This offers a unique perspective into the inner machinations of the justice system—outside of public view—with very bodily, visceral consequences. What happens in these shadowy, discreet spaces is a kind of litmus test for the limits of justice in local and international carceral systems. It falls within the purview of readers to consume this work and act in accordance with the moral imperative. In the case of Syria, thousands of lives continue to be threatened with corporal punishment by the prison system. Not only is it necessary for organizations and activists to act out to prevent further violence; it is necessary for scholars to weave these experiences into a wider web of scholarship on justice and incarceration. For the literary scholar, this means the construction of a poetics that accounts for the urgency and marginality of artistic production in these liminal spaces.

In the case of incarcerated women, the imperative to act and "uncloak" hidden aspects of the prison system is especially urgent. Globally, women comprise an underrepresented population within prison systems.[26] However, incarceration among women is growing at a rate that is twice as fast as that of men.[27] Furthermore, as previously mentioned in the case of Syria, women who leave prison are often stigmatized by their communities. The stakes are quite high individually and collectively. In the next section, I expand this "prison poetics" to account more fully for the experiences of women and creative work beyond text-based narratives—including bodily, visual, and digital arts and crafts. This will enable points of comparative engagement between incarcerated artists in contexts where the written text is not the primary mode of expression—and the male prisoner is not the primary carceral subject. Analyzing work by Syrian women prisoners constructs a more inclusive global network of prison narratives. This pursuit also adds a more acute sense of urgency to the ethical dimension of Larson's work. Syrian women are in brutal prisons today, and the call to action must be acted upon quickly to affect meaningful change. This kind of "prison poetics" must be timely, nimble, and interdisciplinary in order to heed this urgent call.

"Creative Insurgency" in the Arab Spring Uprisings

An inclusive prison poetics must take an interdisciplinary approach to prison art. This includes theorizing the body as excluded from society, inspected and subject to corporal punishment, as well as the site of potential insurgency. Recent scholarship on the Arab Spring uprisings approaches art and activism as intersecting at the locus of the body. Marwan M. Kraidy develops a concept for creative activism—"creative insurgency"—that extends beyond written texts in his 2016 *The Naked Blogger of Cairo*: "[This particular] mixture of activism and artistry characterises revolutionary expression and tracks the social transformation of activism into Art and ensuing controversies. At the heart of these processes is the human body as tool, medium, symbol, and metaphor."[28] "Creative insurgency" hinges on the experience of the body—as both a site of violence and the site of resistance. The body as "tool, medium, symbol, and metaphor" is directly connected to Arab Spring activism since 2010 in Egypt, Syria, and beyond.

In 2010 and 2011, millions of citizens entered the streets to protest violent regimes, and most eventually encountered violent resistance: "Bodies aching for dignity haunt the Arab uprisings and fuel the peculiar aesthetics of insurgent art and culture."[29] The viral image of Mohamed Bouazizi's self-immolation in Tunisia in 2010 is a marker of the beginning of the Arab Spring and serves as a vivid example of the centrality of the body to these uprisings.[30] His self-immolation functions as a counterpoint to the corporal punishment enacted by repressive regimes in Tunisia and beyond. Setting himself on fire after experiencing mistreatment by a government employee, Bouazizi disrupted the punishment structure by transforming his pain into an insurgent visual spectacle to displace corporal punishment by the regime. He burned his body in the street as a kind of parallel statement to the public humiliation he experienced being reprimanded by a female civil servant, Faida Hamdy, issuing him a citation and allegedly slapping him.[31] Kraidy also calls attention to a very different kind of bodily spectacle with the example of Aliaa Elmahdy—the "Naked Blogger of Cairo"—operating in a complicated space of politics and social justice. Elmahdy posted an artistic photograph of her nude figure on Facebook in 2011 to challenge her fellow Egyptians to end the repression and harassment of women (see figure 1.1). The brazen red of her bow and shoes represents a different kind of creative insurgency than Bouazizi's violent self-immolation. She looks directly into the camera with her legs slightly spread to challenge the world to judge her or punish her. This gesture simultaneously challenges the gender norms of her fellow Egyptians and the repressive regime filling the power vacuum left by the resignation of Hosni Mubarak. Elmahdy defied the multiple controls placed upon the female body by turning her own body into a piece of insurgent art and photographing it for the world to see. In the case of Syria too, the body was—and still is—the site of violence, torture, and containment by the regime. Many viral photographs have circulated showing scars across the bodies of former prisoners. The bodies of inmates bear the brutal imprint of the Assad regime—even outside of prison. The punishment on display in these photographs parallels the vibrancy of Mohamed Bouazizi's self-immolation, calling attention to bodily pain as a public spectacle rather than an isolated incident hidden by the shadows of the secret Syrian prison system.

The Syrian tradition of prison art over the past several decades attests to the significance of the incarcerated body as well. One notable example is the poet Faraj Bayraqdar's 2006 memoir, titled *The Betrayals of Language and Silence*, about his experience in the infamous Tadmor prison.[32] In a section titled "portrait of the prison," Bayraqdar uses verse to evoke the language of visual art, more specifically portraiture, to describe a prison he encounters on a daily basis.

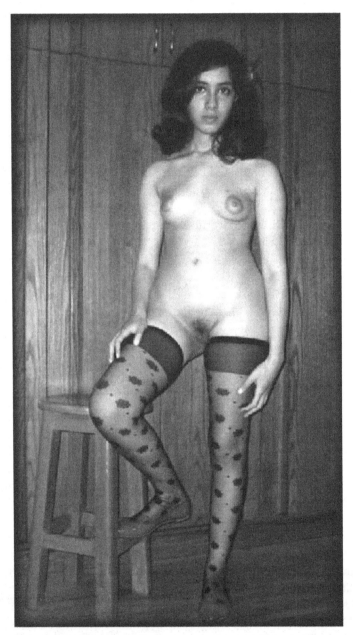

FIG. 1.1 Nude self-portrait (selfie) published on her blog, *A Rebel's Diary*.
Credit: Aliaa Magda Elmahdy, 2011

Again, the focus is the body—this time, the body of the prison that contains the bodies of the incarcerated. The prison is alive, stark, and punishing:

High walls of stubborn cold cement . . .
Observation towers . . .
Minefields . . .
Barriers and checkpoints . . .
Fortifications and highly trained military units . . .
And finally . . . surrounded by lessons of pure, national fear
Oh, names of God!
Even if all of Syria fell,
Surely, it would be impossible for this prison to fall.[33]

The "portrait" Bayraqdar draws with language focuses on the structures of containment, observation, violence, fear—and the enduring quality of the prison to outlive the political turmoil of the present and the Assad regime: "Surely, it would be impossible for this prison to fall." At the same time, the prison is given human qualities like "*stubborn* cold cement" and is able to teach "lessons of pure, national fear." From his vantage point inside its walls, Bayraqdar cannot foresee the imminent 2015 destruction of the prison. It is unwavering, immovable, and likely to cast him into oblivion before the prison itself can be obliterated. The contours of the prison comprise a "betrayal of language and silence" against oblivion. The gestures of the prison's body can be read by the inmates and the outside world through Bayraqdar's poem. Here, the carceral system is no longer completely secrete or silent. Rather, the prison's "portrait" can be read as one strand of a larger poetic web that extends beyond the prison walls and beyond the borders of Syria. The poem calls to be situated within a wider, interdisciplinary poetics inclusive of visual arts and bodily insurgency.

Toward a Poetics of Creative Insurgency in Syria: The Case of Azza Abo Rebieh

Like most traditions of prison writing, the Syrian tradition does not include adequate perspectives from women or gender minorities.[34] In fact, in 2020, it was still considered taboo for incarcerated women to go back to their families. In part, this is because of the fear that they have been raped or tortured. Recently, however, there is an effort, similar to the project of the #MeToo movement in the United States, to destigmatize this abuse by helping women make their stories public on social media.[35] Giving women a platform to share their experiences with a global community of survivors without shame helps reveal previously hidden aspects of the carceral system. Expanding the audience beyond Syria empowers these women to speak even though their local community may not encourage them to do so. One former prisoner who shared her story with the *New York Times*, Azza Abo Rebieh, was held as a political prisoner in 2015 in Adra prison for seventy days. Journalistic advocacy and artistic insurgency overlap in Rebieh's story—as well as overlapping individual and collective actions. Figure 1.2 is a sketch that Rebieh completed of a fellow cellmate in detention named Raeefeh. The portrait of Raeefeh is very different than the portrait of the Tadmor prison in poetic verse by Faraj Bayraqdar. Rebieh drew the women around her to help her community survive their containment—to give dignity back to their abused bodies and psyches:

> There were no mirrors inside the prison, so the drawings I made of the women made them see how they look. They are even more beautiful than the way I draw them.... On New Year's Eve, the guards let us have a party. I drew on the girls' faces, one a cat, one a butterfly. The guards agreed to allow it for one night only. So we wrote them a card, saying "The ladies of Cell Number 4 congratulate you on the New Year."
>
> When the guards saw that we called ourselves "ladies," they went crazy. They said, "You are terrorists, not ladies."[36]

Rebieh dissociates from herself, using her art to give life back to the women around her—turning her gift from serving the health of the singular *I* to the collective *we*. Her portraits and face painting provide a link of solidarity and humanity among the women in her prison community. She wants the women to be able to see themselves in her images, to see their faces. The associative gesture is restricted to the community of women around her while she waits in prison—collaborating through art, dance, and spectacles to survive the abuse they face by highlighting their humanity and joy. Similarly, figures 1.3 and 1.4 illustrate the unvarnished humanity of these women, above all. They see themselves as gendered "ladies" trying to survive the conditions in which they are contained, not genderless "terrorists" who enact violence to disrupt their communities. The simple portraits reveal just how young these women are. They are not hardened criminals but girls who have been incarcerated—in many cases, for no substantiated crime. The poetic gesture of the portraits, in the moment, does not have a larger, political significance to bring awareness to the conditions within the prison. The significance resides inside the prison community and collective survival. She provides them with an experience of their common humanity and the chance to see their faces as young and beautiful even though the prison denies them that luxury. An inclusive prison poetics must account for this kind of humanistic work beyond the written text. Rebieh's creative insurgency is a gesture of life resisting the violent erasure of identity by the Syrian prison system.

Not all prison art by Syrian women is so intensely inward facing. Upon her release, Rebieh has made art that she shares with a global audience. Fearing for

FIG. 1.2 "Raeefeh, Age 22." Credit: Azza abo Rebieh, 2015

FIG. 1.3 "Rama el-Eid, Age 18." Credit: Azza abo Rebieh, 2015

FIG. 1.4 "Tal El Mlouhi." Credit: Azza abo Rebieh, 2015

her life with a case still open against her, she lives in Lebanon and makes art about prison in Syria. In her apartment, she surrounds herself with reminders of her life there—portraits of her cellmates and tiny dolls made of olive pits and bits of wool blanket (see figure 1.5)—to reinforce the message that drives her creative process: "I keep remembering that I am out and they are in."[37] In retrospect, the work she made in prison serves as a reminder to continue fighting and advocating for the women who remain incarcerated—at the edge of oblivion. Surrounding herself with it functions as an imperative to act. After her release, she made etchings of her cellmates (figures 1.6 and 1.7) that differ greatly from the portraits she drew while in prison. The function has shifted radically from preservation of life in her community while incarcerated to advocacy for the women who remain imprisoned in Syria. In these etchings, the focus is on pain and darkness in contrast to the lightness and intimacy of her prison portraits. This work is outward facing and serves to raise awareness of the darkness and misery attending those who remain inside. The details of the women's faces have been blurred to focus more on the darkness of the conditions that surround their bodies. Their bodies melt into the surroundings—their faces nondescript and barely visible in contrast to the glowing portraits of inmates she

FIG. 1.5 Olive pit prison dolls. Credit: Azza abo Rebieh, 2015

sketched while in prison. Here, the dissociative aspect of her creation is even more distanced from the prison community. These etchings are less mirrorlike. She recalls her experience from outside of the prison itself and outside of the Syrian prison state. Rebieh offers viewers a glimpse of her own memory of her prison community. Likewise, the associative gesture connects with a community of other outsiders. Her work advocates for the women who remain incarcerated and serves as a call to action for outsiders. Clearly visible in the images, her concern shifts from enabling the women around her to engage with their humanity, preventing them from disappearing into psychological oblivion, to raising awareness of their collective plight, preventing them from disappearing into oblivion in terms of the international community.

Rebieh's work inside and outside of prison performs different but complementary work. Through her prison portraits, she gives her fellow inmates a glimpse of their own humanity to stave off the internal feeling of oblivion induced by the prison experience in Syria. The dissociative and associative gestures here focus on building a community within the prison walls. Outside of the prison, she dissociates from her personal experience in the prison to advocate

FIG. 1.6 Untitled etching of cellmates. Credit: Azza abo Rebieh, 2016

FIG. 1.7 Untitled etching of cellmates. Credit: Azza abo Rebieh, 2016

for the women who remain. She obscures their identities in her etchings to shed light on the urgency of their condition. The associative gesture connects their experience with a network of concerned global citizens. Inside and outside of prison, she creates art to keep women prisoners alive by putting their bodies in pain on display in acts of creative insurgency.

Ethical Urgency Outside of the Syrian Prison

In the case of Syria, the space of the prison extends far beyond the walls of the institution. Many of the material conditions of living inside a prison—containment, limited communication with the outside world, and the persistent threat of corporal punishment—are a daily concern for generations of Syrians since the 1960s. After the momentum of the Arab Spring uprisings, women like Azza Abo Rebieh have increasingly spoken out about these conditions. Like Rebieh's recent work, calling attention to this grim reality follows them outside of Syria's borders too.

The work of Sulafa Hijazi depicts the country of Syria as a prison trapped in a cycle of violence. Her art is almost exclusively digital because it is more discreet and easier to distribute—inside and outside of Syria. Like Rebieh, she no longer lives in Syria but conveys the Syrian experience through images. Her work depicts physical imprisonment, making military uniforms with human flesh and weapons giving birth to a new generation of prisoners. She describes her particular dissociative and associative gestures as an artist in an essay on her 2012 series, *Ongoing*: "I purposely did not include pictures of the President or any elements related specifically to Syria in the series. I wanted this artwork to be about any conflict situation with accompanying humanitarian issues. However, these illustrations were born out of my experiences in Syria, and I represent an aspect of my identity in the illustrations."[38] Her illustrations develop out of the specific material conditions of her youth, but she intentionally dissociates from them in order to expand the audience of engaged viewers. In a complementary associative gesture, she situates her work in a larger network of oppressed populations struggling to survive under brutal conditions—a "humanitarian issue" that demands action from outside sources.

In *Ongoing*, Hijazi calls international attention to the incredible violence, loss, and containment she experienced in Syria. Figure 1.8 illustrates the futility of trying to fully escape Syria. The eyeless, genderless, nondescript body is punctuated with dots that resemble bullet holes or a rash that has spread across the figure's whole body. It pokes its head through the wall of a cube lined with prison bars or razor wire, but ends up back inside the cube, seeing itself from behind. The incarcerated person seeks freedom outside of the prison's walls, but "outside" is illusory. What seems like outside is a different viewpoint of inside. Hijazi explicitly expands this reading of her work beyond the walls of Syria's prisons to include her entire country. She reflects, "Inside Syria, people live like

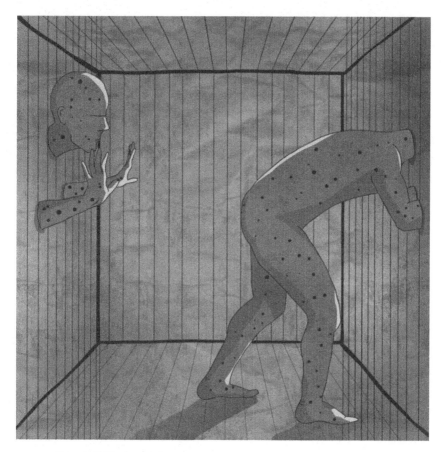

FIG. 1.8 "Untitled." Credit: Sulafa Hijazi, 2012

prisoners inside a huge cell. Once we try to escape from there, we discover that we are still inside."[39] Even from outside of Syria, she feels trapped within the Syrian prison. Hijazi associates with prisoners beyond the borders of Syria, and the moral imperative driving a prison poetic remains an urgent call to action for viewers of these images. The actions of Syrians inside and outside of Syria's prisons or national borders are limited without the support of the international community.

Many of Hijazi's pieces in this series emphasize the human body as contained, mechanized, and devoid of gender or identity. The body becomes complicit with generic, machinelike qualities as a result of the cyclical violence enacted by the Assad regime, but is also radically insurgent and disruptive. In Syria, human bodies become dehumanized as machines of war—their identities disappear into oblivion. Several of her pieces deal with pregnancy and childbirth in graphic, spectacular ways. Figure 1.9 shows an automatic rifle with a subtle outline of breasts gestating a human child out of the tools of war. In this disturbing, dystopic image, a weapon replaces a woman carrying a child. The only characteristics that remain to recall a human woman are the womb and breasts. Women's bodies are written out of the reproductive process and replaced by weapons with mechanized reproductive capacities. This portrait of motherhood out of war does not include any discernible facial features or human identity. However, the child contains a certain amount of insurgent potential to disrupt the war machine, as its body has not yet been mechanized. The child will either perpetuate violence or disrupt the war machine through its humanity.

Figure 1.10 depicts an ambiguously male figure struggling to give birth to an automatic weapon, with other weapons like hand grenades, knives, and handguns scattered around the area where he lies. A human man gives birth to the instruments of violence used to terrorize the Syrian people. Again, the bodies of women are removed from childbirth with horrific results. This suggests that men are responsible for the dehumanization of Syrian women and children and turning people into weapons of war. Hijazi reflects on this gendered distinction: "I also pondered the implications of masculinity in killing, power, dictatorship and domination. I believe that if women were in charge of the world, there would be no more war. Women who give birth know the meaning of life."[40] Syrian women are impacted greatly by the prison system and acts of violence taking place in their country but seem to have little agency in preventing this dehumanization. "The meaning of life" from a woman's perspective is violently erased from considerations over the national war project. Work like Hijazi's and Rebieh's put this objectification and aggression on display by capturing life, violence, and the erasure of women's bodies in their visual art. The two use their work to associate with a community of women around the world who are subject to violence—inside and outside of violent political regimes.

For the vast majority of refugees who have escaped Syria with fewer resources than some of these artists who work in exile, the situation is especially grim. For example, Lebanon has accepted over a million Syrian refugees, and many live under inhospitable conditions. In a report for a 2015 United Nations Development Programme (UNDP) peace-building project, Maya El Helo describes the multiple sources of oppression Syrian refugee women in Lebanon face in an article titled "The Intersectional Faces of Violence against Female Syrian Refugees." For Syrian women in refugee camps, the conditions are like a prison: "There are curfews that have been imposed by some municipalities, inside and outside Beirut, which turned the life of refugees into a prison inside a prison. Many female refugees (depending on their social class) are unable to leave Lebanon to return to their country because of the war, or travel to another country, for financial reasons or the difficulty of obtaining entry visas. . . . There are many questions, but the situation doesn't change; after all these years of crisis and constant war migration flux, there is still no safe place for female Syrian refugees."[41]

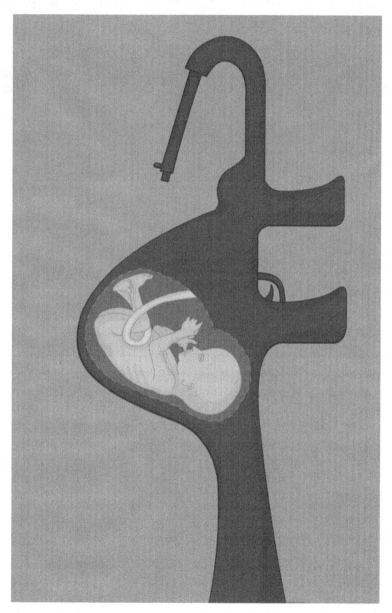

FIG. 1.9 "Untitled." Credit: Sulafa Hijazi, 2012

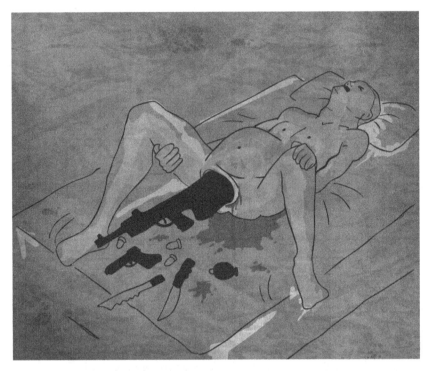

FIG. 1.10 "Birth." Credit: Sulafa Hijazi, 2012

In exchange for fleeing for their lives, Syrian women are essentially imprisoned in the camps. Because many women in these camps lack the means to seek refuge in more accommodating circumstances, they are unlikely to be able to afford to return home. Even if they are not technically incarcerated, Syrian women must choose the danger and oblivion of living in the Syrian prison state or the likelihood of danger and oblivion living abroad—unable to psychologically free themselves from Syria or unable to leave the refugee camps in which they are contained.

Conclusion

Developing a radical, urgent prison poetics that includes women and examines a variety of genres of art—from drawings to crafts to digital images—emphasizes the role of bodies in pain and in captivity and sets the stage for a kind of activism that scholars and teachers can begin to accomplish in classrooms. Studying the various forms of prison art can compel students to bear witness to bodies in pain through texts and images of prisoners in Syria and around the world and take action. This harkens back to the important ethical project underlying Larson's prison poetics: "The incarcerated provide the labor that we ask of no other citizens: the labor of bearing the lash that the rest of us hear cracking at a distance, beating out the rhythm of our own regimented lives. In response, prison writers offer up a chorus that we would be wise to heed."[42] For the scholar of prison art, "to heed" this "chorus" includes articulating a comparative prison poetics that extends beyond the written texts of famous men. It must account for the bodies of marginalized prisoners that experience the pain and oblivion of the carceral state. In this chapter, I push at the boundaries of this poetics to account for women's bodies and the visual arts in the case of Syria—inside and outside prison walls. This is only the first step toward a more inclusive prison poetics that could act as a preventative measure against the oblivion of forcible erasure and provide a foundation for comparative, scholarly work to support social justice efforts outside of the classroom.

The urgency of this kind of scholarly labor is clear in the case of Syria. Until the international community steps up to heed the chorus of Syrians in reports, in art, and on social media, the suffering and injustice will continue. Under the ruthless dictatorship of Bashar al-Assad, hundreds of thousands of Syrians remain locked in prisons with no rights—often being tortured or killed. The kind of psychological and physical oblivion described by Yara Badr and represented in the visual art of the chorus of women including Azza Abo Rebieh and Sulafa Hijazi is a call to act before these voices are forcibly silenced. Without holding Assad to account, this will continue. From December 2019 to December 2020 alone, nearly a million Syrians were displaced from their homes in northwest Syria. One of many problems is that they are trapped in the prison of their homeland, with international refugee quotas decreasing and sources of humanitarian aid drying up. The COVID-19 pandemic, rampant xenophobia, and increased economic inequality is making fleeing from Syria even more difficult. The role of journalists, spectators, and scholars is even more urgent considering the abysmal example set by the American immigration policy. In 2016, under President Obama's guidance, the United States accepted 12,587 Syrian refugees. In 2017, under Donald Trump, that radically decreased to 3,024 and dwindled to only 62 in 2018.[43] Reflected by the official policy of the United States, Americans have failed to see these bodies in pain. These policies prove that like the guards in Tadmor prison, we too see "terrorists," not "ladies."

Notes

1   SCM works "to defend oppressed individuals due to their beliefs or opinions, as well as promoting human rights and supporting and developing independent, critical and professional media." Recent and continuing initiatives include the 2019 launch of the MENA Network for Countering Hate Speech, the maintenance of a robust Violations Documentation Center (VDC) in Syria that documents violations against refugees, and a civilian and noncivilian weekly death count in Syria. "Who We Are," Syria Center for Media and Freedom of Expression, accessed August 30, 2020, https://scm .bz/en/#.

2 Yara Badr, "Lifetimes Stolen," in *Syria Speaks: Art and Culture from the Frontline*, ed. Malu Halasa and Zaher Omareen (London: Saqi Books, 2014), 201.

3 Badr, 200 (emphasis mine).

4 Badr's awards include the 2012 Ilaria Alpi award for brave female journalists and the Alison Des Forges Award for Extraordinary Activism from Human Rights Watch. Darwish's awards include the 2011 Roland Berger Human Dignity Award, the 2014 Pinter International Writer of Courage Award from English PEN, the 2015 World Press Freedom Hero award from the International Press Institute, and the 2015 UNESCO / Guillermo Cano World Press Freedom Prize.

5 The United Nations estimates that over one hundred thousand people have been "detained, abducted, or gone missing" since 2010. United Nations, "Security Council Failing Thousands of People Detained, Abducted in Syria, Civil Society Speakers Say, Demanding Information about Missing Persons' Whereabouts," U.N. Security Council meeting 8593, last modified August 7, 2019, http://www.un.org/press/en/2019/ sc13913.doc.htm#:~:text=Owing%20to%20vetoes%20and%20excuses,whereabouts %20and%20support%20for%20grieving.

6 One exception is Rachel Marie-Crane Williams, "Behind Closed Doors: The Art, Art Making, and Experience of Incarcerated Women," *Visual Arts Research* 27, no. 2 (2001): 79–94.

7 See Maxwell Cotto, "Creative Writing in the Culture of the American Prison," *Salmagundi* 162, no. 3 (Spring/Summer 2009): 160–181; Ioan Davies, *Writers in Prison* (Oxford: Blackwell, 1990); Ileana Sora Dimitriu, "A Bakhtinian Reading of Prison Writing: The Memoirs of Breyten Breytenbach and Wole Soyinka," *British and American Studies* 5, no. 6 (2000): 94–106; H. Bruce Franklin, *Prison Literature in America: The Victim as Criminal and Artist* (New York: Oxford University Press, 1989); Paul Gready, "Autobiography and the 'Power of Writing': Political Prison Writing in the Apartheid Era," *Journal of Southern African Studies* 19, no. 3 (1993): 489–523. Also see D. Quentin Miller's introduction to *Prose and Cons: Essays on Prison Literature in the United States*, ed. D. Quentin Miller (Jefferson, N.C.: McFarland, 2005), 1–11.

8 Dale Tracy, "Metonymy, Poetics, Performance: World-Making and the Real," *Journal of the Midwest Modern Language Association* 15, no. 1 (2018): 7.

9 Doran Larson, "Toward a Prison Poetics," *College Literature* 37, no. 3 (2010): 144.

10 Hugh Macleod, "Syria: How It All Began," Public Radio International, last modified April 23, 2011, https://www.pri.org/stories/2011-04-23/syria-how-it-all-began.

11 United Nations, "Security Council Failing."

12 Miriam Cooke in Daniel Gorman, "From the Outside Looking In," in Halasa and Omareen, *Syria Speaks*, 226. For excellent in-depth analysis of Syrian art under Hafez al-Assad, see Miriam Cooke, *Dissident Syria: Making Oppositional Art Official* (Durham, N.C.: Duke University Press, 2007).

13 The economic situation has been exacerbated by the COVID-19 pandemic. See "Syrian Refugees Profoundly Hit by COVID-19 Economic Downturn," United Nations Refugee Agency, last modified June 16, 2020, https://www.unhcr.org/en-us/news/ briefing/2020/6/5ee884fb4/syrian-refugees-profoundly-hit-covid-19-economic -downturn.html.

14 "As COVID Cases Rise 1000% in Northeast Syria, IRC Calls on UN Security Council to Reopen Critical Yaroubiya Aid Crossing," International Rescue Committee, last modified August 27, 2020, http://www.rescue.org/press-release/covid-cases-rise -1000-northeast-syria-irc-calls-un-security-council-reopen-critical.

15 Lisa Ott and Natacha Hertig, "Family Associations of Disappeared and Missing Persons: Lessons from Latin America and Beyond," Syrian Center for Media and

Freedom of Expression, last modified June 2020, https://scm.bz/en/en-studies/
family-associations-of-disappeared-and-missing-persons-lessons-from-latin-america
-and-beyond-2.

16   "Syria: Female Prisoners Speak Out," Institute for War and Peace Reporting, last modi-
      fied May 29, 2020, https://iwpr.net/global-voices/syria-female-prisoners-speak-out.

17   Badr, "Lifetimes Stolen," 201.

18   See reflections by Martin Luther King Jr. or Nelson Mandela. For a seminal piece of
      scholarship on the "carceral system," see Michel Foucault, *Discipline and Punish: The
      Birth of the Prison*, trans. Alan Sheridan (New York: Vintage, 1995).

19   Larson, "Toward a Prison Poetics."

20   United Nations, "Security Council Failing."

21   Larson, "Toward a Prison Poetics," 145.

22   Miller, introduction, 4.

23   Larson, "Toward a Prison Poetics," 143.

24   Miller, introduction, 5.

25   Larson, "Toward a Prison Poetics," 159.

26   Helen Codd, "Editorial: Women and Imprisonment," *Wagadu, Journal of Transna-
      tional Women's and Gender Studies* 11 (Winter 2013): 1–6.

27   Candice Kruttschnitt, "The Paradox of Women's Imprisonment," *Daedalus* 139, no. 3
      (2010): 32–39.

28   Marwan Kraidy, *The Naked Blogger of Cairo* (Cambridge, Mass.: Harvard University
      Press, 2017), 5.

29   Kraidy, 11.

30   Mohamed Bouazizi's self-immolation is often regarded as the starting point for the
      Arab Spring uprisings. Bouazizi was a Tunisian street vendor who set himself on fire
      after being confronted by a female civil servant for not possessing the proper permit
      in Sidi Bouzid on December 17, 2010.

31   Kareem Fahim, "Slap to a Man's Pride Set Off Tumult in Tunisia," *New York Times*,
      last modified January 21, 2011, www.nytimes.com/2011/01/22/world/africa/22sidi
      .html#:~:text=SIDI%20BOUZID%2C%20Tunisia%20%E2%80%94%20Mohamed
      %20Bouazizi,the%20red%20chilis%20to%20dry.

32   Until 2015, when ISIL militants destroyed it, Tadmor prison was known for its brutal
      conditions, including the 1980 massacre of an estimated one thousand prisoners. An
      Amnesty International report in 2001 describes it as a prison where one could expect
      "despair, torture, and degrading treatment." "Syria: Torture, Despair, and Dehuman-
      ization in Tadmur Military Prison," Amnesty International, last modified Septem-
      ber 18, 2001, http://www.amnesty.org/en/documents/MDE24/014/2001/en/.

33   Faraj Bayrqdar, *The Betrayals of Language and Silence*, quoted in Shareah R.
      Taleghani, "Breaking the Silence of Tadmor Military Prison," *Middle East Research
      and Information Project* 275 (Summer 2015).

34   One notable example of an effort to highlight the experience of Syrian women
      in prison is the 2014 Ramadan drama titled *Qalam humra*. The series cen-
      ters on a female screenwriter in a political detention center. Hatem Ali, dir.,
      Qalam humra [Red lipstick], written by Yam Mashhadi, aired June 29, 2014,
      available at http://www.youtube.com/watch?v=fQCozLnkLKc&list=
      PLLcpeauQVc1u2W4PiNRB9oif2t9iFYwVE&index=2&t=0s&app=desktop.

35   "Syria: Female Prisoners Speak Out."

36   Lina Sinjab and Anne Barnard, "Syria's Women Prisoners, Drawn by an Artist Who
      Was One," *New York Times*, last modified August 7, 2018, http://www.nytimes.com/
      2018/08/07/arts/design/syria-prison-artist.html.

37 Sinjab and Barnard.
38 Sulafa Hijazi, "Ongoing: The Digital Art and Illustrations of Sulafa Hijazi," in Halasa and Omareen, *Syria Speaks*, 15.
39 Hijazi, 16.
40 Hijazi, 15.
41 Maya El Helo, "The Intersectional Faces of Violence against Female Syrian Refugees," *Peace Building in Lebanon Joint News Supplement*, no. 8, July 2015, 6.
42 Larson, "Toward a Prison Poetics," 159.
43 Katie Zezima, "The U.S. Has Slashed Its Refugee Intake. Syrians Fleeing War Are Most Affected," Washington Post, last modified May 7, 2019, https://www .washingtonpost.com/immigration/the-us-has-slashed-its-refugee-intake-syrians -fleeing-war-are-most-affected/2019/05/07/f764e57c-678f-11e9-a1b6-b29b90efa879 _story.html.

Bibliography

Ali, Hatem, dir. *Qalam humra* [Red lipstick]. Written by Yam Mashhadi. Aired June 29, 2014. Available at http://www.youtube.com/watch?v=fQCozLnkLKc&list= PLLcpeauQVc1u2W4PiNRB90if2t9iFYwVE&index=2&t=0s&app=desktop.

Amnesty International. "Syria: Torture, Despair, and Dehumanization in Tadmur Military Prison." Last modified September 18, 2001. http://www.amnesty.org/en/documents/ MDE24/014/2001/en/.

Badr, Yara. "Lifetimes Stolen." In *Syria Speaks: Art and Culture from the Frontline*, edited by Malu Halasa and Zaher Omareen, 192–201. London: Saqi Books, 2014.

Codd, Helen. "Editorial: Women and Imprisonment." *Wagadu, Journal of Transnational Women's and Gender Studies* 11 (Winter 2013): 1–6.

Cooke, Miriam. *Dissident Syria: Making Oppositional Art Official*. Durham, N.C.: Duke University Press, 2007.

Cotto, Maxwell. "Creative Writing in the Culture of the American Prison." *Salmagundi* 162, no. 3 (Spring/Summer 2009): 160–181.

Davies, Ioan. *Writers in Prison*. Oxford: Blackwell, 1990.

Dimitriu, Ileana Sora. "A Bakhtinian Reading of Prison Writing: The Memoirs of Breyten Breytenbach and Wole Soyinka." *British and American Studies* 5, no. 6 (2000): 94–106.

El Helo, Maya. "The Intersectional Faces of Violence against Female Syrian Refugees." *Peace Building in Lebanon Joint News Supplement*, no. 8, July 2015, 6.

Fahim, Kareem. "Slap to a Man's Pride Set Off Tumult in Tunisia." *New York Times*. Last modified January 21, 2011. http://www.nytimes.com/2011/01/22/world/africa/22sidi.html#:~: text=SIDI%20BOUZID%2C%20Tunisia%20%E2%80%94%20Mohamed%20Bouazizi ,the%20red%20chilis%20to%20dry.

Foucault, Michel. *Discipline and Punish: The Birth of the Prison*. Translated by Alan Sheridan. New York: Vintage, 1995.

Franklin, H. Bruce. *Prison Literature in America: The Victim as Criminal and Artist*. New York: Oxford University Press, 1989.

Gorman, Daniel. "From the Outside Looking In." In *Syria Speaks: Art and Culture from the Frontline*, edited by Malu Halasa and Zaher Omareen, 224–233. London: Saqi Books, 2014.

Gready, Paul. "Autobiography and the 'Power of Writing': Political Prison Writing in the Apartheid Era." *Journal of Southern African Studies* 19, no. 3 (1993): 489–523.

Hijazi, Sulafa. "Ongoing: The Digital Art and Illustrations of Sulafa Hijazi." In *Syria Speaks: Art and Culture from the Frontline*, edited by Malu Halasa and Zaher Omareen, 10–16. London: Saqi Books, 2014.

Institute for War and Peace Reporting. "Syria: Female Prisoners Speak Out." Last modified May 29, 2020. https://iwpr.net/global-voices/syria-female-prisoners-speak-out.

International Rescue Committee. "As COVID Cases Rise 1000% in Northeast Syria, IRC Calls on UN Security Council to Reopen Critical Yaroubiya Aid Crossing." Last modified August 27, 2020. http://www.rescue.org/press-release/covid-cases-rise-1000-northeast -syria-irc-calls-un-security-council-reopen-critical.

Kraidy, Marwan. *The Naked Blogger of Cairo*. Cambridge, Mass.: Harvard University Press, 2017.

Kruttschnitt, Candice. "The Paradox of Women's Imprisonment." *Daedalus* 139, no. 3 (2010): 32–39.

Larson, Doran. "Toward a Prison Poetics." *College Literature* 37, no. 3 (2010): 143–166.

Macleod, Hugh. "Syria: How It All Began." Public Radio International. Last modified April 23, 2011. http://www.pri.org/stories/2011-04-23/syria-how-it-all-began.

Miller, D. Quentin. Introduction to *Prose and Cons: Essays on Prison Literature in the United States*, 1–11. Edited by D. Quentin Miller. Jefferson, N.C.: McFarland, 2005.

Ott, Lisa, and Natacha Hertig. "Family Associations of Disappeared and Missing Persons: Lessons from Latin America and Beyond." Syrian Center for Media and Freedom of Expression, June 2020. https://scm.bz/en/en-studies/family-associations-of-disappeared -and-missing-persons-lessons-from-latin-america-and-beyond-2.

Sinjab, Lina, and Anne Barnard. "Syria's Women Prisoners, Drawn by an Artist Who Was One." *New York Times*. Last modified August 7, 2018. http://www.nytimes.com/2018/08/ 07/arts/design/syria-prison-artist.html.

Syria Center for Media and Freedom of Expression. "Who We Are." Accessed August 30, 2020. https://scm.bz/en/#.

Taleghani, Shareah R. "Breaking the Silence of Tadmor Military Prison." *Middle East Research and Information Project* 275 (Summer 2015): 21–25.

Tracy, Dale. "Metonymy, Poetics, Performance: World-Making and the Real." *Journal of the Midwest Modern Language Association* 15, no. 1 (2018): 5–23.

United Nations. "Security Council Failing Thousands of People Detained, Abducted in Syria, Civil Society Speakers Say, Demanding Information about Missing Persons' Whereabouts." U.N. Security Council meeting 8593. Last modified August 7, 2019. http://www.un.org/ press/en/2019/sc13913.doc.htm#:~:text=Owing%20to%20vetoes%20and%20excuses ,whereabouts%20and%20support%20for%20grieving.

United Nations Refugee Agency. "Syrian Refugees Profoundly Hit by COVID-19 Economic Downturn." Last modified June 16, 2020. https://www.unhcr.org/en-us/news/briefing/ 2020/6/5ee884fb4/syrian-refugees-profoundly-hit-covid-19-economic-downturn.html.

Williams, Rachel Marie-Crane. "Behind Closed Doors: The Art, Art Making, and Experience of Incarcerated Women." *Visual Arts Research* 27, no. 2 (2001): 79–94.

Zezima, Katie. "The U.S. Has Slashed Its Refugee Intake. Syrians Fleeing War Are Most Affected." *Washington Post*. Last modified May 7, 2019. https://www.washingtonpost.com/ immigration/the-us-has-slashed-its-refugee-intake-syrians-fleeing-war-are-most-affected/ 2019/05/07/f764e57c-678f-11e9-a1b6-b29b90efa879_story.html.

2

Moving beyond Victimhood

• •

Female Agency in Bangladeshi War Movies

FARZANA AKHTER

Anneke Smelik, in the first chapter of her book *And the Mirror Cracked: Feminist Cinema and Film Theory*, defines cinema as a "cultural practice where myths about women and femininity, and men and masculinity, in short, myths about sexual difference are produced, reproduced, and represented."[1] Indeed, cinema plays a significant role in safeguarding—and many times, perpetuating—some of the flawed ideologies and myths of society. Smelik's utterance cannot be truer than in the case of war movies, where the main focus has always been on masculine prowess and military heroism. Time and again, movies on war have been guilty of conserving gender stereotypes by representing the male body as active agent and the female body as submissive and devoid of any agency. A similar trend is also observed in Bangladeshi movies on the Liberation War of 1971, in which the directors predominantly focus on the valorization of male combatants. Although women have participated in the Liberation War of Bangladesh in multifarious ways, from providing practical support for the combatants to fighting alongside men, their active participation has been surreptitiously pushed to invisibility. Instead, Bangladeshi war movies represent female bodies as passive subjects, either as mothers, or as desolate and helpless rape victims, or at best, as icons of the motherland who need her men to free her from the enemy. Renowned director Nasiruddin Yousuff's award-winning movie *Guerrilla*, however, deviates from the typical war narratives as it subverts the general perception of women's role in the Liberation War of Bangladesh as mere objects or vulnerable subjects and highlights their role as freedom fighters. In this chapter, I argue that the women in the movie *Guerrilla* debunk the stereotypical view of the female body as passive victim and reclaim agency by demonstrating the female body as active agent capable of contributing to the freedom of the country. In doing so, I am primarily invested in showing that women's agency and active participation in war narratives have been intentionally kept invisible to uphold a conventional patriarchal ideology.

Bangladeshi War Movies: An Overview

Right after independence, motivated by the spirit of *muktijudhdho* (liberation war) and nationalism, Bangladeshi film producers and directors started to produce movies on the war of 1971.[2] The very first full-length feature film to be produced in an independent Bangladesh was Chashi Nazrul Islam's *Ora egaro jon* (1972). The film, released in 1972, revolves around the heroic deeds of eleven freedom fighters who fight against the Pakistani enemy to free the country. Another extraordinary war movie, *Alor Michil* (1974), showcases a group of war veterans trying to rebuild the war-torn country. Some of the other noteworthy movies produced in the newly liberated country are Momtaj Ali's *Roktakto Bangla* (1972), Anondo's[3] *Bagha Bangali* (1972), Khan Ataur Rahman's *Abar tora manush ho* (1973), Chashi Nazrul Islam's *Songram* (1974), and Harun Ur Rashid's *Megher onek rong* (1976). Although films centering on war and postwar issues are still produced, their numbers have dwindled over the years. Movies like Shahidul Haque Khan's *Kolmilata* (1981), Nasirudin Yousuff's *Ekattorer Jishu* (1993), Chashi Nazrul Islam's *Hangor nodi grenade* (1997), Tanvir Mokammel's *Nodir nam Modhumoti* (1996), Khan Ataur Rahman's *Ekhono onek raat* (1997), Morshedul Islam's *Agami* (1984) and *Amar bondhu Rashed* (2011), and Zahidur Rahim Anjan's *Meghmallar* (2014) are just a few among the numerous films that have been produced since the postwar era. The movies usually epitomize the heroic and valiant actions of the freedom fighters who not only freed the country from Pakistan's aggression but also rescued the sexually assaulted female body from the Pakistani camp, as can be seen in *Ora egaro jon* and *Roktakto Bangla*. Regiments of male soldiers march to active service on the battlefield, and though in some movies, women are projected as nurses (e.g., *Ora egaro jon* and *Megher onek rong*), they have limited or no agency at all except for taking care of the wounded soldiers. Again, in most of the movies (e.g., *Kolmilata* and *Aguner poroshmoni*), women are shown as staying behind and taking care of home and hearth and waiting for their men to return or, at best, giving shelter to the freedom fighters. Even documentaries like Zahir Raihan's *Stop Genocide* (1971), Alamgir Kabir's *Liberation Fighters* (1971), Babul Choudhury's

Innocent Millions (1971), Nagisa Oshima's *Joi Bangla* (1972), and S. Sukdev's *Nine Months to Freedom* (1975), to name just a few, directed by Bangladeshi and foreign film directors, primarily project monolithic masculinity, completely eschewing women's participation.

Politics of Female Representation in Bangla Movies

Although recent war movies diversified by bringing in varied themes, ranging from collective nation building to unveiling the psychological trauma of war veterans, not much has changed in the general perspective, as these films continue to sustain similar politics of depriving women of agency in order to bolster conventional gender roles. Almost all the movies that have been produced so far, even the documentaries, unfortunately emphasize hypermasculinity and female vulnerability. Even if female characters, though very few in number, take an active part in the war, their on-screen presence is very brief and sidetracked. Film scholar Fahmida Akhter, in her article "Framing Pain as Spectacle: The Aesthetics of Wartime Films of Bangladesh," states that "with regard to portraying female images, these documentary films, particularly by Bangladeshi directors, more or less followed the convention of maintaining the collective interest and traditional outlook. These films did not contradict the patriarchal ideology of the society and its cultural context, and visualized mostly a representation of women as passive and victimized."[4]

In most cases, these documentaries obliterate women's participation in war to showcase masculine prowess. In this regard, Akhter further adds that the few women who took part in frontline battle, even those who carried arms, were not included in these documentaries. Instead, as Akhter writes, "women were projected either as suffering mothers who were fleeing, escaping with their children for a safe place and uprooted by the war, or as the ashamed figures of raped women who represented the ravaging of the nation."[5] Regrettably, in both genres, female bodies are represented as passive subjects and helpless victims.

The majority of the movies represent the female body as docile and devoid of any agency to contribute to the freedom of Bangladesh. However, the most recurring image of the female body that is projected in wartime movies is that of a raped body. Almost all the postindependence war movies have at least one rape scene that reiterates the vulnerability and weakness of the female body. Kaberi Gayen, in her article "Women, War and Cinema: Construction of Women in the Liberation War Films of Bangladesh," claims that starting from 1972, nearly all the war films of Bangladesh contain at least one rape scene or attempt-to-rape scene. In fact, Gayen alleges that "rape scenes were essential parts of earlier films."[6] The raped and oftentimes battered female body is shown on-screen not only to avouch the brutality and viciousness of the Pakistani army but also to glorify man's active participation in war. As the female body is considered a symbol of the motherland, the rape of the female body is symbolically the violation of the nation. According to Joshua S. Goldstein, raping women is also a way to impose domination on a male enemy (by violating his cherished property—that is, motherland, nation),[7] so by showing the rape of the female body, the movies try to glorify the nationalistic and patriotic feelings of the men who risked and sacrificed their lives to defend the motherland or nation. Of course, another purpose of the female body is to arouse emotions of pity and sympathy for the helpless rape victims, which in turn revitalizes the feeling of patriotism and spirit of *muktijudhdho* in the audience.

In addition, the projection of naked, half-naked, and raped female bodies lying here and there in the bunkers of a Pakistani army camp or hanging from the ceiling and branches of trees is motivated by commercial gain. Gayen documents that in postliberation mainstream war movies like *Bagha Bangali*, *Roktakto Bangla*, and *Kolmilata*, images of female rape victims were used for box-office business.[8] The proclivity of using rape scenes can be explained by applying British feminist film theorist Laura Mulvey's analysis on cinema and the female body. Taking a psychoanalytical approach to cinema, Mulvey, in her article "Visual Pleasure and Narrative Cinema," asserts, "According to the principles of the ruling ideology and the physical structure that back it up, the male figure cannot bear the burden of sexual objectification. Man is reluctant to gaze at his exhibitionist like. Hence, the split between spectacle and narrative supports the man's role as the active one for forwarding the story, making things happen. The man controls the film phantasy and also emerges as the representative of power in a further sense: as the bearer of the look of the spectator, transferring it behind the screen to neutralize the extra-diegetic tendencies represented by woman as spectacle."[9]

Mulvey's discussion of the female body as spectacle very aptly explains the function of the raped female body. As the target audience of the movies is mostly men who cannot stand to see themselves as sexualized object, a passive female body serves that purpose. Hence the function of the female body, as Mulvey asserts, is to be the spectacle that holds the look—that plays to and signifies male desire. In Mulvey's words, "In their traditional exhibitionist role women are simultaneously looked at and displayed, with their appearance coded for strong visual and erotic impact so that they can be said to connote *to-be-looked-at-ness*. Women displayed as sexual object is the leitmotif of erotic spectacle,"[10] which often turns to be a subject of male phantasy not only for the men in the film but also for the men present in the theater. Arguably, then, the sexualized female body as a spectacle becomes an object of gaze and erotic desire for the male audience, which in turn ensures the movie's financial success.

On the other hand, the eroticized female body is not only shown as violated and voiceless victim but also rendered absolutely powerless when, after the rape, in most cases, the raped woman is shown to commit suicide, as she is made to think that since she is defiled, she has become impure, and hence, it is better to put an end to such ignominious existence. In this way, the female body's ultimate lack of agency is attained by forcing women to yield to death. The movie *Megher onek rong* is an appropriate example to expose this trend in war movies. In the film, both the leading and supporting female characters are stripped of all sorts of agency as one recedes to a life of domesticity and the other commits suicide after being raped by Pakistani soldiers.

According to Mulvey, in a narrative film, man is always assumed to be active and powerful, while woman is passive and powerless. Her presence in movies, as Mulvey claims, is to ascertain the identity of the male character and thereby the identity of the male viewer, who tends to identify with the male character in the film. Therefore, the presence of the passive female body in movies is necessary to give the male body its meaning: "Woman then stands in patriarchal culture as signifier for the male other, bound by symbolic order in which man can live out his fantasies and obsessions through linguistic command by imposing them on the silent image of woman still tied to her place as bearer of meaning, not marker of meaning."[11] It is such dispositions that drive the directors of Bangladeshi war movies to prescribe women such roles, in which their function is to be the spectacle and augment the glorification of the male characters.

Second, the heroic representation of the male body is used to uphold the cultural ideas about gender and war. Cynthia Enloe, in her book *Bananas, Beaches and Bases*, contends that women are relegated to two minor, symbolic roles in nationalist movements and conflicts; they are represented "either as icons of nationhood, to be elevated and defended, or as the booty or spoils of war, to be denigrated and disgraced so that the real heroes could be men whose responsibility is to defend their freedom, their honour, their motherland and their women."[12] Clearly, then, as Mulvey also posits, women's only role in war is to increase men's heroism. Conversely, as a symbol of nationhood, women have to be protected from the aggression of the enemy, and it is the active male possessing agency who protects the fragile female body or the symbolic nation or motherland that the female body represents. In both cases, the female body is characterized as having no agency to exercise power and save herself, let alone contribute to the freedom of the nation. If the female body is represented as able and having agency, then it would threaten the prevalent concept that it is the responsibility of the men to protect their women and nation. According to Mulvey, "The gender power asymmetry is a controlling force in cinema and constructed for the pleasure of the male viewer, which is deeply rooted in patriarchal ideologies and discourses."[13] It can thus be argued that in Bangladeshi war movies, women's agency and combat experiences are deliberately denied to perpetuate patriarchal hegemony and national masculinity that otherwise would be at stake. Furthermore, counternarrating the gendered history, as stated by Anna Froula, would threaten war's role as an exclusively male rite of passage.[14]

The Movie *Guerrilla*

Unlike most war movies, Yousuff's *Guerrilla* portrays powerful and agentic women who are at the center of all action. Released in 2011, the film narrates the story of Syeda Bilkis Banu (played by Joya Ahsan), a young woman who lives with her mother-in-law in the old part of Dhaka. The movie opens with Bilkis asking her husband, Hasan Ahmed (played by Ferdous Ahmed), a journalist, not to go out that night, as the situation outside is not safe. Indeed, that night—March 25, 1971—was the darkest night in the history of Bangladesh, when the Pakistani military launched an operation and ruthlessly killed thousands of people in Dhaka city. After her husband goes missing, unlike the stereotypical wife shown in many war movies of Bangladesh, Bilkis not only concentrates on an urban guerrilla movement collaborating with the freedom fighters and continues her work with the publication of the secret news bulletin the *Guerrilla*, a magazine that advocates the voices of the freedom fighters, but also takes an active part in armed resistance. Even amid her day-to-day work as an employee in a bank, she collects funds for the *muktibahini* (freedom fighters) and also uses her office as a base to smuggle money and other resources for the freedom fighters.[15] In every step of her work as an informant and messenger, Bilkis risks her life like her male counterparts. What makes *Guerrilla* exceptional from other wartime movies is that, besides focusing the camera for the first time on women freedom fighters, it also highlights the subaltern and peripheral people—women, religious minorities, and the general populace—who in different ways contributed to the freedom of Bangladesh.

Guerrilla: Reclaiming Female Agency

Guerrilla destabilizes gender stereotypes and presents an alternative narrative where, through the main protagonist, Bilkis, the movie redefines the image of Bengali women. The women of this movie, in fact, represent those Bengali women whose dynamic actions in the '71 war have been forgotten in cultural amnesia. Dismantling the general tendency of perceiving women as weak and incapable of carrying out heroic deeds in war, Bilkis, along with the female characters Shahin and Mrs. Khan, carves out a new emblem of the female body possessing agency. Although agency is an integral part of all human beings, women are typically thought to be lacking agentic quality. As Bronwyn Davies says, agency for women is the exception rather than the rule.[16] To have agency, in Davies's opinion, is to have the ability to act in a way that accomplishes one's goals—that is, the capacity to act, to have control over one's circumstances and surroundings. Verily, then, Bilkis, Shahin, and Mrs. Khan assert their agency by exercising their will to work alongside their male counterparts for the independence of the country. War, in fact, mobilized many women like Bilkis and Shahin to cross the threshold of their private sphere (home) and step into the public space (war). Shahin not only is involved with Bilkis in publishing the *Guerrilla* but also works as a messenger for the freedom fighters. She even risks the life of her baby when she goes to Bilkis's office to collect money and a spool of recorded songs of Altaf Mahmud—who, not to mention, was of great value to the Bangladeshis, as his songs were a source of inspiration for the Bengalis.[17] Shahin uses her baby as a decoy to evade suspicion when carrying out the delivery. Here, choosing to contribute to the freedom of the country by risking her baby's as well her own life is an act of choice and courage that establishes Shahin's agency.

Similarly, from her very first scene until the end of her life in the film, Mrs. Khan demonstrates indomitable courage and agentic qualities. Working as a spy, Mrs. Khan not only provides the freedom fighters with money and necessary supplies for their operations but also works as an informant. Mrs. Khan's air of sophistication and elite status earn her easy access to the circles of high-ranking Pakistani officials, whom she exploits to collect information about future schemes and attacks. She is the one who informs Bilkis of a party where Colonel Taj, Major Sarfaraj, and other high-ranking Pakistani officers, their collaborators, and the local elites would be present. Based on Mrs. Khan's information, Bilkis and the guerrilla fighters contrive to blow up the place; however, after the bomb is implanted, when their plan to leave the party goes awry, Mrs. Khan shows tremendous fortitude and stays behind, knowing quite well that along with all the other people in the room, she too will be blown to pieces the moment the bomb blasts. She sacrifices her life not only to save Bilkis but, most importantly, to bring forth the death of the Pakistani soldiers. Mrs. Khan's female body, which in the typical sense is considered a weak body, registers as a powerful agent with her individualized choice to sacrifice herself for the liberation of the country.

The movie reclaims female agency by accentuating Bilkis's strength and resourcefulness rather than her vulnerability and suffering. Bilkis is not considered a freedom fighter in the conventional sense, as she does not participate in war as a direct combatant, yet her involvement in the fight against the enemy is no less than that of a soldier. Bilkis's petite body and innocent look make her work in espionage easy; as she does not appear to be a threat, and she has easy mobility in delivering grenades and explosives to the freedom fighters. In all these cases, Bilkis—the female body—is anything but weak and fragile; instead, she proves to be as active and fearless as her cofighters. Overturning the entrenched view that women are inherently weak and thus incapable of daring actions, Bilkis, in coalition with the freedom fighters, orchestrates a bomb attack at Colonel Taj's party. At the party, Bilkis uses the sensuality of the female body to divert attention and implant the bomb. Here Bilkis manipulates the spectacle of the female body to gain power and agency.

Until the end of her life, Bilkis exercises her autonomy and uses her female body to assert her agency. As Dhaka becomes unsafe for Bilkis, she leaves the capital and makes her way to her village home at Joleswari in Rangpur to meet her brother. On her way, she encounters one of the members of her brother's guerrilla group, Shiraj, who offers to take her to her brother. When Bilkis comes close to her village, she gets the news that her brother has been slaughtered by the Pakistani army, and his dead body, denied a burial, is left to rot. Although the news devastates Bilkis, she determines to find her brother's body and bury it. After enduring insurmountable difficulties, when she finally finds the dead body with the help of Shiraj, both of them are captured and taken to the Pakistani army camp. There, as was the fate of most women who were taken captive by the Pakistani army, Bilkis becomes the target of sexual assault. However, when Bilkis is on the verge of being raped, she uses her body to bring about her predator's downfall. Ousting Captain Shamshad's desire to make her body a venue for "making Muslim baby," Bilkis, contrary to the women seen in most movies who commit suicide to retain their chastity, retrieves her agency by using the same body to kill him.[18] When the perpetrator attacks her, at one point in the struggle, Bilkis frees herself and, showing the safety pin of a grenade, pulls off the safety lever. Bilkis had got hold of the grenade lying on the table and waited for the right moment to detonate it to kill the person who had slaughtered her brother. She uses her body as a pyre to destroy the captain and the entire army camp. Her smile in the last scene, when she shows the safety pin of the grenade to her perpetrator, indicates her power and victory over her enemy and, symbolically, the victory of Bangladesh. Although many critics view Bilkis's last act as a passive submission to death instead of losing her chastity, I read her self-sacrifice as an act of asserting her free will. Bilkis not only kills Captain Shamshad but also shifts the power structure by exerting her power over him. Thus, the last scene of the movie urges us to revise our perception that a battered and sexually threatened body is vulnerable and powerless.

Guerrilla: A Critique of Gender Stereotypes in Traditional War Narratives

Guerrilla, in this sense, unsettles deeply ingrained social understandings of female bodies as vulnerable and devoid of agency and claims a voice in the national narrative for those women whose voices have been muffled. Sadly enough, as Gayen points out, except for Guerrilla, no film has portrayed women as freedom fighters. Researchers who study the war of Bangladesh have also criticized the way women's participation has been systematically sidetracked. In this regard, it is worth bringing in what Yasmin Saikia has said about the absence of women as active agents in the war narratives of Bangladesh. While discussing women's agency and their contribution to the Liberation War of 1971, Saikia, in her book Women, War, and the Making of Bangladesh: Remembering 1971, propounds that although there is an abundance of narratives that were published as memoirs, novels, district-level reports, and accounts of war crimes in Bangladesh about the war, none of these documents mention women's part in the war; instead, all these documents record the war as a narrative of masculine triumph. Saikia remorsefully writes, "We suddenly find we do not know the Bangladeshi women. Our lens was focused on a single vision thus far. We saw

Bangladeshi women as victims of sexual violence and caregivers. We did not encounter Bangladeshi women as aggressive agents desiring to kill and be killed on behalf of territory and nation."[19]

Truly, women's role as active agents of resistance in the '71 war has been clandestinely overshadowed. Going against the traditional war narratives that prioritize male agency and tend to present women as rape victims or as caregivers, Yousuff in *Guerrilla* revises traditional war narratives to uphold the valor and sacrifice of the female fighters. This subversion, in Yousuff's view, is necessary to expose Bangladeshi women's active participation. In Yousuff's words, "In all the eleven sectors throughout the war, countless women actively took part in the war and sacrificed their lives as fearlessly as their male counterparts. But when it comes to documentation, whether historical or artistic, all we find is an incomplete list of rape victims who, too, were badly treated after the war. Well, then what about the real female fighters? Have we ever paid a tribute to their immense contribution? That's why I've cast a strong female fighter as my protagonist."[20] Recognizing war narratives as culturally constructed and definitely gendered, *Guerrilla*, in a way, attempts to right the wrongs done to women not only by the enemy but also by patriarchy. Thus, contradicting the war movies that so far normalized the stereotypical gender roles, *Guerrilla* explodes the myth of gender barriers. Through her last act of killing her perpetrator, Bilkis reclaims the image of "Bangladeshi women as aggressive agents desiring to kill and be killed on behalf of territory and nation."[21]

Bangladesh war narratives have recorded or represented women's participation in war as serving roles more attuned to domesticity because society is more comfortable with images of women as nurses and volunteers, or more appropriately, as keeping the home fires burning for their returning heroes.[22] One cannot but agree with Goldstein that such practice has resulted in the development of a strategy of war whereby "across culture and through time the selection of men as potential combatants and of women for feminine war support roles has helped shape the war system. In turn the pervasiveness of war in history has influenced gender profoundly."[23] Even if women are mobilized to participate in war during times of national crisis, after the war, they are consigned to their private sphere of the home; they are denied entry into the political arena because "in the post-conflict periods, ideas of national security are redefined in terms of safeguarding the political and social quo, rooted in the practical and symbolic mobilization of gender identities, roles, and bodies, in the service of the new polity."[24] Agency is not only the ability to make autonomous choices and the implementation of the choices and decisions made; agency for women, as social economist Naila Kabeer indicates, is also central to empowerment. Kabeer propounds, "Agency in relation to empowerment, therefore, implies not only actively exercising choice, but also doing this in ways that challenge power relations."[25] Clearly, then, there is a correlation between power and agency. Since representing the female body as active agent and having power to resist threatens male authority and institutionalized patriarchy, every attempt is made to undermine female agency. The strategic exclusion of women's agency in war movies is, thus, a political act that perpetuates patriarchal hegemony. Yousuff's *Guerrilla* provides an important cinematic counterpicture of female bodies by empowering them with agentic qualities so as to ascertain their position in the power structure of the society.

The movie at the same time calls into question the issues of historical representation and historical veracity. Bilkis's journey during those nine months of war is a fictional representation of the journeys that many Bangladeshi women made for the freedom of the country. In this regard, Yousuff says, "I did not try to rewrite history. That is the task of a historian. Although I've taken the historical context of 1971 as my subject, I have tried to turn that milieu into an artwork by manipulating the form of film, but also incorporating in the process the various other forms of poetry and painting. In so doing, I've been very loyal to history."[26] Evidently, Yousuff did not alter history; rather, he has been quite faithful to history in representing women with agentic characteristics. In fact, by incorporating the missing voice of the female body, *Guerrilla* challenges the issues of historical accuracy and politics of representation.

That being said, it is not the case that women who did not participate in direct combat are not warriors. Women who stayed behind and helped in every possible way, whether by supplying arms or working as agents or sheltering the freedom fighters, are very much warriors. They may have limited agency—or, in many cases, no agency at all—but that should not deter us from calling them warriors. The act of staying behind and protecting and taking care of the family amid the chaos and uncertainty of war is also an act of bravery. If we move away from the traditional sense of heroism, we will see that such actions can also be considered courageous. A movie that promoted such an idea of gallantry is *Hangor nodi grenade*, in which the mother, despite losing two of her sons to the war, does not hesitate to hand over to the Pakistani soldiers her intellectually challenged son to save the two young freedom fighters she had hidden in her house. The mother's sacrifice here definitely is an act of bravery, but unfortunately, the number of movies that focus on such a concept is sparse. Only by broadening our concept of heroism and making it more inclusive can we deem these women as heroes and thereby acknowledge their contribution. The true essence of the liberation war can be attained only when women's participation, whether active or passive, is recognized and incorporated in the grand narratives of war.

Conclusion

The cinematic portrayal of male heroism in war movies worldwide has repeatedly given testimony that war, indeed, is gendered. In the grand narratives of war and nation building of Bangladesh, masculinity remains almost uncontested.

In glorifying male fighters, women's participation as active agents in the 1971 war has been eclipsed. Just as it is true that countless men have shown unprecedented bravery in the war, numerous women have also played significant roles. While upholding women's agentic contribution to the freedom of the country, I am in no way downplaying the sacrifices and sufferings of the male freedom fighters. Undoubtedly, the freedom fighters along with the general people of the country have exhibited great courage and resolution. However, by showing the female body with agency, my aim here has been to advocate for the acknowledgment of the female body as capable of heroic deeds and the inclusion of female contributions in the national war narratives. Concurring with Bangladeshi liberation war researcher, columnist, and journalist Afsan Chowdhury, who articulated that "unless we develop a new paradigm of describing what went on in that war, for both men and women, we will only view women's participation as victims and helpless dependents,"[27] I too believe that we need a paradigm shift that calls for a revision of our war narratives—that is, looking back at the narratives and making visible women's agentic contribution. *Guerrilla*, in this sense, opens up the possibility of reinterpreting past events and subverts the known trend of male gallantry by underscoring female agency. In order to establish gender equity, it is imperative to recognize women's agentic characteristics. The movie thus compels us to recognize the female body as a site of power and agency, since the failure to recognize women's agentic role leads to the systematic disempowerment of women.

Notes

1   Anneke Smelik, "What Meets the Eye: An Overview of Feminist Film Theory," in *And the Mirror Cracked: Feminist Cinema and Film Theory* (London: Palgrave Macmillan, 1998), 7.

2   The Bangladesh Liberation War of 1971 was fought between Bangladesh, then East Pakistan, and Pakistan, then West Pakistan.

3   Full name not known.

4   Fahmida Akhter, "Framing Pain as Spectacle: The Aesthetics of Wartime Films of Bangladesh," *Bangladesh Film Archive Journal* 7 (2014): 41–42.

5   Akhter, 42.

6   Kaberi Gayen, "Women, War and Cinema: Construction of Women in the Liberation War Films of Bangladesh," *French Journal for Media Research* 3 (2015): 8.

7   Joshua S. Goldstein, *War and Gender: How Gender Shapes the War System and Vice Versa* (Cambridge: Cambridge University Press, 2001), 371.

8   Gayen, "Women, War and Cinema," 10.

9   Laura Mulvey, "Visual Pleasure and Narrative Cinema," in *Film Theory and Criticism: Introductory Readings*, ed. Leo Braudy and Marshall Cohen (New York: Oxford University Press, 1999), 838.

10 Mulvey, 837.

11 Mulvey, 834.

12 Cynthia Enloe, *Bananas, Beaches and Bases: Making Feminist Sense of International Politics* (Berkeley: University of California Press, 1990), 54.

13 Mulvey, "Visual Pleasure," 836.

14 Anna Froula, "Free a Man to Fight: The Figure of the Female Soldier in World War II Popular Culture," *Journal of War and Culture Studies* 2, no. 2 (2009): 154, http://doi .org/10.1386/jwcs.2.2.153_1.

15 *Muktibahini* refers to Bangladeshi freedom fighters who fought against the Pakistani army to liberate the country.

16 Bronwyn Davies, "The Concept of Agency: A Feminist Poststructuralist Analysis," *Social Analysis: The International Journal of Anthropology* 30 (December 1991): 42, https://www.jstor.org/stable/23164525.

17 Altaf Mahmud was an eminent singer, composer, cultural activist, and freedom fighter of Bangladesh. He raised his voice against the Pakistani aggression by composing inspirational and encouraging songs. During the '71 war, he created a hideout for freedom fighters at his house. However, the hideout was discovered by Pakistani occupation forces, and he was abducted on August 30, 1971.

18 See the last scene in Nasiruddin Yousuff, dir., *Guerrilla* (Bangladesh: Ashirbad Cholochchitra, 2011), available at http://www.youtube.com/watch?v= 7QHR16rEt3E&t=6941s.

19 Yasmin Saikia, *Women, War, and the Making of Bangladesh: Remembering 1971* (Durham, N.C.: Duke University Press, 2011), 188.

20 Rifat Munim, "Guerrilla: The Making of an Epic," *Daily Star* 10, no. 17, May 6, 2011, http://www.thedailystar.net/magazine/2011/05/01/cover.htm.

21 Saikia, *Women, War*, 188.

22 Lorraine Dowler, "Women on the Frontlines: Rethinking War Narratives Post 9/11," *GeoJournal: Social Transformation, Citizenship, and the Right to the City* 58, nos. 2/3 (2002): 161, http://www.jstor.com/stable/41147762.

23 Goldstein, *War and Gender*, 9.

24 Haleh Afshar, "Women and Wars: Some Trajectories towards a Feminist Peace," *Development in Practice* 13, nos. 2/3 (May 2003): 185, http://www.jstor.com/stable/ 40295.

25 Naila Kabeer, "Gender Equality and Women's Empowerment: A Critical Analysis of the Third Millennium Development Goal," *Gender and Development* 13, no. 1 (March 2005): 14.

26 Munim, "Guerrilla."

27 Afsan Chowdhury, "Is It Possible to Include Women in the History of 1971?," bdnews24.com, December 15, 2015, https://opinion.bdnews24.com/2015/12/18/is-it -possible-to-include-women-in-the-history-of-1971/.

Bibliography

Afshar, Haleh. "Women and Wars: Some Trajectories towards a Feminist Peace." *Development in Practice* 13, nos. 2/3 (May 2003): 178–188. http://www.jstor.com/stable/ 40295.

Akhter, Fahmida. "Framing Pain as Spectacle: The Aesthetics of Wartime Films of Bangladesh." *Bangladesh Film Archive Journal* 7 (2014): 35–47.

Chowdhury, Afsan. "Is It Possible to Include Women in the History of 1971?" bdnews24.com, December 15, 2015. https://opinion.bdnews24.com/2015/12/18/is-it-possible-to-include -women-in-the-history-of-1971/.

Davies, Bronwyn. "The Concept of Agency: A Feminist Poststructuralist Analysis." *Social Analysis: The International Journal of Anthropology* 30 (December 1991): 42–53. http:// www.jstor.org/stable/23164525.

Dowler, Lorraine. "Women on the Frontlines: Rethinking War Narratives Post 9/11."

GeoJournal: Social Transformation, Citizenship, and the Right to the City 58, nos. 2/3 (2002): 159–165. http://www.jstor.com/stable/41147762.

Enloe, Cynthia. *Bananas, Beaches and Bases: Making Feminist Sense of International Politics.* Berkeley: University of California Press, 1990.

Froula, Anna. "Free a Man to Fight: The Figure of the Female Soldier in World War II Popular Culture." *Journal of War and Culture Studies* 2, no. 2 (2009): 153–165. http://doi.org/10 .1386/jwcs.2.2.153_1.

Gayen, Kaberi. "Women, War and Cinema: Construction of Women in the Liberation War Films of Bangladesh." *French Journal for Media Research* 3 (2015): 1–25.

Goldstein, Joshua S. *War and Gender: How Gender Shapes the War System and Vice Versa.* Cambridge: Cambridge University Press, 2001.

Kabeer, Naila. "Gender Equality and Women's Empowerment: A Critical Analysis of the Third Millennium Development Goal." *Gender and Development* 13, no. 1 (March 2005): 13–24.

Mulvey, Laura. "Visual Pleasure and Narrative Cinema." In *Film Theory and Criticism: Introductory Readings,* edited by Leo Braudy and Marshall Cohen, 833–844. New York: Oxford University Press, 1999.

Munim, Rifat. "Guerrilla: The Making of an Epic." *Daily Star* 10, no. 17, May 6, 2011. http:// www.thedailystar.net/magazine/2011/05/01/cover.htm.

Saikia, Yasmin. *Women, War, and the Making of Bangladesh: Remembering 1971.* Durham, N.C.: Duke University Press, 2011.

Smelik, Anneke. "What Meets the Eye: An Overview of Feminist Film Theory." In *And the Mirror Cracked: Feminist Cinema and Film Theory,* 7–27. London: Palgrave Macmillan, 1998.

Yousuff, Nasiruddin, dir. *Guerrilla.* Bangladesh: Ashirbad Cholochchitra, 2011. Available at http://www.youtube.com/watch?v=7QHR16rEt3E&t=6941s.

3

Structuring Jineology within Global Feminism

• •

Representations of Kurdish Women Fighters in Western Media

LAVA ASAAD

> Enough, mother!
> I want to be a revolutionary
> All of my friends are there
> I'm the only one
> Shamefully staying on the sidelines
> I don't feel right here
> My soul cries out for the mountains
> Mother, please don't cry!
> —Anastasia Trofimova, *Her War:*
> *Women vs. ISIS*

November 25, 2018, marks the date when Jinwar, the "women's village," finally opened in the Autonomous Administration of North and East Syria, commonly known as the Rojava region in northern Syria. This autonomous commune of women is inherently feminist and ecological, and women from all ethnicities and religions are welcomed. The Democratic Federation of Northern Syria has gained its fair share of international recognition since its establishment in 2012. Praised for its secularism, democracy, and gender equality, the federation models its governing policies in the wake of the Syrian civil war on basis of inclusivity in all its spheres. Jinwar is an offshoot initiative of this de facto self-governing region, implanted to be a safe haven for women who survived ISIS and those who escaped repressive gender traditions in the region. While the general, although scant, reaction to the existence of this commune is usually expressed with bafflement and astonishment, these sentiments stem from a lack of understanding of the revolutionary ideological components of the long-established Kurdish militant and political movement headed by the Partiya Karkerên Kurdistanê (PKK; Kurdistan Workers' Party). Admittedly, Western media have followed closely the events in northern Syria since the onset of the Arab Spring and the subsequent emergence of ISIS. Major headlines focus on and glorify Kurdish fighters led by the armed forces of Rojava, divided into the Yekîneyên Parastina Gel (YPG; People's Protection Unit), which mostly consists of men, and the Yekîneyên Parastina Jin (YPJ; Women's Protection Unit), an all-women battalion of mostly Kurdish members. While both these units in Syria are fairly nascent—established around 2011—they are part of the overarching PKK centered in Turkey and Iraqi Kurdistan. Yet these units, and the YPJ more specifically, have succeeded in grabbing much-deserved international attention as they battle a just war in freeing their territory, and the world, from a brutal terrorist group. The female fighters have swept the news and magazine headlines as the West continues to be mesmerized by them, since they defy every expectation and stereotype of Middle Eastern women. The existing scholarship on these Amazonian women is scarce but manages to unveil some of the intricacies of this female militia group. In this chapter, I continue the conversation in an attempt to demystify these fighters and paint them instead as ordinary women who lived through unordinary circumstances that pushed them to bear arms against multiple enemies, although the current one happens to be an Islamist fundamentalist group. Contextualizing the intellectual and ideological aspects of their struggle rather than fixating on their extraordinary physical stamina, as shown in a latter section of this chapter, yields a better understanding of their motivations for joining the fight. Thus, this chapter focuses on analyzing the ways in which these women have been portrayed in documentaries produced in the West. In so doing, I first outline the premise of Jineology, "women's science," into which these female fighters are indoctrinated in addition to their combat training, which most documentaries about these fighters circle around.

The hypervisibility of these female fighters in the media in the last decade coincides with the mobilization of the threat of the Islamic State in the West. Arguably, the fascination with these women will decline once the terrorist threat is contained, which ultimately ignores the fact that ISIS is one of the various enemies the PKK and the YPJ are fighting against. Providing a holistic understating of the "Kurdish question" and the enlistment of female fighters should be of substantial importance to feminist theory, an area of study that has not completely endorsed the ways in which Kurdish women reshape global feminism. The militarized involvement of these women problematizes their cause in feminist studies, which regards combat primarily as stemming from a masculinist tendency to solve a crisis and considers the military institution as antithetical to feminism. For example, in her seminal book on women in the military, *Maneuvers: The International Politics of Militarizing Women's Lives*, Cynthia Enloe sustains the argument that even when women's role is represented as essential in the military, they are still being marginalized, or at best, they are included "to boost morale, to provide comfort during and after wars, to reproduce the next generation of soldiers, to serve as symbols of a homeland worth risking one's life for, to replace men when the pool for suitable male recruits is low."[1] On the other hand, Ilene Rose Fein, in *Citizenship Rites: Feminist Soldiers and Feminist Antimilitarist*, upholds the argument that joining the military is a "women's right and even responsibility to perform martial service, because the military is the *sine qua non* of full citizenship and thus, equality."[2] Generally, there are nuances in how feminist scholarship approaches women in the military, ranging from the right to fight to speculations on whether increasing women's participation in a male-dominated institution really has any effect on women's rights in society as a whole. Nonetheless, there is a collective consensus that brushing off the military as a nonwoman space and falling back to the assumption of women being peacekeepers disregards women's different cultural, political, and historical experiences. In this case, Kurdish women consider joining the nonstate militia, as it offers them emancipatory opportunities on personal and political levels. Recruiting women into the military is yet another controversial angle in the current scholarship. Reed M. Wood provides an explanation in his book *Female Fighters: Why Rebel Groups Recruit Women for War* for why recruiting women can be beneficial for the militia's cause, arguing that militant groups with Marxist leanings tend to be more encompassing of female fighters, as the end result of their political aspirations is to also change social hierarchies. Wood further shows how there are other tactical reasons behind recruiting women; for instance, it enables "domestic and international resources mobilization," and "the novelty and the salience of female fighters increase audience attention to the group and its goals."[3] Indubitably, the PKK has strong Marxists foundations, and the YPJ has certainly arrested the world's attention due to the mass presence of women. Yet to primarily conclude that the PKK and the YPJ increasingly work on recruiting women for international attention is inaccurate and incomplete.

Women's role in the PKK is more encompassing and deeply rooted in a philosophical, intellectual, and historical understanding of women, painstakingly written about by the PKK founding member, Abdullah Öcalan, who is now serving a life sentence in a Turkish prison since 1999. In several of his writings, Öcalan outlines the importance of liberating women and describes the Kurdish national revolution as a women's revolution. Before and during his time in prison, Öcalan witnessed the pivotal role of Kurdish women, and thus, he continued to prolifically publish from prison, which strengthened the ideological establishment of the Kurdish movement as a whole. Öcalan, influenced by Murray Bookchin, unabashedly denounces the idea of a nation-state, considering it to be "a colony of the capital." He says fighting for a separate Kurdish nation-state will only serve the bourgeoisie, not the common people.[4] Instead, he reorients the goals of the PKK to be about establishing a "democratic confederalism," which he defines to be "multi-cultural, anti-monopolistic, and consensus-oriented. Ecology and feminism are central pillars."[5] Democracy for Öcalan entails overturning the existing hierarchies that keep women "as the oldest colonized group."[6] Öcalan's writings paved the way for what is known as Jineology (Kurdish: *Jineolojî*), translated as "women's science," which lays bare the ideological underpinnings of the PKK and the reason why this movement endorses the woman question at the center of its teachings. It is also the reason why the motto "Jin, Jiyan, Azadi!" came to be one of the fundamental mottos for the Kurdish female movement, which translates to "Woman, Life, Freedom!" Essentially, the goal of empowering women is not to separate them from their male counterparts but rather to deconstruct the root cause that denigrates women and esteems men. The process of building a democratic society starts with guaranteeing women's liberation first.

Jineology celebrates the myriad local experiences of Kurdish women and is indebted to feminism in promoting gender equity. Yet Jineology takes a step further "to pursue mechanisms of action in order to implement social freedom and equality."[7] Involvement in the military is something a feminist might label as radical or antipeacemaking; for the Kurdish female guerrillas, however, it presents a different story. While Öcalan's writings and his views on Jineology are taught in the Rojava region as exemplary models for society building, the Kurdish female fighter is the prime encapsulation of this ideology. In "Mother, Politician, and Guerilla: The Emergence of a New Political Imagination in Kurdistan through Women's Bodies and Speech," Nazan Üstündağ studies the role of the female Kurdish guerrilla who has separated herself from family, defined by Öcalan as "man's small state."[8] One of the fundamental creeds in the organization is to prohibit sexual relationships, which transform these guerrilla women "into a collectivity inassimilable to the laws of family, tribe, and kinship." The body of this female guerrilla is the quintessential example of fighting for the movement and bringing social justice. The mysterious reality of this guerrilla, outside the reach of the state, further elevates her status, which has become "omnipresent in Kurdistan life."[9]

The entrenchment of Jineology within the Kurdish movement was not entirely indebted to Öcalan's firm beliefs about women's role. Sakine Cansiz, known as Kurdish Rosa Luxemburg, was one of the cofounders of the PKK in the 1970s. Cansiz (her code name was Sara) worked on regimenting female groups who dedicated their lives to the revolution until she was assassinated in Paris in 2013 by Turkey's Secret Services. While in a Turkish prison (1979–1991), she worked on documenting her life events in establishing the PKK. In her memoir, *Sara: My Whole Life Was a Struggle*, Cansiz writes about how she developed a theoretical and ideological consciousness as a party member and shares her advice on how to be the ideal party member: "To be a Kurdistan Revolutionary was of a whole different order. . . . First one must undergo a mental enlightenment, then embody it more and more in life."[10] The diligent process of undergoing transformation on the intellectual level is a goal embraced by the current Kurdish female fighters in Syria, where their training necessitates an ideological indoctrination before physical training ensues. Cansiz's feminist and Marxist principles revolutionized women's role, and the major goal of the Kurdish movement was "to establish women's equality as a norm within civil society as well as on the battlefield."[11] Because of her encompassing beliefs, the movement was able to attract militants from all sects of the society, where previously it was dominated by more-educated members. Cansiz's pioneer role influenced Kurdish women who would not remain silent under the yoke of patriarchy.

The female Kurdish soldiers of today idealize many feminist leaders in the movement like Cansiz who impacted the shape of resistance ever since the establishment of the Kurdish army in 1992.[12] As a result, Kurdish women in the PKK have not necessarily always functioned under male leadership. Since 1986, women leaders created several organizations and parties, which ultimately led to establishing the Yekitiya Jinen Azad a Kurdistan (YJAK; Free Women of Kurdistan Troops), an entity that was announced by the first women's congress in 1995, which consisted of and was commanded by women fighters.[13] Forming this separate unit was necessary for many reasons, but most importantly, it was to erase gender and class differences between male and female combatants. As mentioned previously, pioneer members of the party were highly educated, while those who joined later were less so due to class differences. Thus, founding a unit solely for women fighters guaranteed that these participants would not be deficient in comparison to members who were already cultivated in Marxist and socialist teachings. The unit, henceforth, worked on establishing unity among its women while also bolstering equal gender and class consciousness.[14] This process of unlearning social and gender inequalities necessitated distributing works by famous feminists from similarly persecuted groups, like bell hooks; thus, to situate the activism of Kurdish women within a feminist context would make them part of third-wave feminism and its reliance on the intersectionality of oppression.[15] These efforts culminated in transforming Jineology into an evolving theory that changes with women's reality. Öcalan opines that Jineology is more comprehensive than feminism and that the latter has several limitations like "not having a strong organizational base; inability to develop its philosophy to the full; and difficulties relating to a militant woman's movement."[16] Additionally, Öcalan emphasizes the importance of women being active in political life because "if success is not attained politically, no other achievement will be permanent."[17] Jineology, then, obliges taking women as the point of departure instead of continuing to deem men as the center of political affairs. These credos definitely influence how male and female soldiers interact, where male leadership and soldiers consider the female soldiers to be "sisters" and henceforth consider sexuality, as mentioned earlier, not to be a physical marker of identity. Assuredly, this extreme defeminization is not in favor of being more masculine; rather, the general goal of the movement is to initiate a holistic social and political change. In fact, by becoming guerrillas, Kurdish women make "the hegemonic notions of masculinity and femininity confusing."[18] In *Blood and Belief: The PKK and the Kurdish Fight for Independence*, Aliza Marcus writes about how the presence of women in the army at the onset of the PKK awakened both men and women to the possibility of transforming gender expectations: "Kurdish villagers often were surprised to discover women among the gun-toting rebels who descended on the villages at night to make propaganda and collect supplies. Aysel Curukkaya, who rejoined the rebels in 1986 after her release from prison, recalled that village women could not believe another woman had gone to the mountains to fight. One young girl insisted on running her hands under Curukkaya's shirt and screamed in surprise when she realized Curukkaya really had breasts. Men, on the other hand, were shamed into action when they realized that women also were fighting."[19]

This initial encounter with a newly independent woman who is a vital member of the party but who is also equally capable of protecting the movement and its ideologies inspired many new recruits to join the army. The road to gender, social, and political emancipation for these female fighters continues to face obstacles, as Middle Eastern social norms are highly patriarchal, which pushes these women to first challenge the norms in their families to finally achieve democratic confederalism, where women's perspective is at the center. While the increasing number of female recruits in the army challenges major stereotypes about women, the hegemonic structure of the society is still rooted in a patriarchal interpretation of women, honor, and homeland and the role of men in protecting them. Consequently, having women join the army does not necessarily imply that emancipation is achieved, especially because "the strict ban on sexual relationships reassured Kurdish families that the PKK would protect their sons' and daughters' honor."[20] This conception was limited to earlier years of forming the PKK, whereas now this ban has been interpreted by Öcalan as women detaching themselves from the influence of men and instead building empowering relationships with one another. Kurdish women continue to actively participate in dismantling man's central role; the turning point in the late 1990s was to equally constitute women's organizations in all sectors. These autonomous organizations grew bolder in decentering men's roles as they closely followed Öcalan's harsh criticism of old Kurdistan, endorsing instead his revolutionary feminist ideologies.

As this chapter has proven thus far, the increasing number of Kurdish female guerrillas is ideologically and ethically predicated on the changing political situations in their areas. The long-established teachings of Öcalan, Cansiz, and other female members of the PKK have allowed for the inclusivity of women not only on the battle ground but also in the decision-making process in all sectors. Yet this rich and complex history of Jineology and the reasons behind motivating women to join the fight are not always priorities in Western-produced documentaries. ISIS's threat has caused a peak in Western media coverage of the Peshmerga in Iraq and the YPG and YPJ in Syria. The fascination with Kurdish female fighters has seeped into the Western culture even beyond media outlets. It should be no surprise, then, that a clothing company like H&M monopolizes these women by designing a khaki jumpsuit similar to what YPJ female fighters would wear, which the company later apologized for. While recent scholarship has addressed the misrepresentation of women in Western newspapers and magazines, it has not focused on how these women are portrayed in documentaries. The general consensus among scholars is that the media coverage of these women has an orientalizing tone. The attention tends to unabashedly hypervisualize the gender of these fighters with extreme astonishment that these assumingly oppressed women would be capable of flipping stereotypes; however, the main attention "belligerently centers their identities as women, in the most superficial and essentialist sense of the category, rather than addressing the more important questions relating to the details of their military incursions or the motivations for their action: elements which would acknowledge the agency underwriting the decision to risk one's life."[21] Not acknowledging the agentic fighter further solidifies stereotypes about these women as victims who join the struggle to topple their patriarchal society. While the patriarchal nature of the area is undoubtedly present, to rebuff the multiple reasons why these women become soldiers and focus mainly on gender roles is incongruous to the theoretical and the philosophical underpinning of the Kurdish movement. To write about their struggle as emitting from "emancipatory motives alone reinforce[s] the stereotypes of victimhood and depreciate female fighters' political agency."[22] Most media outlets have objectified these female soldiers and praised their feminine beauty, even referring to one of the martyrs who died fighting ISIS as the "Angelina Jolie of Kurdistan."[23] In sensationalizing female soldiers, media outlets continue to glamorize their role as women soldiers fighting a brutal group like ISIS, a complete anathema to everything that the female guerrilla stands for. Media outlets label these women as a "novel phenomenon," which intentionally "cheapen[s] a legitimate struggle by projecting their bizarre orientalist fantasies on it."[24] These "badass" women are sensationalized as they march on with their combat gear, brightly colored head wraps, and long braided hair.

While news outlet coverage has been myopic and orientalist, it is not entirely the same case with documentaries. Admittedly, the increase of documentary series on these women also coincides with the rising threat of ISIS, yet the representation oscillates between providing a holistic understanding of these women, explaining Jineology and why they fight, and falling back on the orientalist narrative of Kurdish women transforming themselves from victims to heroines. The number of works will most likely be on the rise as Kurdish women soldiers become more mainstream and less of an anomaly. Documentary, as a genre, offers a unique and more nuanced presentation of activism. Thomas Waugh's seminal book, *"Show Us Life": Toward a History and Aesthetics of the Committed Documentary*, dives into exploring the ways through which documentary makers seek, and thereby commit, to change the status quo through filming those who initiate any type of revolution and resistance. Committed documentary, as Waugh writes, promotes "a specific ideological undertaking, a declaration of solidarity with the goal of radical socio-political transformation" and by doing so, these documentaries endorse "a certain political positioning: activism, or intervention in the process of change itself" whereby the production itself makes the statement of raising awareness and disseminating the filmed message.[25] One might repudiate this act of intervention as being part of a white man's mission with a camera. Nevertheless, the nuances in some productions have saved this intervention from falling into the pitfall of rehashing the savior complex.

The savior complex does make its way through *Fear Us Women* (2017), a documentary following the journey of a Canadian civilian, Hanna Bohman, who decided to join the YPJ as a "volunteer battling ISIS and liberating women in Syria." While the YPJ is renowned for being an all-Kurdish women's army, more Arabs and Western volunteers have joined its ranks. *Fear Us Women* is perorating the same stereotype of Middle Eastern women in need of saving, as seen on the documentary's website: "Hanna's harrowing journey reveals a revolution bigger than the fight against ISIS: a fight for equality and women's liberation in the Middle East. As her status as a former model spreads to the enemy, Hanna becomes a wanted target."[26] Ignoring the deeply ideological war that the women in YPJ are waging reaffirms a neocolonial stance. Chandra Talpade Mohanty elaborates on discursive colonialism, which works on "producing/re-presenting a composite, singular 'Third World Woman'—an image which appears arbitrarily constructed, but nevertheless carries with it the authorizing signature of Western humanist discourse."[27] In the documentary, Hanna highlights the good fortune she has and her privileged position of growing up in a safe country; therefore, she has a responsibility to disseminate liberalism and democracy, all within a "Western humanist discourse." The fight, Hanna acknowledges, is to bring "women's rights to the Middle East," a message that fails to represent the complexities of the movement and why Kurdish women choose to join the army. Situating and analyzing the struggle as purely gender based devalues the intersectionality of oppression that an average Kurdish woman operates within. The documentary is rife with perspectives that escalate the difference between the "West and the Rest." For example, Hanna says, "I believe they deserve to be as free as I am in my country. . . . They are trying to build something that we've taken for granted."[28] The colonial pattern of erasing the local and multifarious experiences of Kurdish women in favor of re-creating a homogenous image of the oppressed women of the Middle East expands the chasm between Hanna's goals and the YPS's overall mission.

Other documentaries also accentuate the feminist leanings of the YPJ, such as *Our Allies: The Kurdish Women* (2017), directed by Anders Hammer, and *Her War: Women vs. ISIS* (2015), directed by Anastasia Trofimova.[29] The directors here are encapsulating the movement as a novel idea, unrelated to the overarching lineage to the PKK, and thus only explaining the establishment of the YPJ to counteract the threat of the increasing influence of the fundamentalist Islamist groups. All these works can be labeled as committed documentaries, as they seek to implement change by documenting the lives of extraordinary female guerrillas. *Our Allies* is a production of Field of Vision, which sponsors and encourages the work of short-term productions, as it "allows filmmakers to respond quickly, take creative risks, reach audiences worldwide, explore new ways of storytelling, and make films with a faster production cycle."[30] The documentary reiterates the YPJ's goals for standing against ISIS. However, it also expands the conversation to include a controversial subject. The PKK has been listed as a terrorist group by the United States, European Union, and NATO for the guerrilla attacks it carried out in Turkey. A commander in the documentary explains how the YPJ aspires to be as big of a movement as the PKK, disagreeing that it is a terrorist movement while also touching upon the shared goals between the two groups. In *Her War*, Trofimova takes a different lane as the documentary follows new recruits in the training camps, diving deeper into why women choose to join the fight.[31] "We saw women in YPJ uniform in town. I was impressed and wanted to join them," says one of the new female recruits, emphasizing that this is "a revolution within a revolution." Additionally, *Her War* highlights class inequality as a main motivator for women joining the fight. As shown previously, in Cansiz's memoir, the movement since the 1980s opened its arms to women who were less educated and hence more impacted by patriarchy. As one commander in the documentary expresses her view, "Those who serve are mostly from poor families. Rich families do other things while poor families send their children to serve the motherland. They fight for a better future . . . they run away from the dirt of society." The intersectional nature of oppression necessitates taking into consideration economic inequity that leaves women even more vulnerable.

There is yet another aspect of filming Kurdish women soldiers that individualizes the movement by following one fighter's journey. *Gulistan: Land of Roses* (2016), directed by Zayne Akyol, and *Commander Arian: A Story of Women, War and Freedom* (2018), directed by Alba Sotorra, adopt the heroine-creation technique that allows viewers to identify with these fighters instead of representing the army as one group of Amazonian women. Cula documents Commander Arian's journey as she leads both female and male units against ISIS in

Syria. Shot multiple times in an ambush and having to stay in a wounded shelter, the documentary humanizes women like Arian who face death and sometimes approach the point of no return. Arian's perspective on the fight centers on an existential drive: "If you are attacked, you have to protect yourself." Her understanding of women's freedom is inseparable from a political view, where freeing Kobane, her city, is essential in eradicating the root cause of women's oppression as well. As a military feminist, Arian's point of view does not have peace-making clichés at its core: "People say we women are taking up arms to make war, but if you are attacked, raped, and cut into pieces, why don't you kill them before they kill you?" As a commander, Arian trains female fighters in their self-worth before allowing them to know how to use weaponry. For her, the struggle for freedom has not been tied to fighting ISIS only, and it will continue long after ISIS disappears: "I always dreamt of becoming a female guerrilla. When I was in the fourth grade, a girl was kidnapped from my neighborhood. They raped her, and she got pregnant. She was twelve or thirteen years old. When her family got her back and realized she was pregnant, they killed her. . . . I wanted to do something to change things. When the revolution started, I saw more women were joining too. They took up arms to fight for freedom."[32] Arian's denouncement of honor killing is echoed in Öcalan's own critique of the Middle Eastern man: "Woman is made to pay for the obliteration of society's honor. Loss of masculinity is taken out on woman. Except for woman's honor, the Kurdish male, who has lost both moral and political strength, has no other area left to prove his power or powerlessness."[33] The Kurdish female fighter finds refuge in the PKK and the YPJ, a place for women who dedicate their lives to righting wrongs and defending those who stay behind. Arian says, "When I rescue a woman that feels defeated—a weak, vulnerable, and humble woman—for me, that is freedom."

While Cula endorses committed documentary ideals that focus on how stereotypical portrayals of gender roles are challenged, Akyol, born in Turkey to Kurdish parents who later escaped to Canada, includes the larger movement, the PKK, which gave women the freedom to deconstruct gender roles and lead the fight. Akyol's documentary is a tribute to a Kurdish activist she had known in Montreal who left to join the women's unit of the PKK.[34] Unable to find her, Akyol redirects her attention to capture the lives and activism of women like Gulistan, to have the documentary become an "homage to feminine heroism."[35] The documentary is a collage of women; each one opens up about her choice and the challenges she faced to join the PKK. However, the senior commander, Sozdar, is the essence of Jineology that the PKK and YPJ potently unveil. Sozdar feminizes war, her body an extension of the land where wars are waged, as a close-up shot follows her hand pulling her hair away from her face to show a scar. "I wish it ran across my cheek," she says. "I think it would be more beautiful." Akyol purposefully alternates between shots of the group discussing the most effective and least heavy pocket knives or the most effective and dangerous bomb—be it Russian or American made, some used by Saddam—and shots of the female fighters helping one another put nettle on their hair "to look younger before they head to Sinjar" to liberate the area from ISIS. This is a woman's war, the documentary seems to suggest, where women do not have to change themselves to be more masculine and where there is no need to hide femininity to be a more "efficient" fighter. After all, ISIS soldiers firmly believe that being killed by a woman will keep them from entering heaven. Additionally, in order to dispel Western ideas of the PKK as a terrorist movement, the documentary closely follows Sozdar and other commanders as they lecture new recruits on the importance of not only using weapons, as they serve political and ideological purposes, but also being fully versed in Öcalan's teachings. "Comrades, it's training that matters above all else. Those who aren't interested in training but only in war have misunderstood the PKK. In fact, the PKK movement fights back through education. It wages a war that is ideological, political, moral, and philosophical," Sozdar states. This egalitarian radical activism comes as a necessity to put a stop to other extremist radicalizations of fundamentalist groups in the region.

All these documentaries have wholeheartedly praised the valiance of these women. While not all of them present the complete picture behind why these guerrillas since the 1980s have dedicated their lives to the movement, the sheer number of representations thus far is a hopeful indication that Western media will grow to acknowledge the political and ideological paradigms and aspirations of these women. The documentary, as a genre, is the closest form of committed engagement with insurgent groups that diligently strive to democratize and proliferate their egalitarian leanings. It is still exhilarating to see how these women are forcibly making their way into Western pop culture. *Girls of the Sun* (2018), a French film directed by Eva Husson, dramatizes a woman-led battalion in Kurdistan fighting the extremists. *Sisters in Arms* (2019) is yet another French film, directed by Caroline Fourest, which shows how two French women join the women's unit and form a close relationship with a female Yazidi survivor. *No Man's Land* (2010) is a TV series that dramatizes the furiousness of YPJ women. More recently, Hillary and Chelsea Clinton are developing a TV series based on Gayle Tzemach Lemmon's book *The Daughters of Kobani: A Story of Rebellion, Courage, and Justice*. The list of titles is growing, and a full understanding of these women will inevitably entail making Jineology an important theoretical lens in global feminist studies. The core principle of Kurdish feminism lies in rethinking what a society can look like, to what degree can women be independent, and the irrevocable importance of sociopolitical freedom before a more just standard for women proceeds.

Jinwar, the democratically led women's village, is a testimony to the ideals of the Kurdish movement and evidence that the main ideologies of Jineology can be actualized. While the jihadists and their threats have been almost eradicated in the region, another threat comes to the scene and vows to suppress what this movement has successfully built. On October 9, 2020, a Turkish-led attack forced these women to leave Jinwar after days of artillery shelling and bombing. Nevertheless, these women returned to the destroyed village and pledged to rebuild it. "Let's defend each other against the attacks of the Turkish state and all other forms of patriarchal violence and oppression," these women assert.[36] Feminist principles in the region will continue to disturb any embedded oppression that works on silencing civilians and depriving them of their human rights. Although current representations of these warrior women capture their courage in the face of ISIS, tomorrow brings another enemy, and there is hope that Western media will continue to fairly portray these women, even if some of the representations are skewed or incomplete.

Notes

1 Cynthia Enloe, *Maneuvers: The International Politics of Militarizing Women's Lives* (Berkeley: University of California Press, 2000), 44.
2 Rose Fein, *Citizenship Rites: Feminist Soldiers and Feminist Antimilitarists* (New York: New York University Press, 2000), 1.
3 Reed M. Wood, *Female Fighters: Why Rebel Groups Recruit Women for War* (New York: Columbia University Press, 2019), 6.
4 Abdullah Öcalan, *Democratic Confederalism* (London: Transmedia, 2011), 13.
5 Öcalan, 21.
6 Abdullah Öcalan, *Liberating Life: Woman's Revolution* (London: Transmedia, 2013), 56.
7 Valentina Dean, "Kurdish Female Fighters: The Western Depiction of YPJ Combatants in Rojava," *Glocalism: Journal of Culture, Politics and Innovation* 1 (2019): 9, https://doi.org/10.12893/gjcpi.2019.1.7.
8 Öcalan, *Liberating Life*, 35.
9 Nazan Üstündağ, "Mother, Politician, and Guerilla: The Emergence of a New Political Imagination in Kurdistan through Women's Bodies and Speech," *Differences* 30, no. 2 (2019): 133, https://doi.org/10.1215/10407391-7736077.
10 Sakine Cansiz, *Sara: My Whole Life Was a Struggle*, trans. Janet Biehl (London: Pluto Press, 2018), 223.
11 SAMINT, "Sakine Cansiz's Double Struggle: Abolition of Patriarchy and Autonomy of Kurdistan," trans. Francine Sporenda, Révolution Féministe, August 23, 2016, https://revolutionfeministe.wordpress.com/2016/08/23/sakine-cansizs-double -struggle-abolition-of-patriarchy-autonomy-of-kurdistan/.
12 SAMINT.
13 Nadje Al-Ali and Latif Tas, "Reconsidering Nationalism and Feminism: The Kurdish Political Movement in Turkey," *Nations and Nationalism* 24, no. 2 (2018): 459, https://doi.org/10.1111/nana.12383.
14 Dean, "Kurdish Female Fighters," 6.
15 Ömer Çaha, "The Kurdish Women's Movement: A Third-Wave Feminism within the Turkish Context," *Turkish Studies* 12, no. 3 (2011): 436, https://doi.org/10.1080/14683849.2011.604211.
16 Öcalan, *Liberating Life*, 55.
17 Öcalan, 54.
18 Bruna Ferreira and Vinícius Santiago, "The Core of Resistance: Recognizing Intersectional Struggle in the Kurdish Women's Movement," *Contexto Internacional* 40, no. 3 (2018): 493, http://dx.doi.org/10.1590/S0102-8529.2018400300004.

19   Aliza Marcus, *Blood and Belief: The PKK and the Kurdish Fight for Independence* (New York: New York University Press, 2007), 172.

20   Novellis Andrea, "The Rise of Feminism in the PKK: Ideology or Strategy?," *Zanj: The Journal of Critical Global South Studies* 2, no. 1 (2018): 119, https://doi.org/10 .13169/zanjglobsoutstud.2.1.0115.

21   Arianne Shahvisi, "Beyond Orientalism: Exploring the Distinctive Feminism of Democratic Confederalism in Rojava," *Geopolitics* 26, no. 4 (2018): 3, https://doi.org/ 10.1080/14650045.2018.1554564.

22   Pinar Tank, "Kurdish Women in Rojava: From Resistance to Reconstruction," *Die Welt des Islams* 57, no. 3 (2017): 408–409, https://doi.org/10.1163/15700607 -05734p07.

23   Jiyar Gol, "Kurdish 'Angelina Jolie' Devalued by Media Hype," BBC, September 12, 2016, https://www.bbc.com/news/world-middle-east-37337908.

24   Dilar Dirik, "Western Fascination with 'Badass' Kurdish Women," Aljazeera, October 29, 2014, https://www.aljazeera.com/opinions/2014/10/29/western-fascination -with-badass-kurdish-women.

25   Thomas Waugh, introduction to *"Show Us Life": Toward a History and Aesthetics of the Committed Documentary*, ed. Thomas Waugh (Metuchen, N.J.: Scarecrow Press, 1984), xiv.

26   "Synopsis," Fear Us Women, accessed June 20, 2021, https://fearuswomen.com/.

27   Chandra Talpade Mohanty, "Under Western Eyes: Feminist Scholarship and Colonial Discourses," *boundary 2* 12/13 (1984): 334–335, https://doi.org/10.2307/302821.

28   David Darg, dir., *Fear Us Women* (Los Angeles: Ryot Films, 2017).

29   Anders Hammer, dir., *Our Allies: The Kurdish Women* (New York: Field of Vision, 2017); Anastasia Trofimova, dir., *Her War: Women vs. ISIS* (Moscow: RT Channel, 2015).

30   "Our Allies: The Foreigners," Field of Vision, August 7, 2017, https://www.youtube .com/watch?v=3p3uRL6nHYk.

31   Trofimova, *Her War*.

32   Alba Sotorra, dir., *Commander Arian: A Story of Women, War and Freedom* (New York: DOC NYC, 2018).

33   Öcalan, *Liberating Life*, 40.

34   Zaynê Akyol, dir., *Gulistan: Land of Roses* (Montreal: Périphéria, 2016).

35   Kate Kennelly, "Movie Review: *Gulistan: Land of Roses*," ECU Film Festival, 2016, https://www.ecufilmfestival.com/movie-review-gulistan/.

36   Jessica Roy, "This Women-Only Village Was Built to Be a Feminist Utopia. Now It's under Threat," Elle, November 5, 2019, https://www.elle.com/culture/career-politics/ a29700409/jinwar-all-women-village-syria-kurdistan/.

Bibliography

Akyol, Zaynê, dir. *Gulistan: Land of Roses*. Montreal: Périphéria, 2016.

Al-Ali, Nadje, and Latif Tas. "Reconsidering Nationalism and Feminism: The Kurdish Political Movement in Turkey." *Nations and Nationalism* 24, no. 2 (2018): 453–473. https://doi.org/ 10.1111/nana.12383.

Andrea, Novellis. "The Rise of Feminism in the PKK: Ideology or Strategy?" *Zanj: The Journal of Critical Global South Studies* 2, no. 1 (2018): 115–133. https://doi.org/10.13169/ zanjglobsoutstud.2.1.0115.

Çaha, Ömer. "The Kurdish Women's Movement: A Third-Wave Feminism within the Turkish Context." *Turkish Studies* 12, no. 3 (2011): 435–449. https://doi.org/10.1080/14683849.2011.604211.

Cansiz, Sakine. *Sara: My Whole Life Was a Struggle*. Translated by Janet Biehl. London: Pluto Press, 2018.

Darg, David, dir. *Fear Us Women*. Los Angeles: Ryot Films, 2017.

Dean, Valentina. "Kurdish Female Fighters: The Western Depiction of YPJ Combatants in Rojava." *Glocalism: Journal of Culture, Politics and Innovation* 1 (2019): 1–29. https://doi .org/10.12893/gjcpi.2019.1.7.

Dirik, Dilar. "Western Fascination with 'Badass' Kurdish Women." Aljazeera, October 29, 2014. https://www.aljazeera.com/opinions/2014/10/29/western-fascination-with-badass -kurdish-women.

Enloe, Cynthia. *Maneuvers: The International Politics of Militarizing Women's Lives*. Berkeley: University of California Press, 2000.

Fein, Rose. *Citizenship Rites: Feminist Soldiers and Feminist Antimilitarists*. New York: New York University Press, 2000.

Ferreira, Bruna, and Vinícius Santiago. "The Core of Resistance: Recognizing Intersectional Struggle in the Kurdish Women's Movement." *Contexto Internacional* 40, no. 3 (2018): 479–500. http://dx.doi.org/10.1590/S0102-8529.2018400300004.

Gol, Jiyar. "Kurdish 'Angelina Jolie' Devalued by Media Hype." BBC, September 12, 2016. https://www.bbc.com/news/world-middle-east-37337908.

Hammer, Anders, dir. *Our Allies: The Kurdish Women*. New York: Field of Vision, 2017.

Kennelly, Kate. "Movie Review: *Gulistan: Land of Roses*." ECU Film Festival, 2016. https:// www.ecufilmfestival.com/movie-review-gulistan/.

Marcus, Aliza. *Blood and Belief: The PKK and the Kurdish Fight for Independence*. New York: New York University Press, 2007.

Mohanty, Chandra Talpade. "Under Western Eyes: Feminist Scholarship and Colonial Discourses." *Boundary 2* 12/13 (1984): 333–358. https://doi.org/10.2307/302821.

Öcalan, Abdullah. *Democratic Confederalism*. London: Transmedia, 2011.

———. *Liberating Life: Woman's Revolution*. London: Transmedia, 2013.

Roy, Jessica. "This Women-Only Village Was Built to Be a Feminist Utopia. Now It's under Threat." Elle, November 5, 2019. https://www.elle.com/culture/career-politics/ a29700409/jinwar-all-women-village-syria-kurdistan/.

SAMINT. "Sakine Cansiz's Double Struggle: Abolition of Patriarchy and Autonomy of Kurdistan." Translated by Francine Sporenda. Révolution Féministe, August 23, 2016. https:// revolutionfeministe.wordpress.com/2016/08/23/sakine-cansizs-double-struggle-abolition -of-patriarchy-autonomy-of-kurdistan/.

Shahvisi, Arianne. "Beyond Orientalism: Exploring the Distinctive Feminism of Democratic Confederalism in Rojava." *Geopolitics* 26, no. 4 (2018): 1–26. https://doi.org/10.1080/ 14650045.2018.1554564.

Sotorra, Alba, dir. *Commander Arian: A Story of Women, War and Freedom*. New York: DOC NYC, 2018.

Tank, Pinar. "Kurdish Women in Rojava: From Resistance to Reconstruction." *Die Welt des Islams* 57, no. 3 (2017): 404–428. https://doi.org/10.1163/15700607-05734p07.

Trofimova, Anastasia, dir. *Her War: Women vs. ISIS*. Moscow: RT Channel, 2015.

Üstündağ, Nazan. "Mother, Politician, and Guerilla: The Emergence of a New Political Imagination in Kurdistan through Women's Bodies and Speech." *Differences* 30, no. 2 (2019): 115–145. https://doi.org/10.1215/10407391-7736077.

Waugh, Thomas. Introduction to *"Show Us Life": Toward a History and Aesthetics of the Committed Documentary*, xi–xxvii. Edited by Thomas Waugh. Metuchen, N.J.: Scarecrow Press, 1984.

Wood, Reed M. *Female Fighters: Why Rebel Groups Recruit Women for War*. New York: Columbia University Press, 2019.

II

Literature and Resistance

● ●

4

All the Female Bodies

• •

Female Resistance and
Political Consciousness in
Testimonies of the Dirty War in
Argentina

LUCÍA GARCÍA-SANTANA

This chapter examines the construction of a female political consciousness in Alicia Partnoy's *The Little School* (1986) and Alicia Kozameh's *Steps under Water* (1987). Both survivors of different stages of the war against political dissidence that led to the last Argentine dictatorship (Kozameh under Isabel Martínez de Perón's government in 1975 and Partnoy under the National Reorganization Process in 1977), they engage in a memory action that, although characteristic of a postdictatorship narrative trend, presents the survival strategies devised in detention camps as mechanisms supporting female empowerment. In this regard, following Michel Foucault's concept of biopower, which pertains to the body as a discourse over which state terror sought to write its disciplining coordinates, women's bodies overcome the victimizing circumstances of their detention and torture to stand as sites of resistance and political reorganization, inscribing in the process new social and gender meanings.[1] In this context, these writers' creative works that surpass the testimonial quality become aesthetic pieces that can mobilize a female readership in a more particular manner by presenting specific challenges and resistance strategies concerning women in the common fight for social equality, thus serving as a strong, compelling legacy that precedes and informs contemporary social movements fighting for women's rights and against gender violence in Argentina. Both then and now, claims focus on the private and social violence in which the body as an expression of self, once again, is under siege and on display.

In this study, I draw on Silvia Federici's explanation of the systemic control of the female body as a capitalist maneuver, according to which "the body has been for women in capitalist society what the factory has been for male-waged workers: the primary ground of their exploitation and resistance, as the female body has been appropriated by the state and men and forced to function for the reproduction and accumulation of labor."[2] In this vein, the body of the female political militant, the so-called rebel female body during the last Argentine dictatorship, is inscribed with the multiple anxieties of a changing society that is questioning capitalist inequalities in the rise of socialist movements inspired by the Cuban Revolution of 1959. In particular, in the 1970s in Argentina, a rhetoric of war against ideological enemies connects to the fight against women's emancipation that was developing with significant intensity since the early 1960s and that pushed women to perform increasing control over their bodies. This emancipatory move becomes a dangerous tool to the patriarchal structure and is soon linked to the contesting forces that are destabilizing the capitalist system all over Latin America, exemplified in Argentina by the figure of "the enemy within."[3] In this context, the left-wing female militants imprisoned by the dictatorship display on their bodies all the marks of a so-called decaying society, exposed in the menace of the dismantling of the traditional family. In contrast, the narratives analyzed here present that individual body under siege as a site of female power by underscoring different instances of resistance performed by the incarcerated and tortured female's physicality. The Semitic nose, the vagina, the self-restraint of the individual body, and the many instances of creativity build the collective body as a solidarity space and a site for concerted claims, and the very process of writing these testimonies becomes a creative tool that asserts the important role of women in writing the history of the national political struggle.

Argentinian Women as Disposable Bodies

In the early 1960s, Argentina witnessed the upsurge of young women's unrest related to the restrictions of the ideology of domesticity. The increased sense of sexual freedom—the gradual acceptance of premarital sexual activity, for instance—and the tensions experienced by young women in a traditional domestic realm led many young women to leave or wish to leave their homes. This trend of the runaway girl exposed the moral menace of the opposition to conservative values and forced the state to rethink the role of its youth in society, which in turn provoked a divergence between progressive educational proposals and the conservative ground that characterized the decade. Simultaneously, the anxieties caused by the expansion of Marxist ideals throughout Latin America after the triumph of the Cuban Revolution became tantamount to the anxieties created by the women's claim for a higher space of freedom.[4] Fearing the dismantling of the conservative patriarchal society as it was known, which, according to Federici, supports the capitalist system and its functioning (2004), the different authoritarian regimes, in collusion with the Catholic Church and other society's sectors, targeted women as the focus of these structural transformations. In particular, the bodies of women militants were read with a double layer of moral deviance for their gender and political adscription. However, notwithstanding their commitment to their political mission, women within active political groups did not enjoy the expected level of acknowledgment and equality, for these groups followed Ernesto Che Guevara's conservative stance in gender matters, fossilizing gender distribution and hierarchy.[5] Thus, the repression of female activists became particularly gruesome, for they represented a challenge to the wide patriarchal system that permeated any social and political group, that encompassed much more than the adduced political justifications, and that therefore translated into a precise experience of gendered violence.

The United Nations Declaration on the Elimination of Violence against Women (United Nations General Assembly 1993) defines violence against women as "any act of gender-based violence that results in, or is likely to result in, physical, sexual or psychological harm or suffering to women, including threats of such acts, coercion or arbitrary deprivations of liberty, whether occurring in public or private life."[6] As these authors observe, violence against women is "shaped by forces that operate at different levels,"[7] and in particular, during the Argentine dictatorship, gender-based violence was a political tool that had powerful ideological roots in the importance of the body to carry out meaning. Under the pretense of identifying gender and left-wing ideology, the repressors exercised their violence upon women with a double implication, enacting what Diana Russell, in her seminal work *The Politics of Rape* (1984), identifies as a correlation between certain masculinity conceptualizations and sexual violence.[8] The ideological underpinnings that supported the regime were also displayed in the way the female bodies were treated as sexual objects, both disposable and desired.[9] In this regard, notwithstanding the state's rhetoric of the Dirty War, the war against dissidence meant war against all forms of difference.[10] The Red Scare that also took over Argentina related ideological threat—mainly, the aforementioned spreading of Marxist ideas—to the weakening of conservative values associated with the family institution, and Jews, gays, and rebel women who opposed the limitations of domesticity were its main targets. However, in the case of women, meaning inscription blurred other identity affiliations, exposing that they were particularly persecuted for their role as agents of social change.

Against this background, female bodies were regarded as linked to nature, out of the logos, and therefore, following Giorgio Agamben's elaboration of the Roman law, they could be killed but not sacrificed.[11] Moreover, as Patricia Fagen remarks about the Southern Cone dictatorships, "The theme of war was merged into the theme of illness, and the enemy came to be portrayed as a cancer to be surgically extracted and destroyed to restore social health."[12] Thus, rebel women were regarded as a malfunction that affected the social body and needed to be repressed and controlled to avoid a dissemination both moral and exemplary—that is, contagious in its ability to transmit ideas to other women—as well as reproductive, creating new generations of subversives. Likewise, these political militants were regarded as disposable citizens within a *necropolitics* dynamic, according to which the state delimits who must live or die.[13] In this regard, Judith Butler points at the vulnerability of a body that is and can be inscribed with a political message, be it by repressing measures or collective claims.[14] This precarious life also represents a resilient site of a political consciousness and activism built on a common struggle.

Authors Alicia Kozameh and Alicia Partnoy belong to the generation of Argentinian women who experienced the trauma of extreme political persecution, and they add to the political account their role as women in a changing society. In a manner like how the militants expose their integrity in protests where they place/expose the body (*poner el cuerpo*) as a political declaration, both authors' testimonials narrate their experiences, presenting the female collective as an embodied political consciousness by diverging their exposition from the conventional witnessing of the torture to witnessing of the resistance. The importance of the literary activity analyzed here consists in presenting this witnessing act not as speaking for or in the name of a community or group, in John Beverley's description of *testimonio*,[15] but as a continuation of their militant role building a collective subjectivity in underscoring the resilience and endurance of female political prisoners. Against the patriarchal structure that blends moral anxieties and political justifications and that incarnates in custodians, doctors, and nurses, male and female alike, the female prisoner stands as a new woman, politically committed and family oriented. What these narratives contest is precisely the institutional assumption that political prisoners were deviant women who wanted to dismantle the traditional family as well as the internal record that their role in the political struggle in collaboration with their male counterparts only occupied a subordinate and marginal space.

Witnessing Resistance

Steps under Water and *The Little School* are narrative structures mixing personal introspection in the form of journal entries and reflections with a sense of shared awareness. The end result is the presentation of internal and external struggles that interact and feed one another, displaying the common suffering particular to the female experience. Moreover, the texts focus on different examples of the female body's stance and reaction to repression as a site of feminine resignification in the midst of a violent patriarchal system that exceeds detention camps' functioning.

In this context, Kozameh's account mixes her alter ego Sara's experience after being released from Villa Devoto, a high-security facility located in a residential neighborhood in Buenos Aires where she was held for four years, and her memories of prison. By chronicling real events and introspections that retell nonexplicitly her suffering in prison, Sara's efforts center on trying to convey sufficient and precise written words to overcome what Elaine Scarry considers the ineffable quality of pain, a circumstance that "does not simply resist language but actively destroys it."[16] Similarly, Partnoy recounts her experience in the so-called Little School (La Escuelita), a detention camp where she was held before being transferred to Villa Devoto, by developing the narrator's perspective that merges the third-person singular with other female consciences. Both authors expand the delimitation of an individual subjectivity into a female collective that demonstrates an increasing feminist political awareness with defined traits, emphasizing, without cosmetic disguises, the dynamics of resistance that placed them in a superior moral position notwithstanding their subordinate circumstances.[17] Far from presenting the physical violence and gender humiliations as a systemic and anonymous overpowering action, they portray the female bodies as places of resiliency and nurture enduring gender violence. In particular, Partnoy's narrative revolves around the core circumstance of her ability to see under the imposed blindfold, this way becoming a chronicler of the endurance of her *compañeras* and the abuses of their captors as much as of her own subjectivity. Likewise, Kozameh's rendering of Sara as a witness of her fellow captives' struggles serves as a way of detaching the personal experience and presenting it as a collective self. Thus, these authors' accounts serve as repositories of an inadvertent feminist political consciousness in the exposition of the gendered underpinnings of their fight and the successes of their insubordination, whose goal seems not to present the truth as a denunciatory act but to give an account of the fruitful creativity of the female prisoners as a resistance strategy.[18]

As explained, under the dictatorship, the female body is particularly targeted as the place where political ideology is also subservient to the subjection of women in a general atmosphere of physical violence and punishment distinctive of a changing sociocultural atmosphere. In the 1960s Argentina, this restriction starts to be more intensely exercised when women begin to demand a new space for freedom.[19] In this context, the body of the female militant is particularly dangerous for its reproduction capacity, for its contesting of the status quo of the motherly figure, and for its representation of an alternative abject femininity both despised and desired.[20] In Kozameh's and Partnoy's narratives, the gender division between the female prisoners and the male guards encompasses a subtle language barrier, and imposing a hierarchical power is problematized by that

unfathomable distance. The subordination to sexual violence proves unfruit-
ful in the unbinding resistance of the female body supported by the group's
identification. In this regard, women activists were trained in the awareness of
the torture and humiliation they would suffer if caught and of the tactics of division that the military would implement against them, and this aspect of collective agglutination is one of the elements that Kozameh and Partnoy emphasize
in their particular way of witnessing. Likewise, *políticas* risked their families in
the intent, propelled by history and the understanding that revolutionary activity was the only way to build a better future for the following generation that
they mothered, as Partnoy declares in the introduction to *The Little School*: "The
coup triggered my rage, and I decided to become more militant.... My daughter, Ruth, was nine months old. My answer to my own fears was that I had to
work for a better society for the sake of my child's future."[21] This wish to build a
community with different rules to acknowledge her daughter's place works
as a symbolic elaboration of the importance of this militancy in creating an
Argentinian feminist consciousness that was different from the political claims
they shared with their male counterparts.

In Partnoy's narrative, her feminist political action starts the moment the
military trespasses into her home in broad daylight to detain her. Despite sleeping all dressed waiting for her captors, the protagonist is caught off guard wearing her home clothes and husband's slippers. She misses these slippers when
trying to escape over the patio wall, leaving her daughter behind, and the pair
of flip-flops decorated with "just one flower"[22] that she is given at the detention center becomes the symbol of her political resistance. That "one-flowered
slipper amid the dirt and fear, the screams and the torture, that flower so plastic, so unbelievable, so ridiculous, was like a stage prop, almost obscene, absurd,
a joke"[23] and represents the beginning of a distinct political female experience.
Precisely, Partnoy's account of the detention camp is built around different
scenes in which she intertwines the personal experience with the collective
consciousness as part of the same whole. The gender difference is patent in all
the scenes, notwithstanding the subtle chronicle of the abuses she suffers, and
it is a conspicuous occurrence how men and women are treated differently in a
behavioral microcosm that responds like a caricature to the outer macrocosms
of the patriarchal state. Thus, "sometimes there were two guards outside [the
latrines]: one handled the men, the other the women,"[24] as if the prison system
respected some conventional decorum in treating the body's functionality in
such a manner that contrasted with its repressive measures in some level of spectacular propriety.[25] The institutional, ideological stance of law and order rooted
in gender distribution tries to overwrite the insubordination and chaos brought
about by the militants in the eyes of the military.[26] However, the disciplining
of the body is contested by an oppositional performance not exempted from
repercussions: "'If you don't hit him, I'll hit you!' I gently patted my friend's
face. *Loro* slapped me twelve times. It almost didn't hurt ... I wasn't going to

hurt a pal." This collaborative gesture contrasts with the continuous abuses with sexual content that make the protagonist falter in her will of resistance, sole instances of her weakness: "Once, last month, I didn't go to the latrine in the afternoon . . . I couldn't stand the guard's hands molesting me when I walked by, hands I couldn't dodge for fear they would know that my loose blindfold allowed me to see."[27] In this vein, as Kozameh explains in an interview with Elsa Pfeiffer, the gender aspect of the violence they suffered in prison was connected to the patriarchal consideration of the female body, at once an object of desire and a symbol of motherhood.[28] The military saw the prisoners as women who had lost their course.[29] Precisely, Kozameh's account emphasizes an alternative fight referring to the domestic realm. She explains, "We had come out of that and they wanted us to go back to that,"[30] thus putting together the political fight for social equality with the struggles of home life. The threat was not that women had left the house, a common moral panic in that decade, as Manzano explains, but that they had taken up arms, hence the need to subjugate them with sexual violence in the detention camps.

In this context, the connection between the gender aspect of the persecution and the ideological opposition in Kozameh's narrative of Sara's imprisonment is presented in the description of a doctor and her staff and clients detained for their connection to a childbirth clinic. Alongside the political prisoners, there are other cellmates who exemplify the systemic control over the female body—to the extent that they become tantamount to the ideological struggle. The similarities and disparities between the different prisoners soon become apparent. The clinic's doctor sarcastically describes the system, in which "*políti-cas* [political prisoners] are really cooked. We just cough up a few pesos. Maybe offer a couple of kids to the police station or court employees, those sterile bastards, and within a month we'll be up and running again."[31] All the types of offenders that Sara encounters when she arrives at the female ward pertain to the subjection of women in society, and the *políticas* seem to represent the new woman who functions outside a failing system:

> That little brunette bitch, instead of getting an abortion, waited until the baby was born and then she drowned it in a bucket of water. . . . The one on the third bed from the back shot her husband three times, except she didn't finish the job. . . . The fake blonde across the way there had a fight with her mother and whacked her over the head with a stick. . . . And it goes on just like that, dear. To that beat. . . . And those two that won't come over here, see them? They're prostitutes. They never fit in anywhere.[32]

The harsh description exposes the individual difficulties in the process of operating as a collective body. The sense of likeness among women does not stand on their personal similarities but on the specific circumstances of their repression. In this regard, Sara's love relationship with her friend Elsa's husband after they are released from Villa Devoto—a circumstance that Elsa, notwithstanding the conflict of interests, considers "just a very tiny part of all this horror"[33]—turns into a successful test of the indelible relationship between both women forged in the tribulations of their political activism. In the conflicting conversations that follow, Sara and Elsa are not fighting for Marco but trying to preserve their relationship amid the convulsion of attempting to return to their normal lives. Their unconventional dynamic stands on a new consideration of sorority, on a precise idea of friendship detached from domesticity and anchored by the historical mission and embodied trauma of those who "day after day exchanged frightened looks with [one another]. Looks of understanding. Looks of farewell in the face of imminent death."[34] They see themselves as other types of women: "Those women. Who defined their enemy. Who concentrated on the fight. Women whom that enemy, having won the battle, physically holds its grip."[35] Friendship and other types of women are one category, a different element of a new taxonomy that the system is trying to suffocate. Interestingly, Marco regards this strong bond as a pitfall in building back a sense of normalcy, and he reproaches Elsa for her apparent indifference when confronted with his infidelity. The disruption of everyday life created by imprisonment and trauma mobilizes other synergies that exclude those outside of the experience. This female common ground is described by Marco as a manifestation of relaxed moral boundaries, as he bluntly explains Elsa's passivity toward his infidelity with her friend as a confirmation that "after four years of sharing almost everything with your cellmates you ended up kind of getting used to it."[36] The language of war and resistance permeating everyday conversations and situations also expresses the menace of that indissoluble bond that Marco cannot fathom and that excludes him. Kozameh elaborates on the powerful coalition of women who become intimidating even to men who are part of the intimate realm. Marco understands that what separates him from those women is not only the experience of torture and repression but something of a vaguer quality. To him, behaving as a regular man in a regular world clashed with the newly acquired experience of his wife and her female friends, which he interprets as a challenge to his family regardless of his own position as a political militant: "I am trying to keep the family together. You can find out, if you have got a couple of minutes, after seeing all those women, your little prison buddies, to build that relationship you all have, which nobody can come between, most of all us men."[37] His affiliation to a gender polarity impedes his understanding and questions his moral place. In spite of his infidelity sanctioned by the systemic double bind, his discourse puts the focus on the unbreakable friendship of these women as a new and enigmatic collective experience.

The Individual Body for the Collective Claim

These narrations present how women's solidarity builds gradually alongside individual tensions, the individual body thus transforming into the repository of collective fight. In *Steps under Water*, the police building more walls to separate the women's space from the guards creates in the prisoners a spontaneous and organized effort to keep their few belongings in a safe place—"in the mattresses, pillows, in their clothes, in their own bodies, space that would preserve the treasures that kept them going: ballpoint refills, slips of paper, little books, a wristwatch or two, minus the band."[38] In this regard, Kozameh explains to Pfeiffer that female prisoners use their bodies to conceal objects and preserve a space for communication and creativity. Likewise, Partnoy's episodes that allude to the realm of the body ("My Nose," "Toothbrush," "The Small Box of Matches") give an account of the importance of the body as a site of resistance. In the episode titled "My Nose," the body that once was under the restraints of conventional trends and beauty canons, as well as ethnic prejudices, becomes a powerful tool to fight repression: "Thanks to it, things have changed. . . . But I recall that I've always detested my nose . . . I never liked its shape. . . . The Semitic curve bothered me."[39] Suddenly, the prisoner realizes that the nose allows her to see because the blindfold rests steeped on the once-despised curve, and that ability connects with her Jewish heritage as a site of resistance. In Kozameh's narrative, the ethnic origin seems to be another reason for targeting and persecution when Sara describes the moment when the police trespass her home in search of her husband, and "one of them painted the walls with five-pointed stars and huge swastikas."[40] The obvious root of ethnic and religious persecution becomes, in the case of the women prisoners, just another form of subjection and abuse, but not the cause of their detention, as the authors expose: "Now that Chiche has come out with the 'discovery' of my Jewishness, I realize this is the first time that subject of my race has come up here. . . . In any case it's not for being Jewish that I was brought to the Little School."[41]

In this regard, the importance of the individual body and its endurance incorporates other women and a common struggle. For instance, the informal chatting among women includes family topics and references to their bodily challenges under exceptional circumstances, as when María Elena and the narrator in Partnoy's novel talk about menstruation alterations: "Remember that none of us are menstruating . . . I don't know, it's as if our bodies were protecting themselves."[42] The explanation that roots in the individual bodies allows the understanding and agglutination of all women under one collective experience, and the trauma associated with the sexual violence is also neutralized in the common intellectual elaboration: "There isn't any way those jerks' filth could stain us. Our bodies might stink, but we are clean inside."[43] The political women's elevation over their captors and other women who are on the other side of the fight is highlighted as a powerful tool to inscribe their place in history and their resistance.

In the same context of the representation of individual body parts, in Partnoy's chapter "The Small Box of Matches," the narrator describes how she breaks her tooth against an iron gate, a tooth that she had lost at an amusement park at the age of twelve. The superimposition of traumas, the importance given to preserving the tooth inside the box of matches, as well as her intent to keep it in place using bread crumbs as support, makes the narrator wonder if "she wasn't to look pretty for the guards, for the torturers," thus exposing the unconscious workings of the conventional gendered dynamics imposed by the system.[44] Moreover, the importance given to this tooth is a reminder of her sense of wholeness, to the point that she continuously places it in her mouth and hides it to avoid losing it. Saving the tooth in a box is also projecting the safe place that she lacks to a part of her body, and this form of resistance—standing on the integrity of the body, not on conventional femininity coordinates—also becomes a powerful metonymy of the preservation of the entire group, a dangerous sign to the repressors: "Sooner or later a guard is going to decide that the box is a dangerous object in my hands."[45] The fear that anything that the prisoners have or do might pose a threat is also the fear of the unknown; these women's maneuvers are hard to understand by the male guards, which showcases how the rebel female body is in itself a powerful site of resistance at both the instrumental and discursive level.

Furthermore, this sense of self linked to the body is an individualization of humanity that in the torture session transforms into the awareness that the brutal action of which the narrator is a recipient constrains her to her instinctive side when she needs to control her mind the most: "I smell like a caged animal. . . . Don't make me believe I'm an animal. . . . Leave my body in peace."[46] This level of control of the self, amplified by the reference to the *I* in the most violent description, emerges as a powerful tool of collective claim not solely by controlling self-condemnation but by showing a shared endurance and support that could disconcert the guards. Moreover, that sense of self multiplies in the common experience of torture, connecting to other bodies in the clothes and things they share. Specifically, when in Partnoy's account the guards take away Vasca, the narrator feels her friend's jacket as an object of motherly protection: "The magic power of the denim jacket came true: the blows almost did not hurt. It was not the jacket's thick fabric, but Vasca's courage that protected me."[47] Likewise, giving the item the quality of the absent body, Kozameh relies on the description of Sara's husband's jacket, worn by his repressor as a way of disseminating fear. What affects Sara is her awareness that her imprisoned husband is "without the slightest idea that this guy had been wearing his jacket for the last four winters. Taking it over. Filling, invading that space which didn't belong to him. Almost like peeling off Hugo's skin and covering himself with it."[48] The gendered experiences as political prisoners become patent when Sara takes the recovered jacket to Hugo in prison as a token of endurance, only to acknowledge the unsurmountable, diverging nature of their ordeal when they reunite in exile and Hugo has left that symbolic item behind. In contrast, Partnoy's account of Vasca's jacket creates in the shared item the metaphor of the collective feminist consciousness that develops in the specificities of their common struggle.

Resistance of the Collective Body

The experiences narrated in these testimonies do not efface the tensions between the individual and the collective claim. As Butler puts it, "When we hear about 'rights,' we understand them pertaining to individuals. When we argue for protection against discrimination, we argue as a group or a class. And in that language and in that context, we have to present ourselves as . . . a community defined by some shared features."[49] In this sense, to Kozameh and Partnoy, the control of individual impulses for the well-being of the group becomes the core of their interpersonal exchanges. The dynamic that supports the individual emotionally and psychologically—the conversation among women, the exchange of gifts and talents—is another level of the creation of the whole group as one political body.

The disassociation of body and mind, as reflected in the use of the third-person singular in the narration of a text of testimonial quality, differs from the effect of the torture and the impact on the bodies, thus alienating it from the mental sphere while creating a collective space made up of the sum of the individual subjectivities. As mentioned previously, the scenes in Partnoy's memory are arranged around items, forming a catalog related to the individual experience of the body; however, they combine events, like "Graciela: Around the Table" or "Benja's First Night," that refer to the connection to the collective. The tangibility of her experience, the inside-outside dynamic of her perception, presents that individual struggle and the ability to connect in solidarity with the struggle of others: "I held Vasca's hand, a handshake of complicity. On my other side, I felt Hugo's firm hand. Our palms conveyed a message: 'Courage. For today and for the rest of the days we will have to endure here.'"[50] Kozameh expresses a similar sentiment in her arrival to Villa Devoto, where she feels that all she needs is "to have a fellow *compañera* nearby,"[51] and the sight of the women's ward becomes a reflection of her own sense of self. Notwithstanding the dramatic act of witness of "twenty, thirty of them. Emaciated and sleeping or moaning," she concludes, "And as she observed the faces from her own parapet, she continued to discover her body a little more, since it seemed that the environment was not hostile."[52] The collective, for the witness, becomes the refuge, the identification, and a reenactment of their political mission. This is why the collective action focuses on distracting the guards to protect other bodies or allow space for communication.

The presence of other bodies brings comfort in the acknowledgment of a common burden. More significantly, the presentation of events in both narratives plays with the building of a collective consciousness in negotiating individual parts. The broken bodies of the individual prisoners become whole in the common strife. In particular, Kozameh's description of the institutional negotiations carried out to treat an ill *compañera*, Patricia del Campo, revolves around a draining argument with the captors that ends up in the prisoner's death, which showcases the collective will to defend their rights under the most strenuous circumstances. When del Campo falls ill, there is an escalation of demands that need to modulate the individual character and the common good of "the whole prison organizing to apply some pressure."[53] The mediators between the institution and the prisoners are female guards, the doctor is also a woman, and Sara suspects that one of the prisoners, Dora—"silent, her eyes ringed, with a tin cup in her left hand but not banging it"[54]—is collaborating with the guards. During the difficult process of negotiation, in which the different "types of women" are exposed, the guards insist on the difficulty of their task, of "being caught in the middle, playing the role of the messenger."[55] This statement provokes a political confrontation, in which one of the prisoners accuses the guards of indolence: "You still haven't tried standing between the sword and the wall. Against that wall between the rifle and the firing squad. But history shows . . . you do know what history is?"[56] The political consciousness of the militant clashes with the gender conscience of their place in history, which they do not share with the female custodians. Eventually, the particular demand is suffocated by "an impatient sign from someone else" that makes the prisoner comply. The collective becomes a site of refuge as well as an uncomfortable ground of another body disciplining for the common good.

In both accounts, control of the body also means a deep awareness that individual weakness could mean the demise of the collective body, a disciplining process that means that individual shortcomings and public vulnerabilities become forms of self-accusation. In *Steps under Water*, the collective exercises a sense of control over the individuals, and Kozameh does not hide the difficulties and tensions among the cellmates who fight to preserve their individuality and use coping mechanisms against the background of militancy training and political expectations. Likewise, they are pressed to perform according to an organized effort of resistance by showing endurance in the eyes of the guards, avoiding presenting themselves as defeated and fabricating a sense of well-being. The act of organization and solidarity in Patricia del Campo's example contrasts with the narration of the chapter "Description of a New Year's Eve," when all women must perform a celebratory mood by mimicking festive rituals. In particular, one of the prisoners, Maura, is described as despicable and conflictive for her opposition to play along, hence a pitfall to the staged joy that summons all the cellmates. Likewise, the narrator is trying to conceal her own repulsion to the faux act: "I'm trying to keep this show of lack of composure under wraps because it's not a question of blowing my image. . . . Because the book on me would be predictable: 'Sara, petite bourgeoise with ideological weaknesses. Blood pressure drops during New Year's get-together.' Very funny."[57] The fear of political pressures is ingrained in the body. Even body functions need to be constrained and controlled. Similarly, Partnoy's narrative insists on the need to stay firm in the face of imminent violence after the narrator is caught in the empowering act of talking with a fellow female prisoner: "She did not indulge in self-pity. The hatred she felt for them shielded her." When the beating starts, "she thought the conversation had been worth it, despite the beatings that could come, despite humiliation."[58] This act of rebelliousness from a feminine space, an act of freedom working for the collective, requires individual compliance in the survival of the group, and the different instances of creativity become the cohesive force that agglutinates the collective body and forestalls individual objections.

Creativity as a Female Space

The embodied act of resistance also seeks to keep intact elements that allow their expression and creativity, their sense of self. Thus, when the guards fulfill one of their never-ending searches, they find, alongside "three pairs of knitting needles made from the wood stripped from the beams of a few bunk beds fell out," a list of items that refer to the literary activity: "They took several notebooks with personal writings and book summaries, synopses and analyses of every kind, detailed diaries and poems, and among those things Sara's notebook . . . the one that contained all her creative writing over the last two months."[59]

In this sense, the women depicted in these narratives transcend their victim condition to become, in Alain Badiou's words, "creator bodies."[60] Badiou problematizes the possibility of justice when the consideration of the victim stems from a logic of spectacle and visibility that turns the body into a "commodity or victim body" for a detached audience to consume. Both Partnoy and Kozameh alter this market dynamic, narrating the many instances of resistance by virtue of which women overcome their strenuous circumstances using their talents and creativity. This strategic creativity as a sense of the collective is reflected, primarily, in the common nurturing. Kozameh narrates the female ward full of children, all being fed and taken care of by all the mothers. Likewise, in this common collective functioning, the power of creativity to articulate their connectivity is present in many instances, such as when women cook a traditional Christmas bread, *pancocho*, with the few ingredients they can afford. The goal is to enact the rituals of celebration to reject their subordinating circumstances, so they wrap up crafts as gifts to be exchanged: "In a corner of the floor over by the bars I see small gifts piled up, which, if tradition is followed, must be an assortment of small knitted, stuffed animals, manufactured clandestinely, and which will disappear for good after the first search of the year."[61] The female prisoners create new traditions to perform in front of the guards as a manifestation of their unbreakable resistance. The importance of this empowering act is exposed in the continuous sweeps that deprived these women of their creations and their possibilities to create.

This powerful space of creativity is presented in Partnoy's narrative in a chapter that opens up with poet Gabriel Celaya's statement that poetry "is a weapon loaded with future."[62] This chapter, titled "Poetry," showcases the close relationship between the body and creativity, to the point that, as the narrator remarks, "when the flesh of poetry is anesthetized, it is impossible to build poems."[63] Once again, this tool in the hands of the prisoners signifies a dangerous weapon to the guards, unable to understand the poetic code of the writings, believing that, as the guard fears, "that poem was written to honor some fucking guerrilla."[64] Notwithstanding the risk, the need for self-expression is stronger and extends to the collective. The moral superiority of the ideological cause combines with the intellectual elevation of poetic writing, a literary genre that the poorly educated sentinels cannot decipher. This sense of danger on the part of those who need to control the captives stands, once again, as a potent example of female resistance.

Conclusion

In an essay about her own testimonial work, Alicia Partnoy mentions the importance of *testimonio* as a writing device that "do[es] not rely on . . . the autobiographical pact, but on a solidarity pact." She goes further to assert her voice as a survivor, arguing against the conventional description of the genre that stands on "two common assumptions: that intellectuals give voice to those without one, and that truth should be the central concern for survivors when engaging in the production of testimonial texts."[65] Her literary work has been criticized for saving the examples of torture and therefore, according to the critics, preventing her creative work from having the social impact it could have otherwise. The lack of explicit descriptions has been interpreted as "deny[ing] that gendered torture greatly affects the women involved," and the author's reluctance to follow this pattern is seen as a lost opportunity to provide "insights into social relations to be used for subsequent political activity."[66] However, in Kozameh's and Partnoy's narratives, as I have analyzed here, the female body is presented as a site of resistance and resilience without erasing the fact of the war for meaning. Both authors perform actions of memory and consciousness-raising that are characteristic of the postdictatorship narrative trend; however, this time, they craft their narrative upon the re-creation of survival strategies by which the female body overcomes its victim circumstances to become a place of political reorganization. They are body creators that overpower their subjugated predicament.

The self-restraint of the individual body creates a body of solidarity that transforms into a strong female political consciousness that overcomes the conservative experience in Argentina's institutions as a whole, including the left-wing political groups, which focused on a social equality that excluded the gender gap of labor and rights distribution. In this regard, the ideological war of the 1970s that obliterated women's self-determination and was present in onerous sexual violence against female political prisoners does not differ substantially from the fundamental claims of contemporary movements that focus on the importance of women's rights on the grounds of defeating the plague of femicides that spreads all over Latin America. Thus, in Partnoy's words, it is not only retelling the experience as a memory action, for "our telling, our writing, can and will make us vulnerable unless a discourse of solidarity is built around our words."[67] It is the importance of building the collective, both contingently and intergenerationally, that creates the change.

Approaching these two texts side by side elevates the affirmation that the female body becomes the repository of a new reading of history. The body as a creator affirms its capacity of re-creating the world, as Jean Franco remarks, expanding on Elaine Scarry.[68] For Partnoy, the individual body overcomes its previous limitations and taboos—the invisibility, the racial profile—to become a new site of power that supports and nurtures other prisoners, other women. For Kozameh, the individual body becomes what Butler regards as the collective *we* of political claim, a solidarity net that creates a female consciousness that expands in contemporary social movements that proclaim that the revolution needs to be feminist.[69] In the context of what Barbara Sutton affirms regarding the centeredness of an embodied female political consciousness in the social movements coming out of the neoliberal turn in Argentina, the narratives analyzed here connect with these contemporary social concerns in their consideration of the female body as the site of a war over meaning—a site targeted with a specific violence that is contested on the grounds of the resilience and resistance built upon women's creativity and collaboration.[70] As Natalia Milanesio explains about current movements like Ni una menos (Not one woman less), "The historical roots of current women's organization and mobilization against femicides can again be traced back to the battle feminists fought in the 1980s.... However, thirty years ago the 'womanhood' of a small group of feminists who took to the streets to demand recognition of their sexual and reproductive rights could be put into question."[71] Thus, what all these contemporary movements for women's rights (Ni una menos, pro-abortion laws, even the COVID-19 pandemic and the social inequalities and state measures) have in common is the need to combat violence against women in its symbolic as well as its embodied dimension as a fundamental step in their fight for equality.[72] All these strategies of resistance that encompass the female body as a meaning carrier, the construction of feminine power spaces upon creative initiatives, and the imagination of a sorority language that reframes the relationship among women by identifying certain specificities regarding their systemic struggle continue working in relation to a lineage of political consciousness with a precedent in the experience, creative elaborations, and endurance of these unwavering precursors.

Notes

1   Michel Foucault, *The History of Sexuality*, trans. Robert Hurley (New York: Vintage Books, 1990).

2   Silvia Federici, *Caliban and the Witch* (Brooklyn, N.Y.: Autonomedia, 2014), 16.

3 Valeria Manzano, *The Age of Youth in Argentina: Culture, Politics, and Sexuality from Perón to Videla* (Chapel Hill: University of North Carolina Press, 2014), 112.

4 Manzano, 114.

5 Manzano, 110.

6 Andrew R. Morrison, Mary Ellsberg, and Sarah Bott, *Addressing Gender-Based Violence in the Latin American and Caribbean Region: A Critical Review of Interventions* (Washington, D.C.: World Bank, Latin America and the Caribbean Region, Poverty Sector Unit, 2004), 25.

7 Morrison, Ellsberg, and Bott, 26.

8 Diana E. H. Russell, *The Politics of Rape: The Victim's Perspective* (New York: Stein and Day, 1984).

9 Concerning sexual violence in clandestine detention centers, Ana Forcinito affirms that it was interpreted as "a form of violence linked to torture and explained by it, therefore, invisible as a crime and as a diverse form of violence," interpretation that correlates to the ominous silence around this practice. Forcinito, *Intermittences: Memory, Justice, and the Poetics of the Visible in Uruguay* (Pittsburgh, Pa.: University of Pittsburgh Press, 2018), 95.

10 The rhetoric of the Dirty War involves the two-demons theory, which equals the crimes against humanity committed by the dictatorship and the guerrilla fight of the left-wing groups. In this context, the National Reorganization Process would allegedly use war tactics to suffocate "the enemy within."

11 Giorgio Agamben, *Sovereign Power and Bare Life* (Palo Alto, Calif.: Stanford University Press, 1998), 43–44.

12 Juan E. Corradi, Patricia Weiss Fagan, and Manuel A. Garretón Merino, eds., *Fear at the Edge: State Terror and Resistance in Latin America* (Berkeley: University of California Press, 1992), 43–44.

13 Achille Mbembe, *Necropolitics*, trans. Steve Corcoran (Durham, N.C.: Duke University Press, 2019).

14 Judith Butler, *Precarious Life: The Powers of Mourning and Violence* (London: Verso, 2004), 25.

15 John Beverley, *Testimonio: On the Politics of Truth* (Minneapolis: University of Minnesota Press, 2004).

16 Elaine Scarry, *The Body in Pain: The Making and Unmaking of the World* (New York: Oxford University Press, 1985), 4.

17 The anthology edited by Viviana Beguán, *Nosotras: Presas políticas, 1974–1983* (Buenos Aires: Nuestra América, 2008), of which Kozameh is a contributor, precisely claims, "This need to be seen as multifaceted, politicized human beings with an important role in the country's history was already recorded in 2002, by historian Margaret Crahan. She conducted extensive interviews with women former political prisoners in Buenos Aires, concluding that they felt that their history has not been accurately recorded to date for, as one of them phrased it 'we are always represented as suffering—the authors are presenting their vision—not our reality'" (19).

18 With regard to the consideration of truth related to the *testimonio* genre, Betina Kaplan states that "alternative sanctions [Mothers of the Plaza de Mayo's protests, demonstrations called *escraches*] produced an inscription. Other cultural productions—literature, film, monuments—, also create an inscription but in a different code. Thus art can take on a social function—different from the denouncing role it assumed during dictatorship—and can be an active participant in the debate about what should be remembered and who and how should be remembered." Kaplan, "Contesting Memories: A Brief Recount of

the Struggles to Talk about the Violent Past in Argentina," *Dissidences* 4, no. 8 (November 2012): 2–3.

19 Barbara Sutton says about her collection of testimonies of violence against women in contemporary Argentina, *Bodies in Crisis: Culture, Violence, and Women's Resistance in Neoliberal Argentina* (New Brunswick, N.J.: Rutgers University Press, 2010), that

> for these women repressive and physically damaging or debilitating forms of bodily control had not become obsolete. They were direct forms of disciplining the body. Women from different social backgrounds interwove complex stories about violence—stories in which, for example, sexual abuse and other seemingly unrelated problems such as negative body image and eating disorders were part of the same matrix. In talking about their bodies, a whole array of violent interventions emerged. Speaking to these issues is particularly important because violence against women in Argentina, as in other parts of the world, continues to be surrounded by an aura of silence and misunderstanding within families, communities, and the broader society. (231)

20 Julia Kristeva, *Powers of Horror: An Essay on Abjection*, trans. Leon Roudiez (New York: Columbia University Press, 1982).

21 Alicia Partnoy, *The Little School: Tales of Disappearance and Survival*, trans. Lois Edwards Athey and Sandra Braunstein (San Francisco, Calif.: Cleis Press, 1998), 13.

22 Partnoy, 27.

23 Partnoy, 28.

24 Partnoy, 30.

25 Frank Graziano's study of the Dirty War's repressive measures emphasizes the importance of certain spectacular formativity that functioned as an economic method of society's control and the regime's rhetorical justification. Graziano, *Divine Violence: Spectacle, Psychosexuality, and Radical Christianity in the Argentine "Dirty War"* (Boulder, Colo.: Westview Press, 1992).

26 As Manzano suggests, the political stance of the revolutionary groups inspired by the Cuban Revolution did not include any reference to alternative participation of female militants, who kept on functioning according to the same rules of the society they were fighting to improve. Manzano, *Age of Youth*, 110.

27 Manzano, 32.

28 It is interesting to point out Nelly Richard's nuanced comments regarding motherhood and female collective protests in the similar context of Augusto Pinochet's dictatorship in Chile, in which "street rebellions were organized during the years of the military regime, whose official policies glorified woman—mother and wife—in her role as defender of the regimented fatherland. Other women (family members of the detainees-disappeared) decontextualized the traditional motherhood home nexus and resignified politically the symbolism of the mother in the public space of the street, traditionally reserved for men." Richard, *Cultural Residues: Chile in Transition*, trans. Theodore Quester and Alan West-Durán (Minneapolis: University of Minnesota Press, 2004), 132.

29 Pfeiffer, *Alicia Kozameh*, 368.

30 Pfeiffer, 369.

31 Pfeiffer, 23.

32 Pfeiffer, 25.

33 Pfeiffer, 70.

34 Pfeiffer, 42.

35 Pfeiffer, 42.

36 Pfeiffer, 45.

37 Pfeiffer, 65.

38 Pfeiffer, 32.

39 Partnoy, *Little School*, 59.

40 Alicia Kozameh, *Steps under Water: A Novel*, trans. David E. Davis (Berkeley: University of California Press, 1996), 11.

41 Partnoy, *Little School*, 63.

42 Partnoy, 70.

43 Partnoy, 71.

44 Partnoy, 8.

45 Partnoy, 90.

46 Partnoy, 94.

47 Partnoy, 112.

48 Kozameh, *Steps under Water*, 79.

49 Butler, *Precarious Life*, 24.

50 Partnoy, *Little School*, 31.

51 Kozameh, *Steps under Water*, 19.

52 Kozameh, 21.

53 Kozameh, 116.

54 Kozameh, 117.

55 Kozameh, 115.

56 Kozameh, 116.

57 Kozameh, 7.

58 Partnoy, *Little School*, 72.

59 Kozameh, *Steps under Water*, 35.

60 Alain Badiou, *Justicia, filosofía y literatura* (Rosario, Argentina: Homo Sapiens, 2007).

61 Kozameh, *Steps under Water*, 128.

62 Partnoy, *Little School*, 103.

63 Partnoy, 104.

64 Partnoy, 106.

65 Alicia Partnoy, "Disclaimer Intraducible: My Life / Is Based / on a Real Story," *Biography* 32, no. 1 (2009): 17, https://doi.org/10.1353/bio.0.0070.

66 Alicia Partnoy, "Concealing God: How Argentine Women Political Prisoners Performed a Collective Identity," *Biography* 36, no. 1 (2013): 135, http://dx.doi.org/10.1353/bio.2013.0006.

67 Partnoy, "Disclaimer Intraducible," 22.

68 In Amy K. Kaminsky, *Reading the Body Politic: Feminist Criticism and Latin American Women Writers* (Minneapolis: University of Minnesota Press, 1993).

69 Butler, *Precarious Life*, 25.

70 See Sutton, *Bodies in Crisis*.

71 Natalia Milanesio, *¡Destape! Sex, Democracy, and Freedom in Postdictatorial Argentina* (Pittsburgh, Pa.: University of Pittsburgh Press, 2019), 243.

72 Contemporary social movements belong to a palimpsest of initiatives, what Nancy Viviana Piñeiro and Liz Mason-Deese point out with regard to the instances of violence and community solidarity in the midst of the COVID-19 pandemic struggle: "Grassroots social movements, neighborhood assemblies, and all kinds of networks have long developed ways of responding to economic and social crises. In the midst of the economic crisis at the beginning of the millennium, people established robust solidarity economies, including barter networks and alternative currencies,

and worker-managed cooperatives, while movements self-organized soup kitchens, schools and health clinics." Viviana Piñeiro and Mason-Deese, "Argentina: Injustices Magnified; Memories of Resistance Reactivated," in *Pandemic Solidarity: Mutual Aid during the Covid-19 Crisis*, ed. Marina Sitrin, Colectiva Sembrar, and Rebecca Solnit (London: Pluto Press, 2020), 235.

Bibliography

Agamben, Giorgio. *Sovereign Power and Bare Life*. Palo Alto, Calif.: Stanford University Press, 1998.

Badiou, Alain. *Justicia, filosofía y literatura*. Rosario, Argentina: Homo Sapiens, 2007.

Begúan, Viviana, ed. *Nosotras: Presas políticas, 1974–1983*. Buenos Aires: Nuestra América, 2008.

Beverley, John. *Testimonio: On the Politics of Truth*. Minneapolis: University of Minnesota Press, 2004.

Butler, Judith. *Precarious Life: The Powers of Mourning and Violence*. London: Verso, 2004.

Corradi, Juan E., Patricia Weiss Fagen, and Manuel A. Garretón Merino, eds. *Fear at the Edge: State Terror and Resistance in Latin America*. Berkeley: University of California Press, 1992.

Federici, Silvia. *Caliban and the Witch*. Brooklyn, N.Y.: Autonomedia, 2014.

Forcinito, Ana. *Intermittences: Memory, Justice, and the Poetics of the Visible in Uruguay*. Pittsburgh, Pa.: University of Pittsburgh Press, 2018.

Foucault, Michel. *The History of Sexuality*. Translated by Robert Hurley. New York: Vintage Books, 1990.

Graziano, Frank. *Divine Violence: Spectacle, Psychosexuality, and Radical Christianity in the Argentine "Dirty War."* Boulder, Colo.: Westview Press, 1992.

Kaminsky, Amy K. *Reading the Body Politic: Feminist Criticism and Latin American Women Writers*. Minneapolis: University of Minnesota Press, 1993.

Kaplan, Betina. "Contesting Memories: A Brief Recount of the Struggles to Talk about the Violent Past in Argentina." *Dissidences* 4, no. 8 (November 2012): 1–15.

Kozameh, Alicia. *Steps under Water: A Novel*. Translated by David E. Davis. Berkeley: University of California Press, 1996.

Kristeva, Julia. *Powers of Horror: An Essay on Abjection*. Translated by Leon Roudiez. New York: Columbia University Press, 1982.

Manzano, Valeria. *The Age of Youth in Argentina: Culture, Politics, and Sexuality from Perón to Videla*. Chapel Hill: University of North Carolina Press, 2014.

Mbembe, Achille. *Necropolitics*. Translated by Steve Corcoran. Durham, N.C.: Duke University Press, 2019.

Milanesio, Natalia. *¡Destape! Sex, Democracy, and Freedom in Postdictatorial Argentina*. Pittsburgh, Pa.: University of Pittsburgh Press, 2019.

Morrison, Andrew R., Mary Ellsberg, and Sarah Bott. *Addressing Gender-Based Violence in the Latin American and Caribbean Region: A Critical Review of Interventions*. Washington, D.C.: World Bank, Latin America and the Caribbean Region, Poverty Sector Unit, 2004.

Partnoy, Alicia. "Concealing God: How Argentine Women Political Prisoners Performed a Collective Identity." *Biography* 36, no. 1 (Winter 2013): 211–241. http://dx.doi.org/10.1353/bio.2013.0006.

———. "Disclaimer Intraducible: My Life / Is Based / on a Real Story." *Biography* 32, no. 1 (Winter 2009): 16–25. https://doi.org/10.1353/bio.0.0070.

Partnoy, Alicia. *The Little School: Tales of Disappearance and Survival*. Translated by Lois Edwards Athey and Sandra Braunstein. San Francisco, Calif.: Cleis Press, 1998.

Richard, Nelly. *Cultural Residues: Chile in Transition*. Translated by Theodore Quester and Alan West-Durán. Minneapolis: University of Minnesota Press, 2004.

Russell, Diana E. H. *The Politics of Rape: The Victim's Perspective*. New York: Stein and Day, 1984.

Scarry, Elaine. *The Body in Pain: The Making and Unmaking of the World*. New York: Oxford University Press, 1985.

Sutton, Barbara. *Bodies in Crisis: Culture, Violence, and Women's Resistance in Neoliberal Argentina*. New Brunswick, N.J.: Rutgers University Press, 2010.

Viviana Piñeiro, Nancy, and Liz Mason-Deese. "Argentina: Injustices Magnified; Memories of Resistance Reactivated." In *Pandemic Solidarity: Mutual Aid during the Covid-19 Crisis*, edited by Marina Sitrin, Colectiva Sembrar, and Rebecca Solnit, 233–248. London: Pluto Press, 2020.

5

The Woman from Tantoura
• •

An Autotheoretical Reading in
the Art of Resistance

DOAA OMRAN

الأم مدرسة إذا أعددتها أعددت شعباً طيب
الأعراق

(A mother is a school—if you prepare her
well, you will have a good nation.)
—Hafiz Ibrahim, *Diwan Hafez Ibrahim*

The plight of the Palestinian people has been ongoing since British attempts
to colonize Palestine began in 1920, and Israeli occupation directly followed
with the *Nakba* (catastrophe) in 1948. A plethora of literary works depict
this plight—a people living in perpetual strife whether in their homeland
or in diasporas across the globe—and women have a grand share in that literary production. Arab women writers have resisted the Israeli occupation
of Palestine through personal narration (whether fictional or nonfictional),
interweaving these narratives into the wider national histories. Among pioneering autobiographies by Palestinian women are Anbara Salam al-Khalidi's
جولة في الذكريات بين لبنان وفلسطين (A tour of memories between Lebanon and Palestine; 1977) and Fadwa Ṭuqan's autobiography, *A Mountainous Journey* (1990).

It has become almost a trend as a plethora of Palestinian memoirs started appearing. Examples of these include *Jerusalem and I: A Personal Record* (1990) by Hala Sakakini, *In Search of Fatima: A Palestinian Story* (2002) by Ghada Karmi, and *Teta, Mother and Me: Three Generations of Arab Women* (2006) by Jean Said Makdisi (Edward Said's sister). This trope, in which the "political becomes personal," is a significant feature of literature on and by Palestinian women who tell the histories of their villages or hometowns, placing those smaller histories into the bigger contextual history of their country and culture.[1] Among the notable works that interweave personal Palestinian daily life into the wider political picture of the occupied land is Radwa Ashour's *The Woman from Tantoura* (2010), a novel that demonstrates characteristics of fictive autobiography.[2] *Tantoura* documents major historical events of the Palestinian *Nakba*, the intifada (the uprising), and diaspora, implementing concepts of postcolonial and feminist theories such as voice, identity, and feminine writing.[3] These characteristics conform with autotheoretical writing. This chapter illustrates how *Tantoura* deploys these characteristics from autotheory in order to present itself as a work of Palestinian resistance. Autotheory has only been applied to Western nonfictive autobiography to date, and the Arabic experience has not been given the required attention. The purpose of this chapter is also to venture into this necessary yet unprecedented attempt of reading Palestinian writing through an autotheoretical lens. I argue that when women write histories that can be easily obliterated due to occupation, fictive autotheoretical writing becomes a tool not only of resistance but also of survival.

Radwa Ashour's (1946–2014) *Tantoura* is a fictionalized historical bildungsroman of Ruqayya, a woman born around 1934 in a Palestinian coastal city, Tantoura. The village suffers from the aftermath of the ethnic cleansing of its inhabitants in 1948. This traumatic event results in the death of two hundred people from Tantoura. Among the deceased are Ruqayya's father and her only two brothers, whose dead bodies she sees piled in a heap with other corpses, the trauma of which leads to her temporary loss of speech.[4] Consequently, Ruqayya and her mother flee to Lebanon and settle there. Ruqayya gets married and gives birth to three sons and adopts a daughter who was orphaned during the Shatila massacre.[5] In an attempt to help her have a "voice," Ruqayya's son Hasan suggests that she record her personal and familial experiences of the Nakba, fleeing to Lebanon, and diaspora. The sons' subsequent migrations to the United Arab Emirates, France, and Canada metaphorically mirror the diasporic journey of Palestine in that all are deprived of owning a collective identity tied to their native land.[6] Hence, the "personal is political," as second- and third-wave feminists would put it.

Palestinian writing is one of resistance, as the author Ghassan Kanafani suggests in his *Literature of Resistance in Occupied Palestine 1948–66* (2015). Kanafani argues that Palestinian literature after the *Nakba* of 1948 continues to be about resistance.[7] Not only does this literature defy Israeli occupation, but it tries to combat the colonialist propaganda that the Israeli counterpart propagates.[8] Kanafani focuses on literature by Palestinian men in his book, as they were the forerunners. These writings and lexicons of resistance began with the *Nakba* in 1948 and continued after the intifada.[9] Palestinian women writers, such as Ashour, however, have taken up this resistance lexicon, embellishing and enhancing its significance for women's identity and role in the struggle. *Intifada* in Arabic "means a shiver, a shudder or tremor, and derives from the trilateral root n-f-d, which connotes shaking." The term *intifada* "is narrative of the revolution," a term that the Israeli government is trying to keep from entering the Hebrew lexicon.[10] The use of the term in *Tantoura* suggests and emphasizes its endurance. *Intifada* has its specificity over the term *thawra* (revolution), according to Abdelwahab Elmissiri, as it is specific to Palestine, whereas *thawra* can be used more broadly.

Barbara Harlow borrows Kanafani's concept of resistance literature in her *Barred: Women, Writing, and Political Detention* (1992), in which she dedicates a chapter to the resistance of Palestinian women, demonstrating parts from Raymonda Tawil's *Women Prisoners in the Prison Country* (1988). Harlow posits, "The narratives that emerged from the concatenation of events in the Occupied Territories were stories, anecdotes, accounts of elderly women confronting soldiers, of neighbors sharing food, and informal classes held in homes when the schools were closed, that circulated by word-of-mouth, acquiring in the telling renewed impetus, new settings in different villages and refugee camps, and alternate casts of characters."[11] However, the recording of the term *intifada* in *Tantoura* suggests and emphasizes its endurance as an act of resistance in itself. One of the main characters in *Tantoura* is Wisal, who "would open up when we were talking about this or that and the subject of the *Intifada* came up unexpectedly, and the talk turned to what happened. The strange thing was that Wisal always laughed when she told her *stories*, always choosing comical incidents. Was it because she gained strength from laughter? Or was it that despite the sacrifices, *the Intifada was like the resistance* when it entered the Lebanese camps after 1967, when it filled the residents with pride and confidence?"[12] Thus, narration becomes an act of resistance in *Tantoura* and a form of intifada. Telling one's story is an act of rebellion against aggression.

Another key element associated with intifada is *atfal al hijara*, or "children of stones," who can only counterattack the occupier through flinging stones at them. Ruqayya reports what she sees in the news; she "follow[s] the pictures of the young men throwing stones at the soldiers of the occupation. A woman facing an enlisted man, her hands in his face, shouting. Enlisted men wearing armor firing their rifles or pursuing kids down the side streets."[13] In addition to verbally confronting the aggressive soldiers who attack their children, Palestinian women can also throw stones at them. The narrator in *Tantoura* recounts, "I would think a lot about Wisal and her children, and look closely at the pictures whenever a woman appeared in an embroidered peasant dress, raising her hand with determination to throw a stone at one of the army cars, or to quarrel with the soldiers in order to release one of the children they had arrested. She seems to be Wisal. She looks like her, but it's not Wisal."[14] Throwing *hijarah*, or "stones," as an act of resistance has also been adopted by women. If the illiterate Palestinian peasant woman can resist through flinging stones, her educated sister can resist through writing and recording her story in a theoretical and historical framework just as Ashour does.

Autotheory provides a theoretical framework for decoding the voice and identity of Palestinian women's resistance writing. Stacey Young introduced *autotheory* and coined the term in her *Changing the Wor(l)d: Discourse, Politics, and the Feminist Movement* (1997). Lauren Fournier published her *Autotheory as Feminist Practice in Art, Writing, and Criticism* in 2021. Young argues that female academics intersperse reflections of theory in their intellectual work when telling their own personal stories or autobiographies.[15] Fourier posits that in autotheoretical works, "master discourses are fused with self-reflection and self-representation" and that autotheory transforms existing colonial discourses of philosophy and theory, interweaving the personal with the critical.[16] Thus, autotheoretical biography goes a step further than a mere recording of one's story, as the author self-reflects on critical theory as an integral part of the writing. Both Young and Fournier focus on autobiography and theory and how they intersect. Both scholars study autotheory as witnessed in actual autobiographies, but I argue that a fictive autobiography in Arabic such as *Tantoura* is also autotheoretical.

In *Changing the Wor(l)d*, Young argues that, among other reasons, women write their stories to inspire other women in similar situations. It is the "power of women telling their stories, and placing their experiences within political contexts, in order to help other women to imagine and act on options they did not previously realize existed."[17] Ever since Ṭuqan pioneered in writing her autobiographies in 1985 and 1993, Palestinian women have been offering a new edge to coloniality, apart from French and British versions, as well as giving insights into Middle Eastern autotheoretical postcolonial feminism.[18] Fournier develops the idea that the "personal is political," positing that "the personal is theoretical" as women write their "plight in patriarchal and colonial societies."[19]

Autobiographies can be accused of being subjective. Stefan Herbrechter affirms that the very nature of autobiography is subjective: "The very idea of autobiography relies on a subject (or a narrator) who is capable of remembering, interpreting and identifying with his or her life story. It is a very specific form of embodiment that usually convey trust in the impression that the subject of the narration is identical to the subject of the narrative. This is, in fact, what guarantees self-sameness, that is an assurance that 'I' am 'me.'"[20] That may not be particularly the case in fictive autobiographies. As readers, we know that the book between our hands is a fictive autobiography of the invented Ruqayya, whose fictional autobiography materializes as *The Woman from Tantoura*. Some of the events described in the novel are, however, historically recorded ones, such as the four ethnic cleansing massacres of Deir Yassin (1948), Tantoura (1948), and Sabra and Shatila (1982). Furthermore, we know that Palestinian cultural icons mentioned in the novel, such as Anees al-Sayigh and Ghassan Kanafani and the renowned Palestinian caricaturist Naji al-'Ali, were real and, in the case of al-'Ali, were Ashour's compatriots. Ashour's views on these real people and events are evident in *Tantoura* as well as in her more strictly autobiographical work لكل المقهورين أجنحة (*All the Oppressed Have Wings*), a cluster of essays by Ashour published posthumously in 2019.[21] Reading two of her works simultaneously thus presents compelling evidence of the autotheoretical nature of *Tantoura*.

Ashour was an Egyptian professor teaching at Cairo University who critiqued Western hegemony and its support of Israel. Her long-lasting marriage to the prominent Palestinian poet Mourid Barghouti (1944–2021) gave her a firsthand experience of his dislocated Palestinian family. In her *Wings*, Ashour dedicates four pages to *The Woman from Tantoura*. She reflects on writing the novel and makes connections to her Palestinian experience, saying, "I thank Mourid Barghouti, to whom I dedicate this book. Had it not been for the forty years of shared life, I would not have had the courage to approach the topic the way I did. After forty years of my marriage to a Palestinian and my closeness to numerous Palestinian family and friends, it seemed to me that I was capable of transferring the rhythms of this life. I dared. I hope I was not impulsive. I leave the decision to you."[22] Barghouti was a renowned diasporic Palestinian poet whose works focus on the plight of the Palestinian people. Because of his political opinions about the Egyptian government, he was expelled from Egypt for seventeen years and separated from his wife and son. Ashour's life has been affected because of the nationality of her husband. Ashour places the setting of her book in the colonized land and focuses on her husband and his motherland.

Ashour defies the notion that writing a people's history and documenting culture is the purview of only the men of that society. In *Tantoura*, Ashour provides a road map for non–college educated Palestinian women like Ruqayya, empowering them to write their own history and decolonize Western hegemonic theory. Voice also becomes the tool for resistance and agency for Palestinian women in combating the Israeli attempts of obliterating their stories, their history, and even their very existence on their native land. Ashour gives Palestinian women power through narrating a personal story in a wider national context. However, the novel is more than that: the fictional Ruqayya sets an example for real-world women in occupied territories to record their own stories and to reflect on them within their own families and among one another. Ruqayya's son Hasan asks her to record her storytelling in an intimate gesture of honoring her voice and its sound over the actual details of the incidents in her stories.[23] Throughout the novel, one of Ruqayya's main challenges lies in finding her "voice" to write. It is worth noting here that Ruqayya literally lost her voice when she saw the corpses of her father and brothers. The novel, hence, is not merely a historical fiction but also a literacy/literary narrative in its depiction of Ruqayya's education and the struggles that she faces in the process of writing. This is reminiscent of the autotheory propositions of Young and Fourier.

As an academic, Ashour has always leaned into a mission of writing about marginalized people. Her dissertation, titled "The Search for a Black Poetics: A Study of Afro-American Critical Writings" (1975), is representative of this resistance that aims at giving visibility to underprivileged people.[24] Ira Dowrkin, in his "Radwa Ashour, African American Criticism, and the Production of Modern Arabic Literature," seconds this. He states,

> [Ashour] explains, "The issues raised by Afro-American writers were very relevant to me because they helped me answer some of the critical questions related to modern Arabic literature." Ashour's transnational formulation of Arabic literature is precise. As a geopolitical venue, it expands beyond her Egyptian homeland to include, centrally, Palestine, which is essential to her work and consciousness, and no doubt further reinforced by her marriage to and partnership with Palestinian writer and activist Mourid Barghouti. Ashour not only acknowledges the value of African American criticism for understanding Arabic literature, but she also understood the importance of her two years in the United States well enough to make them the exclusive subject of an autobiography.[25]

The congruency between the African American experience and its Arabic counterpart is evident in *Wings*, in which Ashour dedicates more than fifty pages to reflecting on Palestine. She makes connections to the African American folkloric story "All God's Children Have Wings," which is about the growing of wings of African American slaves and their flight after being abused by their callous white masters. Ashour reflects on the story and makes a connection to the Palestinian cause: "This is not merely a folktale that the collective memory of the African slaves produced . . . it is also an exemplary tale that represents a rule of communal struggle for liberation; where *memory* is a prerequisite for such a liberatory act. I follow the news detailing the Palestinian Intifada, in the West Bank, Gaza Strip and occupied Palestine since 1948, I go back to this folktale, I murmur: all the oppressed have wings."[26] The essential role that memory plays is crucial in liberation movements according to Ashour, be it for Palestinians or for African American slaves. It is no wonder, then, that the protagonist of *Tantoura* is currently a grandmother who is remembering her story, lest the future generations forget.

Tantoura is a woman's story of writing her autobiography. The seventy-something Ruqayya struggles to remember, relive, and record the events of her past. It drains her. Her son Hasan, who is a lawyer, is the one who encourages her to do this and gets her a notebook, on the cover of which he writes, "The Woman from Tantoura." Hasan is also collecting the testimonies of the villagers of Tantoura who survived the massacre. When Ruqayya tells Hasan that writing and remembering will kill her, he responds, "Memory does not kill. It inflicts unbearable pain, perhaps; but we bear it, and memory changes from a whirlpool that pulls us to the bottom, to a sea we can swim in. We cover distances, we control it, and we dictate to it."[27]

In *Tantoura*, Ruqayya mentions her grandchildren fleetingly but concludes her autobiography with mentioning her encounter with a talented child named Naji and offering homage to her friend, the caricaturist al-'Ali. As such, memory is deployed in *Tantoura* not only to remember but to wish and emphasize that there is hope, or "wings," for the oppressed Palestinian children—one day. The past is present in the current time as well as in the future, as the events of 1948 continue to have repercussions in the present day that ripple into contemporary Palestinians who are remembering and honoring the histories of their families.

Marianne Hirsch, in her *The Generation of Postmemory: Writing and Visual Culture after the Holocaust* (2012), coins the term *postmemory* to denote the repercussions of traumatic past events on future generations even if those future generations have not witnessed or lived those events directly.[28] Postmemory, however, is not exactly the case for Palestinian young people who suffer from the events of *Nakba* even now. Postmemory becomes more concerned with archiving the stories of individuals left out of official archives, which is a main goal of autotheory. Autotheory not only gives the personal reflection of theory but also, at least in Ashour's case, brings in entangled strands of disparate traumatic histories into more intimate connection for future generations. Body writing is also an essential part of autotheory, as women often experience life through their bodies much more than men do. Ruqayya refers to her body as a woman and as a mother several times in the novel. The occupation of her native land reflects on her body; in turn, her body resists the occupation by giving birth to three sons, two of which she names after her two deceased brothers. The act of reproduction becomes a means for resisting the occupation through bringing to the world more Palestinians who may one day retrieve the occupied land. Her sons, thus, are representatives of those displaced Palestinians engaged in postmemory experiences of history and culture. Hence, the novel's autotheoretical action of recording history transcends the national and becomes personal.

Ashour's *Tantoura* tells us the story of earlier events in the Palestinian struggle through the voices of fictional witnesses to nonfictional events. Additionally, she references other genres, such as the songs and cartoons of al-'Ali.[29] Arab readers are already familiar with the fictional character of Handhalah, who is the main character of al-'Ali's cartoons. Ashour uses her imagination to archive historical details and enrich actual historical events, and thus, new media and new strategies of memorization are introduced. As a feminist, she gives voice to the oft-silenced female Palestinian subject. Ruqayya becomes a figure for real-world resistance and agency. It is through works like *Tantoura* that actual Palestinian women today can be visible and empowered in spite of the sustained political efforts to keep them invisible and victimized.

Ashour writes in order to resist. She has an interesting essay in *Wings* about her novel in Arabic. She posits that the Industrial Revolution and bourgeoisie circumstances that led to the birth of the novel in the West did not exist in the East, as people from the Middle East were more invested in writing poetry. She argues that the rise of the novel in Arabic was primarily due to postcolonial reasons.[30] I posit that postcoloniality is also contingent on resistance. *Tantoura* is a perfect example of this, as the novel is at once a great story, a literacy narrative, a historical document, an act of resistance, a postmemory, and a road map for contemporary Palestinian men and women. Through being an autotheoretical novel and a fictive autobiography, it preserves Palestinian history and educates generations to come. It is through women that the history of Tantoura is preserved through generational narration. Ashour, among other pioneers such as Anbara al-Khalidi and Ṭuqan, set an example for younger Palstinian writers to record their stories that document Palestinian plight. In a "country" where it is impossible to ascertain accurate statistics of deaths and daintiness, recording the stories of individuals—even if fictive—might be the only way to record events that cannot be obliterated by occupying forces. These personal stories might even convey the catastrophe better than the huge numbers of deaths that could have been recorded. Through her autotheoretical writings, Ashour becomes a foremother for emerging ones. In that sense, she is a pioneer in educating the nation about erased historical struggles.

Notes

1 Fadwa Ṭuqan, *A Mountainous Journey: An Autobiography*, trans. Olive E. Kenny and Naomi Shihab Nye (St. Paul, Minn.: Graywolf Press, 1990). Ṭuqan as well as Susan Abu al-Hawa, in her *Mornings in Jenin*, narrate their personal stories as Palestinians.

2 Radwa Ashour, *The Woman from Tantoura*, trans. Kay Heikkinen (Cairo: American University in Cairo Press, 2014). This work was written in Arabic as الطنطورية in 2010 and translated into English in 2014.

3 Feminist literary scholars Lauren Fournier and Stacy Young have developed autotheory as a theoretical framework for the analysis of women's autobiography. See Fournier, *Autotheory as Feminist Practice in Art, Writing, and Criticism* (Cambridge, Mass.: MIT Press, 2021); and Young, *Changing the Wor(l)d: Discourse, Politics, and the Feminist Movement* (New York: Routledge, 1997).

4 Ashour, *Woman from Tantoura*, 53.

5 Ashour, 219–226.

6 Ashour, 18.

7 Ghassan Kanafani, *Literature of Resistance in Occupied Palestine 1948–66* [in Arabic] (Beirut: Dār al-Rimāl, 2015), 11.

8 Kanafani, 71.

9 This refers to the Palestinian popular uprising against Israeli occupation of the West Bank and Gaza Strip that began in 1987.

10 Barbara Harlow, *Barred: Women, Writing and Political Detention* (Middleton, Conn.: Wesleyan University Press, 1992), 104.

11 Raymonda Tawil, cited in Harlow, *Barred*, 106.

12 Ashour, *Woman from Tantoura*, 287 (emphasis mine).
13 Ashour, 293.
14 Ashour, 288.
15 Young, *Changing the Wor(l)d*, 13–20.
16 Fournier, *Autotheory as Feminist Practice*, 313.
17 Young, *Changing the Wor(l)d*, 13.
18 The Egyptian Hoda Shaarawy's *Harem Years* (1987) and the Lebanese Anbara Salam-Khaldy's autobiography, *Memoirs of an Early Arab Feminist* (1978), preceded Ṭuqan's, but Ṭuqan was the first purely Palestinian woman in the modern age to write her life narrative.
19 Fournier, *Autotheory as Feminist Practice*, 20–21.
20 Stefan Herbrechter, "Posthumanism, Subjectivity, Autobiography," *Subjectivity* 5, no. 3 (September 1, 2012): 331.
21 Radwa Ashour, *All the Oppressed Have Wings: The Professor Speaks* [in Arabic] (Cairo: Dar al-Shorouq, 2019), 261–274.
22 Ashour, 51 (my translation).
23 Ashour, *Woman from Tantoura*, 205–207.
24 Radwa Ashour, "The Search for a Black Poetics: A Study of Afro-American Critical Writings" (unpublished doctoral dissertation, 1975, University of Massachusetts Amherst, university microfilms).
25 Ira Dworkin, "Radwa Ashour, African American Criticism, and the Production of Modern Arabic Literature," *Cambridge Journal of Postcolonial Literary Inquiry* 5, no. 1 (2018), 1–19.
26 Ashour, *Wings*, 11.
27 Ashour, *Woman from Tantoura*, 208.
28 Marianne Hirsch, "An Interview with Marianne Hirsch," by Columbia University Press, accessed July 2021, https://cup.columbia.edu/author-interviews/hirsch-generation-postmemory.
29 For a comprehensive archive on Handhalah, see http://handala.org/handala/.
30 Ashour, *Wings*, 18.

Bibliography

Ashour, Radwa. *All the Oppressed Have Wings: The Professor Speaks*. [In Arabic]. Cairo: Dar al-Shorouq, 2019.
———. "The Search for a Black Poetics: A Study of Afro-American Critical Writings." Unpublished doctoral dissertation, 1975. University of Massachusetts Amherst, university microfilms.
———. *The Woman from Tantoura*. Translated by Kay Heikkinen. Cairo: American University in Cairo Press, 2014.
Dworkin, Ira. "Radwa Ashour, African American Criticism, and the Production of Modern Arabic Literature." *Cambridge Journal of Postcolonial Literary Inquiry* 5, no. 1 (2018): 1–19.
Fournier, Lauren. *Autotheory as Feminist Practice in Art, Writing, and Criticism*. Cambridge, Mass.: MIT Press, 2021.
Harlow, Barbara. *Barred: Women, Writing and Political Detention*. Middleton, Conn.: Wesleyan University Press, 1992.
Herbrechter, Stefan. "Posthumanism, Subjectivity, Autobiography." *Subjectivity* 5, no. 3 (September 1, 2012): 327–347.
Hirsch, Marianne. "An Interview with Marianne Hirsch." By Columbia University Press.

Accessed July 2021. https://cup.columbia.edu/author-interviews/hirsch-generation
-postmemory.

Kanafani, Ghassan. *Literature of Resistance in Occupied Palestine 1948–66*. [In Arabic.] Beirut:
Manshūrat al-Rimāl, 2015.

Ṭuqan, Fadwa. *A Mountainous Journey: An Autobiography*. Translated by Olive E. Kenny and
Naomi Shihab Nye. St. Paul, Minn.: Graywolf Press, 1990.

Young, Stacey. *Changing the Wor(l)d: Discourse, Politics, and the Feminist Movement*. New
York: Routledge, 1997.

6

South Asian Women and Hybrid Identities

• •

Narratives of Abduction and
Displacement in Partition
Literature

MARGARET HAGEMAN

On August 15, 1947, the Partition of India created a humanitarian crisis that involved thousands of South Asian women who were abducted from their homes and subjected to rape, torture, and murder. Women who inhabited villages that became border towns between India and Pakistan were particularly vulnerable to extreme acts of violence. While the Abducted Persons (Recovery and Restoration) Act, implemented on December 19, 1949, attempted to rectify these events, these women were forever changed by their experiences.[1] These displaced women, belonging neither to their country of origin nor their country of occupancy, embody Homi Bhabha's concepts of hybridity and the third space by occupying multiple cultural spaces at once without fully belonging in any single state. Expanding on Bhabha's scholarship on hybridity and the third space, I examine gendered portrayals of abduction, displacement, and violence against South Asian women in literature.

Significantly, the women who experienced the Partition belonged to various religious and ethnic groups, resulting in a marginalized population with little in common other than their respective differences. These women's various religious, ethnic, and class statuses only contributed to their hybridity and further prevented them from occupying the space of either their homeland or their country of residence. Additionally, South Asian women's cultural hybridity made them appear exceptionally threatening to men, putting them in danger of being physically attacked, sexually assaulted, and killed in order to be subjugated and controlled in an overwhelmingly patriarchal society. The hybridity of women during the Partition is further explored in contemporary literature, including Amrita Pritam's novella *Pinjar* and Shobha Rao's short story collection *An Unrestored Woman*. In their compelling portrayals of South Asian women, Pritam and Rao also address the ongoing struggle that women have continued to face in coping with the complicated aftermath of the Partition. While Partition narratives have historically been male dominated and have represented women as passive victims of violence, I argue that the aforementioned writers present poignant depictions of women as survivors of abuse who, having traditionally been silenced, reclaim their voices and their agency.

Bhabha's Third Space and Hybrid Identities

For the purposes of my analysis, I will be using Bhabha's conceptualization of hybridity as the theoretical basis for my analysis of South Asian women's literature. While Bhabha discusses hybridity as a general theme in postcolonial studies, hybridity is particularly notable in discussions of the Partition, an unprecedented event that divided religious and ethnic groups who had previously coexisted in colonized India. In *The Location of Culture*, Bhabha writes, "The discriminatory effects of the discourse of cultural colonialism, for instance, do not simply or singly refer to a 'person,' or a dialectical power struggle between self and other, or to a discrimination between mother culture and alien cultures. Produced through the strategy of disavowal, the *reference* of discrimination is always to a process of splitting as the condition of subjection: a discrimination between the mother culture and its bastards, the self and its doubles, where the trace of what is disavowed is not repressed but repeated as something different—a mutation, a hybrid."[2]

If Bhabha refers to a metaphorical splitting, then Partition represents a literal splitting of the self and the other, or the "mother culture and alien cultures."[3] As Denise L. Spitzer has written, elaborating upon Bhabha's theory of hybridity, "Transnational linkages between homelands and lands of resettlement further contribute to hybridized identities in which multiple versions of self are constructed under conditions of inequity."[4] Expanding upon these previous theories, I argue that in Partition literature, the South Asian woman represents an exceptional example of a literary figure with a hybridized identity who occupies the third space in subcontinental Asia. Belonging to neither India nor the newly formed Pakistan, the South Asian woman falls into an ambiguous third space.

In his work, Bhabha addresses the "range of other dissonant, even dissident histories and voices—women, the colonized, minority groups, the bearers of policed sexualities" in relation to hybridity and in-between spaces.[5] Partition narratives offer insight into the lives of individuals who occupied multiple categories in Bhabha's discussion, or women who were simultaneously colonized people and members of minority groups. Prior to the Partition, women of various religions occupied the colonized space because of British rule; indeed, judging by the extreme violence committed against women before and after the Partition, women remained colonized subjects in the eyes of society long after India and Pakistan gained independence.[6]

Significantly, Bhabha writes, "The productive capacities of this Third Space have a colonial or post-colonial provenance."[7] In other words, India's extensive history as a colonized nation provides a prime example of the third space in action and how it has affected and continues to affect women. Moreover, although women may outnumber men in population groups, they are often treated as a minority subject rather than a majority. To paraphrase Bhabha, South Asian women, both before and after the Partition, would have been considered a colonized minority group whose sexualities were overtly controlled and policed. This makes them a compelling subject within discussions of hybridity and postcolonialism. Essentially, Bhabha's conceptualization of the third space will be vital to my historical and literary analysis of women and hybrid identities in South Asia.

Amrita Pritam's *Pinjar*

Originally published in 1950, Amrita Pritam's novella *Pinjar* is one of the earliest literary responses to the Partition of India.[8] Significantly, Pritam offers a feminist perspective on the traumatic effects of the Partition on women. The narrative's protagonist, Pooro, is abducted from her Hindu village at fifteen years old; her abductor, Rashid, is a Muslim man who forces Pooro to marry him against her will. Although the abduction and forced marriage occur eleven years before the Partition,[9] Pritam acknowledges that at this time, members of religious groups were becoming increasingly aggressive toward one another.[10] Eventually, Rashid reveals to Pooro that he abducted her out of revenge for an ongoing familial dispute between their two families. Because Pooro's uncle had previously abducted Rashid's aunt and held her captive for three days, Rashid's family encouraged him to take action for this injustice. Pooro escapes from Rashid and returns to her parents, although they explain there is little they can do for her, since her family will be in danger should they accept her back into their home. In fact, Pooro's mother tells her, "Daughter, it would have been better if you had died at birth!"[11] The text highlights the ways in which women were perceived by both their families and society. Additionally, Pritam provides historical background for the tumultuous events leading up to the Partition while also foreshadowing the additional conflicts to come.

After marrying Pooro by force, Rashid renames her Hamida and has her new name tattooed on her arm. Six months after her forced marriage to Rashid, Pooro becomes pregnant. Because this baby is the result of rape, Pooro does not want to give birth to the child growing inside her. Instead, "she felt as if her body was a pea-pod inside which she carried a slimy, white caterpillar. Her body was unclean. If only she could take the worm out of her womb and fling it away! Pick it out with her nails as if it were a thorn! Pluck it off as if it were a maggot or a leech!"[12] Eventually, after a difficult birth, her son is born, and Pooro grows to love the child and seemingly disregards her prior feelings. While Pritam does not further examine Pooro's change in attitude toward her son, she successfully portrays Pooro's growing hybrid identity. To highlight this concept, Pritam writes that "in her dreams, when she met her old friends . . . everyone still called her Pooro. At other times she was Hamida. It was a double life: Hamida by day, Pooro by night."[13] While Pooro still remembers her previous name, no one refers to her by this name, not even Pritam. Instead, Pooro is henceforth referred to as Hamida and is, for all intents and purposes, a Muslim woman, wife, and mother.

Later on in the narrative, Pooro learns of the violence against women that has occurred as a result of the Partition. She concludes, "It was a sin to be alive in a world so full of evil. . . . It was a crime to be born a girl."[14] After helping various women who have been abducted and displaced from their homes, Pooro learns that her sister-in-law, Lajo, has been abducted from her brother's home and is being held in a nearby village. She implores Rashid to help her rescue Lajo, and together they devise a plan to help Lajo escape from her captors. As Bede Scott aptly describes, "In an act that simultaneously replicates and reverses the novel's inaugural transgression," Rashid assists Pooro in rescuing Lajo from her abductors and reuniting her with her family.[15] Significantly, although Pooro is given the chance to escape to India with her family, she decides to remain in Pakistan with Rashid and her children. She tells her brother, "When Lajo is welcomed back in her home, then you can take it that Pooro has also returned to you. My home is now in Pakistan."[16] Although Pooro contemplates joining her brother and sister-in-law in their journey to India, she realizes that her true home is in Pakistan with her new family. While Pritam does not state this explicitly, it seems that Pooro cannot seriously consider leaving Pakistan because it is the home of her children. As the mother of Muslim children, she cannot leave Pakistan and return to her old home in India.

Pritam provides a compelling portrayal of Pooro's hybrid identity that forms after she is abducted from her family home. Initially, Pooro is hesitant to claim her new identity as Hamida, a Muslim wife and mother. However, when she is ultimately given the choice to leave her children in Pakistan and escape with her brother and sister-in-law to India, she refuses. While Pooro previously longed to return to her familial home, she cannot fathom leaving her two young children behind. In her nuanced portrayal of Pooro, Pritam suggests that, following the Partition, in order to survive and thrive in their new homes, women could eventually come to embrace their hybrid identities while also showing agency and independence. Although Pooro stays in Pakistan, she seems determined to continue helping other displaced women return to their homes while making the most of her new life. As one of the first literary responses to the Partition of India, *Pinjar* offers insight into the plight of abducted and displaced women while providing audiences with an optimistic perspective. However, not all Partition narratives necessarily present positive outlooks; rather, a more contemporary literary representation of the Partition portrays an abducted and displaced woman who experiences a decidedly bleaker outcome.

"The Lost Ribbon"

Shobha Rao's story "The Lost Ribbon" is a compelling representation of the horrors of the Partition as well as the pervasiveness of memory and trauma. As an older woman, the unnamed female narrator is haunted by memories of her past, in which she, at fourteen years old, was abducted by a Muslim man who forced her to relocate to Pakistan with him. After experiencing recurring rapes, she becomes pregnant and bears a little girl, who, poignantly, is named Noora, or light. Noora is the woman's only companion at the darkest moment of her life until she encounters a male soldier from the Indian Army who intends to rescue her and return her to her home country of India. However, after he leaves to obtain approval from his superiors, a senior officer and middle-aged woman return in his stead. The woman emphasizes that the narrator cannot take Noora with her, as the baby is a child of Pakistan. Although, or perhaps because, the narrator loves Noora dearly, she strangles her six-week-old child to death with a ribbon so that she will never undergo the same trauma that her mother has experienced. The narrator escapes to India but remains deeply affected by her memories of Noora and her abductor. Rao provides readers with an important narrative that explicitly addresses the consequences of the Partition and the difficult decisions women were forced to make at this time.

In addition to the female narrator, Rao presents another intriguing female character: an old woman who acts as a midwife and assists in delivering Noora. The narrator describes how, during the delivery, the old woman is cold and standoffish, stating the baby will "'die anyway. . . . I had seven myself. Only three lived. All that trouble for nothing.'"[17] However, after the delivery is successful and Noora is born a healthy baby girl, the narrator notes, "Something like apology swept over [the old woman's] face. 'One of them lived only for a day. A girl.' She paused and I thought she might sigh but she didn't; she wasn't a woman who sighed. 'Smart too,' she said. 'She knew a day of this was more than enough.'"[18] The woman, although unnecessarily harsh earlier, has been hardened by her own traumatic experiences of the Partition. By giving the reader some insight into this side character's story, Rao highlights how the extreme violence of the Partition affected thousands of South Asian women.

While infanticide was undoubtedly a reality of the Partition, many fictional narratives have not addressed this theme; however, Rao approaches this taboo subject with respect and deliberation. Significantly, the narrator struggles with her own decision of killing her child, and the choice appears to be an act of extreme desperation after she is told by the older woman, "But she's a child of Pakistan. She's a Muslim."[19] Noora must remain in Pakistan, even if the narrator, a Hindu, wishes to return to India. In her work, Lopamudra Basu explains, "abducted women had to leave children born of their former captors behind when they were rescued and these children became wards of the state."[20] If the narrator had chosen to abandon Noora in Pakistan, Noora could have become a ward of the state. However, the narrator understands that it is more likely that her daughter would have experienced the same physical and sexual violence that she had endured. Like her mother, Noora is a female character who embodies a hybrid identity by being both Indian and Pakistani or, respectively, Hindu and Muslim.

In her struggle to make a decision to leave or stay, the narrator describes how she must remind herself, "If you don't kill her, he will," keeping in mind her abductor's cruelty and the likely possibility that he will harm or kill her child anyway.[21] Unlike other fictional narratives of Partition written by men, Rao examines the agency that women embody, despite their limited options. Rao depicts these women as active storytellers, allowing them to tell their own stories in their own words; the majority of the narratives in *An Unrestored Woman* feature female protagonists, and many are written in the first-person perspective. At the same time, however, Rao acknowledges that none of the choices these women had, including infanticide and abortion, are ideal and should not be discussed in simplistic terms or approached thoughtlessly. Like Pritam, Rao provides readers with an enriched and detailed female perspective of the Partition of India and its lasting effects.

Although Pritam's narrative is optimistic in its portrayals of female solidarity in the aftermath of abduction and displacement, Rao's story is grim in its depictions of women snubbing other women in need. The older women who interact with the narrator of "The Lost Ribbon" are far less compassionate than Pooro is to Lajo and the other women she assists. As the narrator of Rao's story asks herself after the older woman tells her that Noora must remain in Pakistan, "How could she say such a thing? A woman, and a Hindu?"[22] Moreover, Pritam's novella ends on a bittersweet note, with Lajo returning to her husband and Pooro bidding a final farewell to her family. However, Rao's story concludes with the narrator remaining isolated and alone, bereft of companionship. Significantly, in her discussion of the Recovery and Restoration Act, Shobha Rao writes, "Though the commonly used term for these women is *recovered* women, I have chosen to refer to them as *restored* [as in the title *An Unrestored Woman*]. The distinction may seem trivial, but it is necessary, for I believe that while the recovery of a person is possible, the restoration of a human being to her original state is not."[23] Even though some abducted women were recovered and reunited with their families, they were by no means restored to their former selves. Instead, these women continued to be affected by the physical and psychological trauma they experienced for the rest of their lives.

Conclusion

While estimates vary, the total number of women abducted from their communities during the Partition ranges from seventy-five thousand to one hundred thousand.[24] In her discussion of the violence against women that occurred during the Partition, Haimanti Roy writes that "the confluence of violence and the identity formation" was crucial for the "abducted women and their forcible recovery by the Indian and Pakistani states."[25] To paraphrase Roy, the links between violence and the formation of identity during the Partition are most overt when examining the prevalence of abduction and displacement experienced by women at this time in history. Literature by writers like Pritam and Rao presents audiences with carefully crafted and nuanced perspectives of hybrid identities that form as a direct result of abduction and displacement. Moreover, these fictional narratives examine the continued effects of the Partition upon South Asian individuals and families without appropriating these narratives. Pritam draws on her own firsthand experiences of the Partition, while Rao relies on her family members' retellings to re-create narratives that are as accurate as possible. In order to further examine the prevalence of violence against women in modern South Asian society, we must consider the figure of the South Asian woman and her role in literature within the historical contextualization of the Partition.

Notes

1 Yasmin Khan, *The Great Partition: The Making of India and Pakistan* (New Haven, Conn.: Yale University Press, 2007), xxi.

2 Homi Bhabha, *The Location of Culture* (New York: Routledge, 2004), 159.

3 Bhabha, 159.

4 Denise L. Spitzer, "Immigrant and Refugee Women: Recreating Meaning in Transnational Context," *Anthropology in Action* 14, nos. 1/2 (2007): 54.

5 Bhabha, *Location of Culture*, 6.

6 M. Javaid Akhtar, Azra Asghar Ali, and Shahnaz Akhtar, "The Role of Vernacular Press in Subcontinent during the British Rule: A Study of Perceptions," *Pakistan Journal of Social Sciences (PJSS)* 30, no. 1 (2010): 71–84; Meredith Borthwick, *The Changing Role of Women in Bengal, 1849–1905* (Princeton, N.J.: Princeton University Press, 1984); Shahida Lateef, "Ethnicity and Social Change," *Economic and Political Weekly* 15, no. 50 (1980): 2086–2087; Shahida Lateef, "Whither the Indian Women's Movement?," *Economic and Political Weekly* 12, no. 47 (1977): 1948–1951; Bharati Ray, "Women of Bengal: Transformation in Ideas and Ideals, 1900–1947," *Social Scientist* 19, nos. 5/6 (1991): 3–23.

7   Bhabha, *Location of Culture*, 56.
8   While the novel was initially published in Punjabi, I have used Khushwant Singh's English translation for my analysis. Singh translates the title *Pinjar* to "the skeleton," while others indicate that in Hindi, *pinjar* translates to "the cage." See Paroma Chanda and Diptarka Chakraborty, "Bordered in an Interrogated Identity: A Study of Amrita Pritam's *Pinjar*," in *Border, Globalization, and Identity*, ed. Sukanta Das et al. (Newcastle upon Tyne, U.K.: Cambridge Scholars, 2018), 156–162.
9   Rosemary Marangoly George, *Indian English and the Fiction of National Literature* (Cambridge: Cambridge University Press, 2013), 199.
10 Amrita Pritam, *Pinjar: The Skeleton and Other Stories*, trans. Khushwant Singh (New Delhi: Tara Press, 2009), 6.
11 Pritam, 22.
12 Pritam, 1.
13 Pritam, 25.
14 Pritam, 86.
15 Bede Scott, "Partitioning Bodies: Literature, Abduction, and the State," *Interventions* 11, no. 1 (2009): 35.
16 Pritam, *Pinjar*, 125.
17 Shobha Rao, *An Unrestored Woman* (New York: Flatiron Books, 2016), 114.
18 Rao, 115.
19 Rao, 118.
20 Lopamudra Basu, "The Repetition of Silence: Partition, Rape, and Female Labor in Bapsi Sidhwa's *Cracking India*," *South Asian Review* 28, no. 2 (2007): 9.
21 Rao, *Unrestored Woman*, 106.
22 Rao, 118.
23 Rao, xii.
24 Scott, "Partitioning Bodies," 35.
25 Haimanti Roy, *Partitioned Lives: Migrants, Refugees, Citizens in India and Pakistan, 1947–65* (New Delhi: Oxford University Press, 2012), 154.

Bibliography

Akhtar, M. Javaid, Azra Asghar Ali, and Shahnaz Akhtar. "The Role of Vernacular Press in Subcontinent during the British Rule: A Study of Perceptions." *Pakistan Journal of Social Sciences (PJSS)* 30, no. 1 (2010): 71–84.

Basu, Lopamudra. "The Repetition of Silence: Partition, Rape, and Female Labor in Bapsi Sidhwa's *Cracking India*." *South Asian Review* 28, no. 2 (2007): 5–26.

Bhabha, Homi. *The Location of Culture*. New York: Routledge, 2004.

Borthwick, Meredith. *The Changing Role of Women in Bengal, 1849–1905*. Princeton, N.J.: Princeton University Press, 1984.

Chanda, Paroma, and Diptarka Chakraborty. "Bordered in an Interrogated Identity: A Study of Amrita Pritam's *Pinjar*." In *Border, Globalization, and Identity*, edited by Sukanta Das, Sanatan Bhowal, Sisodhara Syanbo, and Abhinanda Roy, 156–162. Newcastle upon Tyne, U.K.: Cambridge Scholars, 2018.

George, Rosemary Marangoly. *Indian English and the Fiction of National Literature*. Cambridge: Cambridge University Press, 2013.

Khan, Yasmin. *The Great Partition: The Making of India and Pakistan*. New Haven, Conn.: Yale University Press, 2007.

Lateef, Shahida. "Ethnicity and Social Change." *Economic and Political Weekly* 15, no. 50 (1980): 2086–2087.

———. "Whither the Indian Women's Movement?" *Economic and Political Weekly* 12, no. 47 (1977): 1948–1951.

Pritam, Amrita. *Pinjar: The Skeleton and Other Stories*. Translated by Khushwant Singh. New Delhi: Tara Press, 2009.

Rao, Shobha. *An Unrestored Woman*. New York: Flatiron Books, 2016.

Ray, Bharati. "Women of Bengal: Transformation in Ideas and Ideals, 1900–1947." *Social Scientist* 19, nos. 5/6 (1991): 3–23.

Roy, Haimanti. *Partitioned Lives: Migrants, Refugees, Citizens in India and Pakistan, 1947–65*. New Delhi: Oxford University Press, 2012.

Scott, Bede. "Partitioning Bodies: Literature, Abduction, and the State." *Interventions* 11, no. 1 (2009): 35–49.

Spitzer, Denise L. "Immigrant and Refugee Women: Recreating Meaning in Transnational Context." *Anthropology in Action* 14, nos. 1/2 (2007): 52–62.

7

Writing Solidarity

• •

Women in Bapsi Sidhwa's
Cracking India

CAROLYN OWNBEY

Born in Karachi in 1938, Bapsi Sidhwa immigrated to the United States in the early 1980s. Her third novel, *Cracking India* (1991), was her first written in North America. While both of her earlier novels, *The Crow Eaters* (1978) and *The Bride* (1982), concentrate on family matters and village settings, *Cracking India* expands its scope, focusing on Lahore and its surroundings and traversing more explicitly political terrain. Representing the subcontinent through the 1940s, *Cracking India* "is in fact one of the few Pakistani novels on the subject of Partition, and the first Partition anglophone novel from the subcontinent that tells the female version of the story."[1] While many critics have claimed it as a metaphor for the Partition, the book's original title, *Ice-Candy-Man*, suggests an interest both in gendered violence—the character Ice-candy-man perpetrates one of the central violations of a woman—and in the complicated moral quandary that the Partition necessarily generates. Imbued with ambiguity, rife with contradictions, and populated with deeply flawed characters, Sidhwa's novel invites us to ask, How do guilt and innocence signify in the landscape of the Partition? What do rehabilitation, recovery, and reparation mean when seemingly none are innocent? And to what extent are solidarity and community possible in this context?

The novel is narrated in hindsight by a child named Lenny, a disabled Parsi girl living with her upper-middle-class family in Lahore. Lenny narrates the Partition from a limited vantage point. The novel opens in the early 1940s, when Lenny is just four years old, and continues into her adolescence post-Partition. As the new border is created, Lenny witnesses violence in Lahore and hears stories about violence in nearby villages. One central intrigue is the kidnapping of her nanny, a Hindu woman named Shanta who is referred to almost exclusively by her occupation, Ayah, throughout. Scenes of spectacular violence are often kept out of sight—Ayah's rape and subjugation by Ice-candy-man, for instance, or the slaughter and dismemberment of women on a train. While Sidhwa does at times draw gruesome scenes, neither sympathy nor horror is the goal. Instead, the story focuses on the matriarchs of Lenny's family who recover and rehabilitate women who have either been kidnapped or crossed the border from India to escape violence.

Cracking India is often read as a feminist text that highlights violence against women during the Partition.[2] Some critics expand this reading to consider the "portrayal of violence as a more long-term phenomenon in the lives of its women."[3] Others fixate on deviant sexualities (Ayah's sensuality, Lenny's bisexual attractions) and how "Partition was a process of eradicating multiple and playful forms of desires."[4] Some readings touch on the concept of solidarity and argue that "Sidhwa portrays a version of solidarity among women across classes"[5] that "debunks class and religious borders."[6] In contrast, Ambreen Hai argues that *Cracking India* fails in its "attempt to empower and exhort a notoriously apathetic middle-class society of Pakistani women to forge cross-class, cross-ethnic gender alliances."[7] My reading allows for both possibilities: I aim to uncover both the affordances and the limits of solidarity in the moment of border creation.

While much criticism names Ayah a heroine, I contend that the structure of narration—narrated by a child ignorant of the significance of much of what she witnesses—teaches us to look beyond Lenny's fixation on Ayah to see a coalition of characters materialize, each adding nuance to what it means to be a citizen or a member of a community. Lenny's narrative voice privileges Ayah and elides other stories; reading past Lenny's impressions provides a complex vision of Partition Lahore and its surroundings. I aim first to establish parameters of citizenship in the context of the Partition. Second, I turn to a reading of the novel, demonstrating how the narrative explicitly interrogates and implicitly exposes the terms of inclusion in the new state and the complexity of guilt and innocence in the face of Partition violence. Lastly, I examine the liberatory potential exposed through the actions of *border women*—women living on the border of a new nation at Partition, especially those participating in the recovery and rehabilitation of others—and I outline the limits of that potential, arguing that Sidhwa's text provides a potent yet incomplete blueprint for solidarity writ large.

On Citizenship: The Nation after Partition

The practice of defining citizenship—the inclusion of those who are to be members of the nation-state and the exclusion of those who are not—is a foundational aspect of nation building: Who can (and cannot) be imagined as belonging within the new state? Citizenship is "deeply embedded in state formative practices," as Anupama Roy explains, because "fixing territorial boundaries and making [the state's] inhabitants legible . . . make the 'citizen' a stable and enumerable category, amenable to specific practices of rule."[8] In the context of Pakistan, the legal apparatus of citizenship—the Pakistan Citizenship Act—materialized in 1951. By this point, what we might call the social act of citizenship formation had been well underway for years. Operating under the understanding that India was to be a majority Hindu/Sikh nation and Pakistan majority Muslim, many individuals were forced to cross the newly drawn border, while others targeted groups who did not belong in the new scheme of things. Mass migrations and violence characterize this period of South Asian history. Women especially were targets of violence. This section outlines the practice of citizenship in the pre- and post-Partition contexts, with a focus on how women are excluded from full citizenship and left vulnerable to violations both legal and extrajudicial. The actions of the Pakistani and Indian governments to rectify the latter violations paradoxically serve further to inscribe women within their disciplinary power rather than providing citizenship rights or allowing women to choose for themselves.

On the one hand, citizenship describes a legal category and "the legal relationship between the individual and the polity";[9] on the other, there are gradations within citizenship. Many scholars such as Ariella Azoulay have described limitations of citizenship or "impair[ments] of civic status,"[10] wherein "socioeconomic equality,"[11] as Seyla Benhabib states, and "race, ethnicity, religion, sex, sexual orientation, and other 'identities,'"[12] as Saskia Sassen describes, exclude some citizens from full rights despite official citizenship. Women often inhabit the liminal space of not-quite-citizenship: they are legally citizens but set apart in terms of being both more subject to legal surveillance than their counterparts and particularly vulnerable to extrajudicial harm. In other words, women "as a class are a group to be protected on the one hand, and violable on the other."[13] In neither circumstance do women qualify as autonomous, fully protected legal actors.

The dual exposure of women—to governmental control and to extrajudicial harm—is a hallmark of South Asian society in colonial *and* postcolonial contexts. Whereas one might presume postcolonial nationalism would reject colonial logics and legalities, often such nationalism organizes around heteropatriarchal conceptualizations of nation and citizenship. Therefore, "heteropatriarchal nationalist law has not sufficiently dislodged the major epistemic fictions constructed during colonial rule . . . neither has it dislodged any of the received notions of womanhood."[14] This is the case in the context of the subcontinent, where codes of honor and other heteropatriarchal ideologies exist on a continuum that crosses both sides of the temporal break of the Partition.[15] These "received notions of womanhood" require purity, submission, and heterosexuality.[16] Under such a framework, women's behaviors and their significances and legalities are overdetermined in advance by the heteropatriarchal nation-state.

The trope of women's suicide—on the funeral pyre of one's husband or to avoid rape in the context of large-scale violence—as an honorable choice through which to secure a place in the national imaginary persists. Gayatri Chakravorty Spivak elucidates the structure of the former, wherein the social significance and purpose of sati change the social understanding of suicide. "The general scriptural doctrine is that suicide is reprehensible," she explains. "Room is made, however, for certain forms of suicide which, as formulaic performance, lose the phenomenal identity of being suicide."[17] In the act of sati, she identifies a "profound irony in locating the woman's free will in self-immolation." Her reading of such irony extends to suicide in response to communal sexual violence, or *jauhar*, as well:

> Although jauhar is not, strictly speaking, an act of sati, and although I do not wish to speak for the sanctioned sexual violence of conquering male armies . . . female self-immolation in the face of it is a legitimation of rape as "natural" and works, in the long run, in the interest of unique genital possession of the female. The group rape perpetrated by the conquerors is a metonymic celebration of territorial acquisition. Just as the general law for widows was unquestioned, so this act of female heroism persists among the patriotic tales told to children . . . when the status of the legal subject as property-holder could be temporarily bestowed on the female relict, the self-immolation of widows was stringently enforced.[18]

Legalities and moralities bend in the face of violence against women. The possibility of a woman owning property reverses the legality of suicide; the possibility of a woman's "pollution" through rape reverses the morality of it. Women, therefore, are both hypergoverned and uniquely violable.

In the Partition context, *jauhar*, rather than sati, predominates. Veena Das explains, "In family narratives on Partition riots which I collected, the heroic sacrifices made by women have a special place. By choosing a violent death for themselves rather than submitting to sexual violence by men of other communities, women are enshrined in these narratives as saviours of family honour."[19] The passive voice, "are enshrined," is telling: the women who made this "choice" cannot testify, so these stories are primarily told by (and for) men. Whereas "in the male versions of these narratives, the voluntary choice made by their women is emphasized," women are far more ambivalent about "the burdens of a heroic death": "women's stories show that they experienced the burdens placed upon them not only as a form of violence from men of other communities, but also as a form of violence emanating from their own."[20] The choice these women make in response to the imminent threat of violence is merely between different kinds of violation: "honorable" suicide or rape and murder. The immaterial consequence of each choice—beyond the materiality of harm in either instance—is her status in terms of the nation: if she chooses the former, she "can be accommodated within the narrative of the nation as a legitimate and pure—albeit dead—citizen"; if she chooses the latter, she is "refused entry into the domestic space of the new nation."[21] The imbrication of narratives of honor/shame in the new national imaginary necessarily means that full citizenship, in terms of (living) participation in the affairs of the nation-state, is not available to these women, regardless of their choices.

In 1948, responding to large-scale violence, the governments of India and Pakistan jointly took action to recover individuals who had been kidnapped. The Abducted Persons (Recovery and Restoration) Act of 1949 could perhaps be described as too little, too late: "The single most important point about the Abducted Persons (Recovery and Restoration) Bill was that it needed to be legislated at all, since the maximum number of recoveries had been made between 1947–49, before the Bill was introduced."[22] Moreover, the legislation—ostensibly meant to protect women—in fact extends their subjugation, entrenching it in law. The act creates a new legal category, an "abducted person," defined as "a male child under the age of sixteen years or a female of whatever age."[23] All women are hereby legally made minors, whereas men come of age into autonomous citizenship. Additionally, "once the problem came into the domain of state legislation, it took away the freedom of women to make their own choices"[24] Women become subject to a law that further removes their ability to choose. The law stipulates, "If any question arises whether a person detained in a camp is or is not an abducted person . . . it shall be referred to, and decided by, a tribunal."[25] Denied the right of choice, women are inscribed within the decision of the law—of, specifically, a tribunal made of men.

The Pakistan Citizenship Act of 1951 does little to ameliorate the plight of "abducted persons." There is only one category within the act that accounts for women—section 10, on "Married Women," which ties a woman's citizenship to her husband's. In the Partition context wherein forced marriages were not uncommon, the act does not provide any accounting for whether the married woman has chosen that marriage—and if such choice was brought into question, the Abducted Persons Act would require the matter decided before a tribunal rather than by the woman. As Ritu Menon and Kamla Bhasin argue, "The Abducted Persons act was remarkable for the impunity with which it violated every principle of citizenship, fundamental rights and access to justice, and for contravening all earlier legislation with regard to marriage, divorce, custody, and guardianship."[26] Under either law—the Citizenship or Abducted Persons Acts—women are excluded from citizenship and made subject to men.

Narrating Partition: Lenny as Incomplete Witness

The scene laid out in the previous section forms the sociopolitical backdrop of *Cracking India*. Sidhwa's novel approaches the subject from the perspective of child narrator Lenny, who watches as the landscape around her changes drastically. She hears stories of violence from others and witnesses gruesome scenes firsthand. As tensions escalate, Lenny muses over her mother's illicit activities—smuggling petrol in the family car, for instance—not understanding their significance (she believes her mother is committing arson; her mother actually is aiding Hindu and Sikh women to cross the border). At nearly the center of the novel, Lenny becomes aware of her new national identity: "I am Pakistani. In a snap. Just like that."[27] Most critics understand Lenny's perspective as innocent, even neutral. "The naïve perspective allows Lenny to ask questions that would otherwise be unacceptable," argues Kamran Rastegar, "and to interrogate the foundations of the communitarian violence around her in ways clearly unavailable to her older family members."[28] Sidhwa herself suggested that Lenny's position gives her some sort of impartiality: "I wrote from a Parsi child's perspective, because I felt it could bring some sort of fairness on the issue of Partition."[29] While I agree that Lenny's perspective allows a different kind of narrative to emerge because of her innocence (or ignorance) and her Parsi identity, this is only part of the narrative function of the novel. Lenny herself, precisely *as* an innocent and ignorant narrator, easily falls prey to propaganda and to stories that adults and older children tell her, no matter how suspect. Lenny is trained to believe certain stories—including nationalist ones, wrapped up in the heteropatriarchal discourse of honor—but the reader is invited to see nuance beyond Lenny's perspective. Reading against the general critical consensus that Ayah is the primary victim, I contend that the text complicates violence, victimhood, guilt, and responsibility through the readable partiality of Lenny's perspective.

Lenny falls victim to what Ariella Azoulay calls "planted pictures." Azoulay explains, in the context of her own adolescence, "an entire world of moving freely through space and its related adventures had been gradually placed beyond my reach, because these had always involved walking at night, entrance halls, and public parks. Each one of us carries with her an album of these planted pictures about the subject they designate and about their sense."[30] While Lenny does have a window into such prohibited scenes—namely, through Ayah, with whom she sits among men in the public park—she is conditioned by narratives that older relatives plant. Her mother blames the lower-class nannies for Lenny having contracted polio: "'I neglected her—left her to the care of ayahs. None of the other children who went to the same park contracted polio.'"[31] While Lenny personally views her disability as akin to "being born under a lucky star,"[32] the implication of her mother's words is clear: such an affliction is—or *should be*—a lower-class affair. The novel confirms that Lenny has absorbed such stories when she accompanies Godmother to the red-light district to find Ayah: "None of the women here is veiled. The bold girls, with short, permed hair, showing traces of stale makeup, stare at us as if we are freaks. They whisper and burst into giggles when we pass and bury their faces in each other's shoulders and necks. Their crumpled kamizes are too short and the *pencha*-bottoms of their shalwars too wide. Even I can tell they are not well brought up. I have never seen women of this class with cropped and frizzed hair: nor using the broad and comfortable gestures of men."[33]

Lenny internalizes the classist, heteropatriarchal narrative of how these women signify in terms of honor. She demonstrates that she is what Sara Ahmed calls a "good citizen": "one who watches (out for) suspicious persons and strangers, and who in that very act, becomes aligned, not only with the police (and hence the Law), but with the imagined community itself, whose boundaries are protected in the very labour of this look."[34] Lenny is not capable of separating herself from these planted pictures and hence from complicity. Not only is she Pakistani, but she is a *good Pakistani citizen*. The critical work of "examining the social relationships that are concealed" in what Ahmed terms "stranger fetishism" is left up to readers: "We need to consider how the stranger is an effect of processes of inclusion and exclusion, or incorporation and expulsion, that constitute the boundaries and bodies and communities."[35]

Part of this critical work is to read beyond Lenny's fetishization of Ayah. Despite her best intentions and clear devotion to Ayah, Lenny is unable to comprehend the full scope of Ice-candy-man's violation *as well as* the inequality of civil status between herself and the servant. When Lenny and Godmother meet with Ayah and Ice-candy-man, Lenny is told that Ice-candy-man "'has christened our ayah Mumtaz.'"[36] Lenny realizes the name change has come with a chance of countenance: "Where have the radiance and animation gone?" she asks, meeting Ayah's eyes for the first time. "Can the soul be extracted from its living body?"[37] Lenny does not understand the implications of this new "christening"—sexual violence and forced marriage—but through the narrative, she protests the change nonetheless. In the paragraphs following, Lenny refers to Ayah by both names, Ayah and Mumtaz (importantly, *not* Shanta), but uses the former increasingly and insistently, culminating in a frenzy of "Ayahs"—eight times on a single page as the scene closes.[38]

Lenny's devotion to Ayah and her partial awareness of harm done determines how she narrates—explicitly in this instance but also implicitly. As a result, many critics read Ayah as the novel's central figure: "Ayah is the heroine of the novel," Najia Zaidi claims.[39] She "comes to stand for the innocent victims of all violence," according to Paul Brians, and she "becomes the silent representative of female violation in this text," in Hai's reading.[40] Reading the novel in alignment with Lenny's perspective has consequences: a focus on Ayah's as *the* body upon which violence occurs lends itself to certain readings, obscuring others. For one, the explicit physical violence against Ayah is kept out of sight, which, if read as the primary instance of violence, causes problems. Hai reads "the manifold troubling implications of this narratival unspeakability" and argues that "silence about certain kinds of violation [. . .] acquiesces to, indeed, reinforces, the cultural system that dictates that rape signifies a woman's shame and the dishonor of her male protectors."[41] Certainly, there is much other violence that is unspeakable or unspoken. Lenny's father's abuse of her mother, for instance, is merely suggested. Deepika Bahri explains, "Her father, too, has betrayed her mother; that story of infidelity [and physical abuse] must remain shrouded in silence, its only permitted sign the telling bruises on her mother's body."[42] However, if we expand our reading of violence in the novel—against women, and against others—its "unspeakability" comes into question.

The explicit violence in the novel includes the deaths of strangers and familiars to Lenny. She sees "a naked child, twitching on a spear"[43] and watches as a man is tied to two jeeps and forcibly torn in half—an act that she, traumatized, replays with one of her dolls.[44] Lenny is present when the dead body of Masseur, a favorite suitor of Ayah's, is found: "The sack slowly topples over and Masseur spills out—half on the dusty sidewalk, half on the gritty tarmac."[45] Lenny also witnesses implicit violence, beyond Ayah. The wedding of child bride Papoo, occurring in the narrative immediately after Ayah's abduction, is one example. At the wedding, "it takes [Lenny] a while to realize that the crumpled heap of scarlet and gold clothes flung carelessly in a corner is really Papoo."[46] Her friend, drugged into compliance, is being married off to a much older—in Lenny's view, hideous—man. Lenny recoils when she sees him: "He is no boy! He is a dark, middle-aged man . . . the smirk lurking about his thin, dry lips gives an impression of cruelty."[47] The scene is reminiscent of an earlier moment when Lenny meets Gandhi. Surrounded by women, gaunt and smaller than expected, Gandhi nonetheless commands respect. Over time, Lenny's image of Gandhi changes: "It wasn't until some years later—when I realized the full scope and dimension of the massacres—that I comprehended the concealed nature of the ice lurking deep beneath the hypnotic and dynamic femininity of Gandhi's non-violent exterior."[48] Lenny learns, slowly and not completely within the novel, to understand the signs of concealed or future violence, particularly against women.

There are many other incidents of violence in the novel, both explicit (Ranna's story)[49] and implicit (the harassment of Himat Ali, formerly Hari; Lenny's cousin promising "I'll show you someday" when she asks what rape is).[50] Lenny understands the significance of some, missing others—and so too might the reader. I contend that the stage set by Sidhwa—wherein Ayah is not the only victim—makes any straightforward conception of responsibility, solidarity, or even community impossible. Perhaps the best example of the quandary of victimhood, villainy, responsibility, and guilt comes in the novel's original namesake: Ice-candy-man.[51] We know, of course, that Ice-candy-man is responsible for the kidnapping, serial rape, and forced marriage of Ayah, and we are led to believe he has been involved in other violence. His cruelty is only curbed by the force of the state, in two instances. First, the Abducted Persons Act, never named explicitly in the novel, is implied: "On discovering the rescue mission undertaken by the two governments for abducted women, Ice-candy-man promptly marries Ayah."[52] Officially made a citizen of Pakistan (as a woman now married to a citizen), Ayah-as-Mumtaz is no less vulnerable to harm despite the change in her civil status. The second act that checks Ice-candy-man's cruelty is the forcible recovery of Ayah by the police at the behest of Lenny's godmother.

At the same time, readers have seen Ice-candy-man experience trauma on multiple occasions—some Lenny registers, some she does not—which must inform our understanding of him as a pivotal character in the novel's imaginary. One instance is worth quoting at length:

> And just then, in the muted rustle, we hear the rattle of a bicycle hurtling up our drive at an alarming speed. We grow still, expectant. And emerging from the night like a blundering and scraggy bird, scraping his shoe on the veranda step to check the heedless velocity of his approach—Moti and Muccho scramble out of his way—Ice-candy-man comes to an abrupt and jolted halt. He is breathless, reeking of sweat and dust, and his frantic eyes rake the group. They rest for an instant on the Sikh, and flutter back to us. "A train from Gurdaspur has just come in," he announces, panting. "Everyone in it is dead. Butchered. They are all Muslim. There are no young women among the dead! Only two gunny-bags full of women's breasts!" Ice-candy-man's grip on the handlebars is so tight that his knuckles bulge whitely in the pale light. The kohl lining his eyes has spread, forming hollow, skull-like shadows: and as he raises his arm to wipe the perspiration crawling down his face, his glance once again flits over Sher Singh. "I was expecting relatives . . . For three days . . . For twelve hours each day . . . I waited for that train!"[53]

Ice-candy-man's trauma and fear (his glance toward the Sikh suggests his awareness that the violence was likely committed by Sikhs), are evident.[54] He is "breathless" and "frantic." Lenny registers the trauma explicitly. "What I've heard is unbearable," she says in the moment; she later refers to the incident as "the evening he emerged from the night and almost crashed into us with the grim news of the trainload of dead Muslims," describing him as having a "darkly grieving look."[55] But another trauma occurs out of sight, out of Lenny's consciousness, that the reader may not register. Following the train incident, Ice-candy-man disappears for several days. When he "visits at last," he is changed, with "an unpleasant swagger" and "full of bravado."[56] What we do not see, what Lenny does not intuit, is what happened to cause the change. We learned earlier that Ice-candy-man has a wife living in a nearby village. A reader with a sense of Partition violence can piece together the events that followed Ice-candy-man's feverish bicycle ride: having gone to his wife's village, he has either found her dead or not found her at all. Traumatized, honor insulted, Ice-candy-man rejects grief and turns toward retribution. What are we to make of such a scenario? In a context where his villainy is underwritten by victimhood, Ice-candy-man's guilt and responsibility are not straightforward. The novel models several responses to his behavior: Godmother's chastisement and "cold rage,"[57] Lenny's ultimate forgiveness, Ayah's refusal to acknowledge him altogether.

By way of an answer, this chapter's final section argues that Sidhwa's representation of the border women and their allies—the women in Lenny's family and the men serving as collaborators—constitutes the novel's political message, insofar as it has one. This coalition, far from uncomplicated heroes or intersectional champions of women's rights, work within difficult confines and toward nebulous goals. Nonetheless, the coalition itself signals a possibility within the complex landscape of Partition: a different kind of citizenship or community, something perhaps akin to solidarity.

The Possibility of Solidarity

In the context of Partition—where none are innocent, not even a disabled child (Lenny, after all, is the one who betrays Ayah)[58]—the question of what ordinary people can do to rectify harms done is a difficult one. That difficulty lies not only in the issue of whose harm—what about Ice-candy-man's?—but also in what constitutes repair and reparation. The novel does not answer these questions. It does nonetheless capture some of the (primarily women's) work of harm reduction that occurred during the Partition. What is perhaps most remarkable about Sidhwa's story is the reversal of community mentality that her coalition undergoes: far from the "hunt with the hounds"[59] mentality that the Parsi community adopted under colonial rule, the actions of the coalition represent a possibility of solidarity.

The matriarchs of Lenny's family correspond to real-life women. Menon and Bhasin explain, "The real work of rehabilitating women fell to women . . . not just those whose names can be found in government records and ministry reports; not the score or more with whom we spoke but countless others."[60] While these women worked in good faith, they operated "within patriarchal structures, often displayed rather patriarchal attitudes and were influence by urban middle-class conceptions of socially appropriate roles for women and men."[61] The same is true of the women in *Cracking India*. Before arranging her recovery, Godmother suggests to Ayah that living as Ice-candy-man's wife might be better than an uncertain future: "What if your family won't take you back?"[62] Ayah chooses to leave, and where the Abducted Persons Act might require the matter come before a tribunal, Godmother instead employs the law to fulfill Ayah's wish. In this way, "women's agency is situated in a contradictory way, as both complicit and transgressive."[63] Godmother is complicit in the abuses of the act because she leverages its authority, but she also undermines its power of subjugation, letting Ayah choose for herself; Godmother is complicit in heteropatriarchal structures and narratives of honor in her understanding of options open to Ayah, but she also undermines their power of decision. There is no possibility for her to work outside the parameters of the law; she must call upon the police to recover Ayah, as her coalition would be unable to challenge Ice-candy-man's (now legal, since their marriage) claim on Ayah.

To a limited extent, we can understand the actions of this coalition as work *in solidarity*: the novel draws a community at work toward a common cause. However, it fails to present a broader-minded, longer-term solidarity: none in the coalition challenges the heteropatriarchal order *as such*, even when individual actions undermine its structures; none dismantles class hierarchies or social understandings of honor. Yet they take risks on behalf of lower-class women with different religious and cultural affiliations, who are seen as sullied after violence has been committed against them. This coalition works to find places within a national imaginary for fallen women who have otherwise been written out.

Partition is an exemplary site to analyze citizenship—its moment of definition and creation. It is also an exemplary site to analyze how exclusionary discourses—including citizenship—might be imagined differently. Benhabib argues, "We must be ready to imagine forms of political agency and subjectivity which anticipate new modalities of political citizenship."[64] What the women in *Cracking India* provide is a preliminary model for how to do so: they work to make the recovery of women a recuperation of some semblance of citizenship. This solidarity, limited as it is, transcends their previously held opportunistic group mentality and presents a model of better citizenship.

The novel demonstrates kinds of (partial) community and solidarity that can be enacted by those excluded by new nationalisms. The women are not political or social activists, nor will their activities continue into the post-Partition future. However, in the moment of crisis, they choose not to remain above the fray. Perhaps the novel would have been more successful had their activities signified more clearly as social activism or had they not been privileged and heteropatriarchal-conforming. Certainly, there were a large number of women—not wealthy, victimized themselves, even radical—whose lives could have taught us something different. Within Sidhwa's story, however, we still learn something about solidarity. While the novel does not valorize their work as ideal—the women who are able to leave the abducted persons camp still find themselves in difficult situations—the actions of the coalition in this violent interregnum nonetheless provide a glimpse of what might be possible, what citizenship and solidarity might look like outside of the impositions of state and society.

Notes

1 Deepika Bahri, "Telling Tales," *Interventions: International Journal of Postcolonial Studies* 1, no. 2 (1999): 227, https://doi.org/10.1080/13698019900510321.

2 See Kamran Rastegar, "Trauma and Maturation in Women's War Narratives: *The Eye of the Mirror* and *Cracking India*," *Journal of Middle East Women's Studies* 2, no. 3 (2006): 22–47; Sangeeta Ray, *En-gendering India: Woman and Nation in Colonial and Postcolonial Narratives* (Durham, N.C.: Duke University Press, 2000); and Bahri, "Telling Tales."

3 Hakyoung Ahn, "Queer Eyes and Gendered Violence in Bapsi Sidhwa's *Cracking India*," *Journal of Postcolonial Writing* 55, no. 5 (2019): 602, https://doi.org/10.1080/17449855.2019.1627570.

4 Rani Neutill, "Bending Bodies, Borders and Desires in Bapsi Sidhwa's *Cracking India* and Deepa Mehta's *Earth*," *South Asian Popular Culture* 8, no. 1 (April 2010): 75.

5 Ahn, "Queer Eyes," 604.

6 Arunima Dey, "The Female Body as the Site of Male Violence during the Partition of India in Bapsi Sidhwa's 'Ice-Candy-Man,'" *Complutense Journal of English Studies* 26 (2018): 38, http://dx.doi.org/10.5209/CJES.54661.

7 Ambreen Hai, "Border Work, Border Trouble: Postcolonial Feminism and the Ayah in Bapsi Sidhwa's *Cracking India*," *Modern Fiction Studies* 46, no. 2 (Summer 2000): 402, https://doi.org/10.1353/mfs.2000.0028.

8 Anupama Roy, "Gender and Citizenship in India," in *Routledge Handbook of Gender in South Asia*, ed. Leela Fernandes (New York: Routledge, 2014), 56.

9 Saskia Sassen, "The Repositioning of Citizenship and Alienage: Emergent Subjects and Spaces for Politics," in *Displacement, Asylum, Migration: The Oxford Amnesty Lectures 2004*, ed. Kate E. Tunstall (Oxford: Oxford University Press, 2006), 180.

10 Ariella Azoulay, *The Civil Contract of Photography* (New York: Zone Books, 2008), 14.

11 Seyla Benhabib, *The Rights of Others: Aliens, Residents and Citizens* (Cambridge: Cambridge University Press, 2004), 111.

12 Sassen, "Repositioning of Citizenship," 185.

13 Kathleen R. Arnold, *Homelessness, Citizenship, and Identity* (Albany, N.Y.: SUNY Press, 2004), 43.

14 M. Jacqui Alexander, "Erotic Autonomy as a Politics of Decolonization: An Anatomy of Feminist and State Practice in the Bahamas Tourist Economy," in *Feminist Genealogies, Colonial Legacies, Democratic Futures*, ed. M. Jacqui Alexander and Chandra Talpade Mohanty (New York: Routledge, 1997), 97.

15 As Jill Didur explains, "The economy of meaning within elite, patriarchal, and racist national imaginaries circulating at the time conflated the sacredness of the nation with the sacredness of Woman, making women both an object of protection and a target of violence—both physical and discursive." Didur, *Unsettling Partition: Literature, Gender, Memory* (Toronto: University of Toronto Press, 2006), 7.

16 Alexander's argument comes in the context of what she calls "erotic autonomy"; she argues, in short, that the possibility of women controlling their own sexualities—queer or otherwise—threatens the nation-state.

17 Gayatri Chakravorty Spivak, "Can the Subaltern Speak?," in *Marxism and the Interpretation of Culture*, ed. Cary Nelson and Lawrence Grossberg (Champaign: University of Illinois Press, 1988), 299.

18 Spivak, 303.

19 Veena Das, *Critical Events: An Anthropological Perspective on Contemporary India* (Delhi: Oxford University Press, 1995), 62–63.

20 Das, 63.

21 Ray, *En-gendering India*, 135.

22 Ritu Menon and Kamla Bhasin, *Borders & Boundaries: Women in India's Partition* (New Brunswick, N.J.: Rutgers University Press, 1998), 122.

23 Abducted Persons (Recovery and Restoration) Act, 1949. This was a legislative agreement signed by India and Pakistan in 1948, allowing Muslim girls and boys under age sixteen from India to be sent to Pakistan to reunite with their migrated families. The bill was enacted to ensure the safe recovery and restoration of women and young Hindu and Muslim girls and boys, who were victims of violence. See Gyaaneshwar Joshi, "Abducted Persons (Recovery and Restoration) Act, 1949," Pleaders, November 26, 2021, https://blog.ipleaders.in/abducted-persons-recovery-and-restoration -act-1949/.

24 Das, *Critical Events*, 67.

25 Abducted Persons Act.

26 Menon and Bhasin, *Borders & Boundaries*, 125.

27 Bapsi Sidhwa, *Cracking India: A Novel* (Minneapolis: Milkweed Editions, 1991), 150.

28 Rastegar, "Trauma and Maturation," 27.

29 Bapsi Sidhwa, "Making Up with Painful History: The Partition of India in Bapsi Sidhwa's Work," interview by Isabella Bruschi, *Journal of Commonwealth Literature* 43, no. 3 (2008): 143.

30 Azoulay, *Civil Contract of Photography*, 13–14.

31 Sidhwa, *Cracking India*, 25.

32 Sidhwa, 20.

33 Sidhwa, 271.

34 Sara Ahmed, *Strange Encounters: Embodied Others in Post-coloniality* (New York: Routledge, 2000), 30.

35 Ahmed, 6.

36 Sidhwa, *Cracking India*, 271.

37 Sidhwa, 272.

38 Sidhwa, 275.

39 Najia Zaidi, "Glimpses of the New Woman in Sidhwa's Novels," *Pakistan Journal of Women's Studies: Alam-e-Niswan* 18, no. 1 (2011): 66.

40 Paul Brians, *Modern South Asian Literature in English* (London: Greenwood Press, 2003), 106; Hai, "Border Work," 401.

41 Hai, "Border Work," 401.

42 Bahri, "Telling Tales," 226.

43 Sidhwa, *Cracking India*, 144.

44 Sidhwa, 145, 148.

45 Sidhwa, 185.

46 Sidhwa, 197.

47 Sidhwa, 198–199.

48 Sidhwa, 96.

49 Sidhwa, 207–220.

50 Sidhwa, 192, 278.

51 In an interview with Preeti Singh, Sidhwa calls Ice-candy-man a character who "represents so many themes of the novel" (qtd. in Dey, "Female Body," 42). The book's title only changed at the insistence of her American publishers, who "found the title off-putting" (Brians, *Modern South Asian Literature*, 104).

52 Dey, "Female Body," 36.

53 Sidhwa, *Cracking India*, 159.

54 A number of U.S. Department of State telegrams indicate rumors of a large Sikh mob on the Indian side of the border responsible for a great deal of violence,

including attacks on trains. See U.S. Department of State incoming telegram no. 727, August 24, 1947, from New Delhi to Secretary of State, signed Howard Donovan, counselor of embassy; and no. 906, October 1, 1947, from New Delhi to Secretary of State, signed Henry F. Grady, ambassador at New Delhi.

55 Sidhwa, *Cracking India*, 159, 164.
56 Sidhwa, 164–165.
57 Sidhwa, 259.
58 Sidhwa, 194–195.
59 Sidhwa, 26.
60 Menon and Bhasin, *Borders & Boundaries*, 169. They explain, "As we travelled through Punjab and Haryana and talked to people in Delhi who had worked on rehabilitation, we realized just how many women had been instrumental in resetting other women" (183).
61 Menon and Bhasin, 192.
62 Sidhwa, *Cracking India*, 274.
63 Menon and Bhasin, *Borders & Boundaries*, 199.
64 Benhabib, *Rights of Others*, 179.

Bibliography

Ahmed, Sara. *Strange Encounters: Embodied Others in Post-coloniality*. New York: Routledge, 2000.

Ahn, Hakyoung. "Queer Eyes and Gendered Violence in Bapsi Sidhwa's *Cracking India*." *Journal of Postcolonial Writing* 55, no. 5 (2019): 602–613. https://doi.org/10.1080/17449855 .2019.1627570.

Alexander, M. Jacqui. "Erotic Autonomy as a Politics of Decolonization: An Anatomy of Feminist and State Practice in the Bahamas Tourist Economy." In *Feminist Genealogies, Colonial Legacies, Democratic Futures*, edited by M. Jacqui Alexander and Chandra Talpade Mohanty, 63–100. New York: Routledge, 1997.

Arnold, Kathleen R. *Homelessness, Citizenship, and Identity*. Albany, N.Y.: SUNY Press, 2004.

Azoulay, Ariella. *The Civil Contract of Photography*. New York: Zone Books, 2008.

Bahri, Deepika. "Telling Tales." *Interventions: International Journal of Postcolonial Studies* 1, no. 2 (1999): 217–234. https://doi.org/10.1080/13698019900510321.

Benhabib, Seyla. *The Rights of Others: Aliens, Residents and Citizens*. Cambridge: Cambridge University Press, 2004.

Brians, Paul. *Modern South Asian Literature in English*. London: Greenwood Press, 2003.

Das, Veena. *Critical Events: An Anthropological Perspective on Contemporary India*. Delhi: Oxford University Press, 1995.

Dey, Arunima. "The Female Body as the Site of Male Violence during the Partition of India in Bapsi Sidhwa's 'Ice-Candy-Man.'" *Complutense Journal of English Studies* 26 (2018): 27–45. http://dx.doi.org/10.5209/CJES.54661.

Didur, Jill. *Unsettling Partition: Literature, Gender, Memory*. Toronto: University of Toronto Press, 2006.

Hai, Ambreen. "Border Work, Border Trouble: Postcolonial Feminism and the Ayah in Bapsi Sidhwa's *Cracking India*." *Modern Fiction Studies* 46, no. 2 (Summer 2000): 379–426. https://doi.org/10.1353/mfs.2000.0028.

Joshi, Gyaaneshwar. "Abducted Persons (Recovery and Restoration) Act, 1949." Pleaders, November 26, 2021. https://blog.ipleaders.in/abducted-persons-recovery-and-restoration -act-1949/.

Menon, Ritu, and Kamla Bhasin. *Borders & Boundaries: Women in India's Partition*. New Brunswick, N.J.: Rutgers University Press, 1998.

Neutill, Rani. "Bending Bodies, Borders and Desires in Bapsi Sidhwa's *Cracking India* and Deepa Mehta's *Earth*." *South Asian Popular Culture* 8, no. 1 (April 2010): 73–87.

Rastegar, Kamran. "Trauma and Maturation in Women's War Narratives: *The Eye of the Mirror* and *Cracking India*." *Journal of Middle East Women's Studies* 2, no. 3 (2006): 22–47.

Ray, Sangeeta. *En-gendering India: Woman and Nation in Colonial and Postcolonial Narratives*. Durham, N.C.: Duke University Press, 2000.

Roy, Anupama. "Gender and Citizenship in India." In *Routledge Handbook of Gender in South Asia*, edited by Leela Fernandes, 55–69. New York: Routledge, 2014.

Sassen, Saskia. "The Repositioning of Citizenship and Alienage: Emergent Subjects and Spaces for Politics." In *Displacement, Asylum, Migration: The Oxford Amnesty Lectures 2004*, edited by Kate E. Tunstall, 176–203. Oxford: Oxford University Press, 2006.

Sidhwa, Bapsi. *Cracking India: A Novel*. Minneapolis: Milkweed Editions, 1991.

———. "Making Up with Painful History: The Partition of India in Bapsi Sidhwa's Work." Interview by Isabella Bruschi. *Journal of Commonwealth Literature* 43, no. 3 (2008): 141–149.

Spivak, Gayatri Chakravorty. "Can the Subaltern Speak?" In *Marxism and the Interpretation of Culture*, edited by Cary Nelson and Lawrence Grossberg, 271–313. Champaign: University of Illinois Press, 1988.

United States Department of State. Incoming telegram no. 727, August 24, 1947, from New Delhi to Secretary of State. Signed Howard Donovan, counselor of embassy.

———. Incoming telegram no. 906, October 1, 1947, from New Delhi to Secretary of State. Signed Henry F. Grady, ambassador at New Delhi.

Zaidi, Najia. "Glimpses of the New Woman in Sidhwa's Novels." *Pakistan Journal of Women's Studies: Alam-e-Niswan* 18, no. 1 (2011): 63–72.

8

Sri Lankan Postcolonial Inversion and a "Thousand Mirrors" of Resistance

• •

MOUMIN QUAZI

> Only an extremely close detonation would pop a head off a body like that. It makes me ponder this woman, girl really. What could have led her to this singularly terrible end? What secret wound bled until she chose this most public disassembly of herself? Just moments earlier she had been just another nameless woman in the teeming crowd; now, blown to bits, she was either a martyr or mass murderer, according to one's taste. Either way she had attained instant immortality. But what had led her to that moment? That is the question that haunts me.
> —Nayomi Munaweera, *Island of a Thousand Mirrors*

Alexandra Heller-Nicholas, in her *Rape-Revenge Films: A Critical Study* (2021), critiques the dissolution of the rape survivor as seen in Dario Argento's film *La*

sindrome di Stendhal (The Stendhal syndrome; 1996) by noting that "the protagonist's [Anna's] struggle is not just against her rapist, but against a long, unre-
lenting history that allows the rape survivor only a limited number of choices
regarding how she can be artistically configured."[1] One of those configurations
has been written by Nayomi Munaweera, through her fictional response to the
Sri Lankan Civil War,[2] who has resisted war violence by offering a narrative that
spurs understanding of the postcolonial ruptures through a variety of mimic-
ries that reframe the paradoxes inherent to the Sri Lankan conflict. Particularly,
she uses the trope of inversion (in the sense of something being inside-out) to
reframe the absurdity of war violence and its aftermath.[3] Munaweera's debut
novel, *Island of a Thousand Mirrors* (2012), is a diasporic imagining of the island
nation of Sri Lanka and its thirty-year civil war.[4] Told from the perspective of a
writer born in Sri Lanka who then immigrated to Nigeria and then the United
States, the novel has become an important fictional voicing of the horrific effect
of war violence against Sri Lankan women, who are both victims and perpetrators of violence, some even becoming victims of their own violence in the
form of suicide bombings.[5] Munaweera uses inversion along with mirroring and
mimicry throughout the novel to engage the hybrid fluidity of the postcolonial
consciousness. Her parodying of the sex act becomes a trope that accentuates
the dual nature of hybridity. A forced hybridity produces dissolution and dis-
integration, even as it promises birth and homogeneity through a complicated
death, while an unforced one causes a complicated life. These two conditions
become distorted mirror images of each other, inverting the expected order.
Munaweera's title of her novel lends a clue to this pattern in that its imagery,
actions, and title highlight "a thousand mirrors" of resistance to the war violence that plagued her homeland from 1987 to 2009.

Like a teardrop dripping from the eye of South Asia, Sri Lanka is an island
with a storied colonial and now postcolonial history.[6] Beginning the narrative
action in what was then called Ceylon in 1948, Munaweera tells the story—as
she calls it, "one possible narrative"[7]—of two families, one a Tamil family (culminating its focus on the woman Saraswathi, who becomes a suicide bomber[8])
from the north, and the other a Sinhala family (narrowing its focus on Yasodhara whose sister dies in a suicide bombing) from the south, primarily in the
two cities of Hikkaduwa and Colombo, the capital.[9] The Sinhala are believed
to be the descendants "from the lovemaking between an exiled Indian princess
and a large jungle cat,"[10] while the Tamil are represented by a tiger, resulting in
flags featuring "a rifle-toting tiger [and a] sword-gripping lion."[11] Not that tigers
and lions are inversions of each other; they are, in a sense, distorted mirror
images, both big cats. Inversion and mirroring become the dominant patterns
in *Island of a Thousand Mirrors*. Munaweera uses this pattern to craft a narrative that resists war violence. She structures her novel in two main parts, with
a prologue and an epilogue bookending those two parts. In this way, even the
novel has this mirror structure. In the first part, the background of one of those

two family parts (Yasodhara's) is highlighted, whereas in the second part, the background of the other of those two family parts (Saraswathi's) is brought to light. Part 2 is where those two families' plotlines converge. The second part is where Munaweera details the "spoiling" of Saraswathi through rape and its aftermath.

The term *spoil* is one pregnant with meaning: it can refer to being damaged, going bad, or being plundered. The term can refer to the plunder, the plundered, or the act of plundering. Idiomatically, it can even refer to being desirous of or eager for something.[12] Munaweera uses the term to describe the effect that rape has on a woman not only in a war context but in a marriage context as well. She describes the process, after the consummation of marriage, of examining the bedsheet for the blood of the supposed virginal wife: "When afterward, her husband looks carefully at the sheet to find the splotch of blood that indicates her honor, she turns her head away . . . all the family will know that he has married a good girl, an unspoiled girl."[13] In a war context, the effects of rape are punctuated in the following scene: "If you are a girl, there is always the chance that the soldiers will spoil you or that people will say that they did. I don't know what 'spoiled' means exactly, but it must be something truly terrible. It happened to my friend Parvathi. She was coming home from school when a soldier grabbed her, dragged her into the chili fields, and spoiled her. People stopped talking to her as soon as it happened, but they never stopped talking *about* her. . . . One day last year she jumped into a well."[14] A raped woman is both the spoils and the spoiled.

The novel's primary narrator, Yasodhara, has a reverse-image shared narrator, Saraswathi, who is a kind of inverted Yasodhara. They are both studious. Yasodhara is a self-confessed bookworm,[15] and Saraswathi is on a trajectory to become a teacher. In fact, she is named after "the serious-eyed and studious goddess of learning."[16] Saraswathi's plans are horribly derailed when she is viciously raped by Sri Lankan armed forces members, thus causing her to be considered to be "spoiled":

The soldiers break in . . . they push me into the yawning maw of a white van, . . . two soldiers come for me, they grasp my upper arms, pull me, my legs and feet dragging useless against the earth . . . I see the rifle butt coming before it smashes into my face. Gushing red, teeth spilling, I fall hard onto my wrists, then they are upon me. *Tiger bitch.* . . . I am pulled apart, uncovered, exposed. They hold me down. . . . They tear me open with their nails, bite me with their fangs, their spittle falls thick across my breasts. They break into me. Break me. Break into me. Break me. Burying their stench deep inside my body while they pant like dogs over me. Until I no longer smell like myself. Until this body is no longer mine. Until I am only a limp, bleeding, broken toy. *Tiger bitch! Tiger! Bitch! Tiger! Bitch!* I pull my eyes onto that perfect square of sky. High above, a crane passes slowly. . . . This is what it means, then, to be spoiled.[17]

In this horrifying experience, Saraswathi is violated not only physically, verbally, and mentally but also in ways that words cannot convey, yet her violation is not over. Now she has been cast into the realm of the spoiled. Later, she says, "I cannot meet her [Amma's] eyes, cannot explain to her the shame of what has happened."[18] She has been raped into a hyperliminality: "I've slipped into some other place that exists alongside this one, a place no one else knows about where men can take girls, rip them open, and bury a kind of corruption in their flesh."[19] Payel Mukherjee describes Saraswathi's rejection: "Stereotyped as a rape victim, her violated body was subjected to multiple rejections, both within her family and in society."[20] One of the aftermaths of this "dishonor" is that Saraswathi's mother pushes her into the Liberation Tigers of Tamil Ealam (LTTE). She asks, "What will you do here? What man will take what the soldiers have spoiled? . . . If you don't go, you will ruin us all. . . . We will lose face with everyone."[21]

As a result, Saraswathi will embrace suicide as her way out of this condition: "There is one way out, Parvathi's way [suicide]."[22] With nothing left to lose, she is transformed into an inverted tabula rasa (but not really a "clean" or "empty" slate). She claims, "The soldiers have left me a blank page. They used me, spoiled me, and then threw me away like a piece of refuse. They did not expect me to survive. They should have killed me, but they didn't, and this is their mistake. Now the Tigers write upon my surfaces."[23] She is transformed into a stealthy weapon of war: "I am becoming slowly but surely a jungle cat."[24] Describing her first kill, her tone is unflappable: "I hear that click and I pull the trigger. / The back of his head explodes; blood, bone, gray stuff splatters across my boots, splashes along my pants leg, even onto my hands. . . . We are Tigers now."[25] She boasts, "I am fearless. I am free. Now, I am the predator."[26] She continues, "Now I *am* the Shiva Nataraja, the dancing face of death. / In this way I will never again be prey, small, trembling, and weak."[27] Shiva is "the god who performs the dance of destruction as well as creation."[28]

Through all the bluster of proclaimed fearlessness, Saraswathi admits that her recollections go back to the night of her rape: "Fear wraps its fingers around my throat, bile rises into my mouth. The uniforms materialize. . . . I am struggling. . . . I will forever smell of him so that all will know when I enter a place bringing unending corruption. . . . I fight then, struggle with all my strength, smashing myself from side to side, trying to throw him off. . . . Moans spill out of me. They wrench me awake."[29] Her narration continues,

> Know that night after night, the faces of the soldiers change into the face of the one I love the most in the world. Know that, now, nightly, it is not the soldiers who rip me apart, but our Leader himself. . . . When I sleep the dream comes and it is unbearable. The Leader is our Father. He has done everything for us. He has devoted his life to us, and yet I cannot rid myself of this grotesque nightmare. I know then that something is wrong with me. I am flawed, defective. I

am corrupted. I am beyond the help of all who lie sleeping peacefully, innocent, around me.[30]

In this corruption, the memory of the perpetrator in Saraswathi's violation is blurred and then replaced by new images of "The Leader." In real life, the actual leader of the LTTE did conduct last suppers with his bombers. Daya Somasundaram describes the ritual of eating a last dinner with the supreme leader the night before carrying out a suicide bombing: "Prabhakaran himself is reported to have a last supper with the cadres before their mission, a picture of which is released posthumously."[31] Bhatia and Knight theorize that this ritual "was probably followed to further ignite passion for the 'cause' as we as to assess the determination of the candidates before they embarked on their final mission."[32]

The next day, though, Saraswathi believes she will achieve a type of immortality as one of the martyrs for the cause of progress toward a Tamil homeland. Her immortality will be through memory, she thinks: "My portrait, miles high, will hang everywhere extolling my bravery, . . . Amma and Appa will be proud. Luxshmi [her sister] will be the sister of a martyr. She will be honored by all the rebels for this. I cannot give them more than this."[33] She feels a sense of hope. When she sees her reflection in the mirror (the ultimate mimicry), Saraswathi claims that she is a "ghost from a different time and place. Useless to me. Beyond her gaze, I search for my own eyes. In them I see Hope . . . and that is Everything."[34] Now Munaweera reveals that whereas Sri Lanka is the island of a thousand mirrors,[35] Saraswathi "will explode in a hundred directions, send a thousand pieces of shrapnel to lodge in all this soft, pliant flesh."[36]

What has motivated this transformation in Saraswathi? Yasodhara meditates on a suicide bomber who prefigures Saraswathi: "Just moments earlier she had been just another nameless woman in the teeming crowd; now, blown to bits, she was either a martyr or mass murderer, according to one's taste. Either way she had attained instant immortality. But what had led her to that moment?"[37] Rape becomes one of the prime motivations behind Saraswathi's accession into suicide bombing. In this way, Munaweera is mimicking the motivation that was offered by the LTTE when they made it known that "Dhanu [the suicide bomber who killed former Indian premier Rajiv Gandhi] had avenged herself because she had been raped by members of the IPKF sent to Sri Lanka under Gandhi."[38] Saraswathi's penultimate thoughts are of her rape and the refrain *Tiger Bitch* repeated nine times, finally culminating in an eruption of anger, memory, and violence: "I cannot tell where the walls end and the sky begins—*Tiger Bitch*—and where the voices begin and the hands end, and where I begin or end, and I am tearing into shreds and something buried deep is erupting like a land mine, like rage buried in my flesh, something settled—*Tiger Bitch*—and burrowed under my heart like a fetus raising its head. *Tiger bitch Tiger bitch Tiger bitch!*"[39] And then the bomb explodes, and Saraswathi sees herself in her final thoughts as a dancing Shiva Nataraja who "*is watching and I am dancing, swirling and stamping. My fingers opening like the petals of the lotus bud. . . . I am in motion. Unstoppable and Immaculate.*[40] Memories of being raped are woven throughout Saraswathi's stream of consciousness.[41]

Inasmuch as a person's consciousness can be studied, especially one who has perished, Mia Bloom, in her "Female Suicide Bombers: A Global Trend," studies the phenomenon of female suicide bombers. In her 2007 article, she acknowledges a "growing trend of women bombers." While noting a "long history of female involvement in political violence," she observes that the traditional expectation was to give birth to more insurgents, but in 2007, "women are now taking a leading role in conflicts by becoming suicide bombers"—using their bodies as human detonators for the explosive material strapped around their waists.[42] Bloom demonstrates, "The IED is often disguised under a woman's clothing to make her appear pregnant, and so beyond suspicion or reproach," noting as an example the Sri Lankan woman Kanapathipillai Manjula Devi, who used this "tactic to penetrate a military hospital in Colombo, Sri Lanka, posing as the wife of a soldier on her way to the maternity clinic."[43]

Often, the motivation for suicide bombing is rape,[44] even rape that hasn't happened to the woman herself: "In fact, the atrocities need not even hurt a Tamil woman directly for her to join the LTTE, as long as they affect the Tamil community as a whole: Witnessing rape . . . hearing about rape from other villagers and the Army's killing of Tamil youth . . . and the feeling of helplessness in not being about to defend against the Sri Lankan Army are the main reasons for the girls joining the LTTE."[45] Edmar Salem, in his "Attitudes towards Female Suicide Bombers in Palestine and Tamil Sri Lanka," makes two important observations for this present study: (1) "portrayals of female operatives tend to produce specific images of the perpetrators as improved versions of traditional women—as sexually pure virgins, brides, mothers, or in ways that interlink women with nature," and (2) "research into the personal lives of female bombers suggests that women are often compelled to forsake their lives once they deviate away from patriarchal norms." In this sense, female suicide bombers operate out of "shame" and "dishonor" in order to redeem fallen reputations, such as being barren, divorced, defiled, unchaste, and so on.[46] Bhatia and Knight assert that "rapes and molestations made a bitter impact" on attracting women to the LTTE.[47] Elizabeth Jean Wood, in her "Armed Groups and Sexual Violence: When Is Wartime Rape Rare?" explains that in Sri Lanka, "the LTTE relied on recruitment based on sexual violence by enemy forces."[48] Bloom asserts, "The spectacle of female suicide bombers doesn't challenge the patriarchy as much as provide evidence of its power. The message female suicide bombers send is that they are more valuable to their societies dead than they ever could have been alive."[49] Neloufer de Mel has analyzed suicide bombing extensively. He asserts, "A suicide bombing also carries symbolic meaning of life and death. It contains the powerful paradox in the self-annihilation that is simultaneously regarded as life-giving to a community. It is to die while seeking immortality as a hero-martyr to the cause."[50]

Later, in 2012, Robert J. Brym and Bader Araj studied suicide bombers, and their article "Are Suicide Bombers Suicidal?" catalogs a wide range of factors previously understood to have motivated suicide bombers, including "religious fanaticism, the desire to liberate occupied territory, the craving for revenge against occupiers, inter-group competition aimed at attracting recruits and supporters, desperation originating in material deprivation, and irrational urges grounded in psychopathology,"[51] but they note that nobody really knows what's going through a bomber's mind because analysts "lack direct access to the cognitive and limbic processes occurring in actors' minds,"[52] so the problems with understanding motives involve sampling and diagnostics.[53] Brym and Araj assert the "importance of focusing on the political and social roots of the phenomenon rather than a psychological approach."[54]

Yet in 2018, Marco Krstić, in his "Personality Profile of a Suicide Bomber," does just that, positing that "terrorist suicide is a product of psychological implications," which include trauma, humiliation, social exclusion, ideological reasons, and social pressures.[55] He asserts that three key elements are needed for suicide terrorist attacks: "strongly motivated individuals, access to organizations whose goal is to create suicide bombers and a community that glorifies perpetrators as heroes and accepts their acts as noble acts of resistance."[56] He continues, "Terrorist acts are not the product of mental illness (hence, experts often state that 'terrorists are built, they are not born')."[57] He concludes that "there is no unambiguous answer or individual motivation that could fully explain why people become terrorists."[58] This conclusion makes Munaweera's novel important as resistance to war violence; she brings insight to possible motives for Saraswathi's transformation from innocent, aspiring schoolteacher to cutthroat killer of innocents as a Tamil Tiger Black Widow. Daya Somasundaram describes the roles and responsibilities of the members of the Tamil Tigers: "In joining the Tamil Tigers, the cadres commit themselves to die and wear a cyanide capsule (usually on a necklace) at all times to be used in the event of imminent capture, ostensibly to avoid giving information under torture."[59] Somasundaram clarifies, "According to the LTTE and their sympathizers, these were not suicide (*thatkollai*), but self-sacrifice, the Tamil term being *thatkodai*."[60] "One of the distinguishing marks of the LTTE," according to Bandarage, "that made it a prototype of 21st-century global terrorism was the popularization of suicide bombing."[61] She continues, "The LTTE 'perfected' the use of women in combat" and "is known to have invented the suicide bomb belt and used women suicide bombers extensively. One-third of Black Tigers—the Tigers' suicide unit—was composed of women" recognized for their "ferocious participation in many major battlefront operations and their competent execution of ambushes, sabotage, suicide bombings, and so on."[62] Granting women such a prominent role, the Black Widows (a.k.a. Black Tigers) are not denied a "direct relation to national agency."[63] The power of that agency outlasts death, according to the mythos. For example, in the novel, Saraswathi's head is later placed in a plastic bag by a policeman. She is reduced to being called by Yasodhara, "Vanquished Medusa, death dealer, serial killer."[64] Later, Lanka (Yasodhara's sister) is described in her death as "transformed into stone."[65] Like Medusa's bewitching power, Saraswathi's is able to transform into stone. As Bandarage observes, women play multiple roles in war, "as victims, perpetrators, and peacemakers, albeit recognizing that there are not always mutually exclusive categories."[66]

Shamara Ransirini makes a strong case that the woman suicide bomber is "an assemblage of affects, intensities, and multiple becomings that resists identification."[67] Ransirini traces Saraswathi's becomings, in particular, as a militant, dancer, and suicide bomber.[68] In the end, Saraswathi envisions her own end as a form of an island of a thousand mirrors: she imagines her body "disintegrating into a thousand tiny pieces that will birth and nurture a sapling that grows into a tree, a non-human, organic form of life."[69] In this way, her death is not "just as transformation but as a transfiguration."[70] Bloom asserts, "The advent of women suicide bombers has thus transformed the revolutionary womb into an exploding one."[71] In fact, the Tamil Tiger chief Velupillai Prabhakaran invoked that imagery in 1993 when he wrote, "The ideology of women's liberation is a child born out of the womb of our liberation struggle."[72]

In the early part of the novel, Munaweera foreshadows the power of hybridity, even if it is borne out of barrenness: "Unable to conceive, my aunt delves into the sex lives of plants. Pulling apart tender flower lips with pollen-dusted fingers, she exposes fleshy stamens, produces hybrids and variations never before seen on the island. . . . Every year, she walks away from the Colombo Garden Show with the biggest trophies and the envy of other horticulturally minded ladies."[73] There is a sort of victory in Sri Lanka's heterogeneity. Maryse Jayasuriya and Aparna Halpé, in "Contestation, Marginality, and (Trans)nationalism: Considering Sri Lankan Anglophone Literature," observe that one of its paradoxes "is the way Sri Lankan Anglophone literature straddles the conventional boundaries between a minority and majority literature, between nationalism and diaspora, between ethnic identity politics and human rights advocacy."[74] Munaweera's fiction does more than straddle boundaries; it blends them, blurs them, and in some cases, obliterates them. The novel ends with a recalling of the many victims of the war, numbering eighty thousand at least.[75] Munaweera writes, "It is a number beyond comprehension. I must mourn for them. I shall cry for a long time. And then when my weeping is spent, when I have no more sorrow to give, I shall celebrate peace. . . . I shall wake up from these long decades of war and begin to see what we can do in peace, what sort of creatures we are when the mask of lion or tiger falls from us."[76] Whereas Saraswathi's violence aims toward giving birth to an Ealam for the Tamil people, the inverted image of that is Yasodhara, who becomes a birthmother with her now deceased sister's widower husband, Shiva. About her pregnancy, she meditates, "I had not known that mothering would replicate falling in love so intimately, but I have learned that it is the biology in us that reacts to both states. She has transformed us in unexpected, unimaginable ways."[77] The *she* here is referring to the new baby, Samudhra, whom they call Sam. Yasodhara and Shiva's daughter "represents the unification of both the Sinhala and Tamil ethnicity."[78] She is a female, though her nickname downplays her gender.[79] From the perspective of a post–civil war diaspora writer, the promise of peace can now be reframed differently. Rather than conveying a sense of precarity,[80] Munaweera, at the end of her novel, describes Yasodhara and her husband's lovemaking as a "homecoming."[81] Their child, Sam (a name that is not gender specific), is "both American and Sri Lankan, but beyond this, also Tamil and Sinhala."[82] There is hope in Sam's hybridity. Yasodhara sees her child as one "of the peace, the many disparate parts of her experience knit together in jumbled but peaceable unity."[83]

Through her fictional use of inversion and mirroring, Munaweera has resisted the postcolonial paradox of yearning for home and not feeling at home, especially for the diasporic dweller. Lovemaking is couched as a violent act, and violence is used to describe the most familial of acts. Munaweera has endeavored to expose some of the root causes of war violence while giving voice to those who are so misunderstood in that diasporic homeland for resisting war violence, especially that of rape. Robin E. Field, in her *Writing the Survivor*, has emphasized that "rape is unknowable except to victim-survivors. Rapists erase their victims by their very presence as well as through their violent actions."[84] Field has rightly predicted that in the twenty-first century, "many more stories—both real and fictional—of female, male, transgender, and genderqueer victim-survivors will be told."[85] In her own, unique way, through inversion and mirroring, Munaweera has unerased the rape victim in *Island of a Thousand Mirrors*, as a form of resistance to war violence, even as that victim then erases herself and others through the act of suicide bombing. This paradox emblematizes the dilemma of suicide as resistance to oppression while hopefully shedding light on the underlying violence of oppressive systems that place unbearable weight on women not to be "spoiled."

Notes

1 Alexandra Heller-Nicholas, *Rape-Revenge Films: A Critical Study*, 2nd ed. (Jefferson, N.C.: McFarland, 2021), 178.

2 According to Sepali Guruge et al., "Intimate Partner Violence in the Post-war Context: Women's Experiences and Community Leaders' Perceptions in the Eastern Province of Sri Lanka," *PLOS One* 12, no. 3 (2017): 1–16, Sri Lanka's civil war had strong ethnic and geographical dimensions: it was driven by demands from a separatist, predominantly Tamil, ethnic minority group in the northern and eastern region of the country for a "state independent from the Sinhalese majority" (2). Furthermore, "Sri Lanka has a population of approximately 20 million consisting of an

ethno-religious mix of Sinhalese [Buddhists] (75%), Tamils [Hindus] (11%), Moors [Muslims] (9%), and other groups such as Burghers and Malays (5%)" (3). According to Human Rights Watch, "Since 1983, between 80,000 and 100,000 people—the majority of them Tamil, Sinhalese, and Muslim civilians—have been killed due to the conflict" (qtd. in Asoka Bandarage, "Women, Armed Conflict, and Peacemaking in Sri Lanka: Toward a Political Economy Perspective," *Asian Politics & Policy* 2, no. 4 [2010]: 653). The war finally ended with the "Sri Lankan government's military defeat of the secessionist Liberation Tigers of Tamil Ealam (LTTE) in May 2009" (Bandarage, 653).

3 In her collection of essays entitled *The Reversible World: Symbolic Inversion in Art and Society* (Ithaca, N.Y.: Cornell University Press, 1978), Barbara A. Babcock broadly defines "symbolic inversion" as "any act of expressive behavior which inverts, contradicts, abrogates, or in some fashion presents an alternative to commonly held cultural codes, values, and norms be they linguistic, literary or artistic, religious, or social and political" (14). She adds, "Since the early Renaissance at least, the word 'inversion' has been used to mean 'a turning upside down' and 'a reversal of position, order, sequence, or relation' (OED: 1477)" (15). Ultimately, she notes, "symbolic inversion is central to the literary notions of irony, parody, and paradox" (16). Her anthology concerns itself with the ways symbolic inversions "affect the ways we perceive, group ourselves, and interact with others," especially "the ways and means and purposes for manipulating and upending sociocultural orders" (31). This chapter is concerned with how inversion is used in a postcolonial context, as a means of presenting a subjectifying version of a female suicide bomber as a form of resistance to Sri Lankan civil war violence.

4 Nayomi Munaweera, *Island of a Thousand Mirrors* (New York: St. Martin's Press, 2012). Maryse Jayasuriya and Aparna Halpé outline the ways many writers (they mention no fewer than seventy) have responded to the thirty-year conflict and its phases: "The separatist struggle by militant groups such as the Liberation Tigers of Tamil Ealam (LTTE), which turned into terrorist brutality; the second JVP insurrection in the late 1980s; and the brutal repression of the insurgents by paramilitary forces associated with the government; which led to countless deaths and disappearances. The acceleration of the diaspora due to the war and violence resulted in many new writers emerging outside Sri Lanka," one of which is Nayomi Munaweera. Jayasuriya and Halpé, "Contestation, Marginality, and (Trans)nationalism: Considering Sri Lankan Anglophone Literature," *South Asian Review* 33, no. 3 (2017): 20.

5 Vandana Bhatia and W. Andy Knight refer to the condition of women suicide bombers as being victims of "zombification," for "having failed to uphold the standards of the patriarchal society as virgins, chaste characters and bearers of children, they are then considered aberrations of the that patriarchal society." Bhatia and Knight, "Female Suicide Terrorism in South Asia: Comparing the Tamil Separatists and Kashmir Insurgents," *South Asian Survey* 18, no. 1 (2011): 22. See also Brite Heidemann, "The Symbolic Survival of the 'Living Dead': Narrating the LTTE Female Fighter in Post War Sri Lankan Women's Writing," *Journal of Commonwealth Literature* 54, no. 3 (2019): 387.

6 Heidemann explains that three different empires—the Portuguese, the Dutch, and the British—"reshaped the island [known today as Sri Lanka] into a multi-ethnic society par excellence, consisting of Sinhalese, Tamils, Muslims, and Christians by the time the British left in 1948" (385).

7 Munaweera, *Island of a Thousand Mirrors*, 7.

8 Maryse Jayasuriya, in her "Exploding Myths: Representing the Female Suicide Bomber in the Sri Lankan Context in Literature and Film," *Journal of Postcolonial*

Cultures and Societies 4, no. 1 (2013): 233–257, argues that Munaweera, in her fleshing out of subjectivity o fa woman's process of becoming a suicide bomber, undermines the tendency "to exoticize or sensationalize women who kill" (238).

9 See Bibhuti Mary Kachhap and Aju Aravind, "Narration of the Displaced: A Study of Female Characters in the Novel *Island of a Thousand Mirrors*," *Forum of World Literature Studies* 9, no. 1 (2017): 1–9, in which the authors provide the following plot summary:

> The story begins in Colombo, the capital of Sri Lanka, where a Sinhalese family resides and houses a Tamil family as tenants upstairs. The Sinhalese children in the family, Yasodhara and Lanka, grow along with the tenant's children, including Shiva Shivalingam, the Tamil son. After the death of Yasodhara's and Lanka's uncle in the Sinhala-Tamil riot, they leave for the United States. Their uncle Ananda is already settled in America. The other story line involves Saraswathi, a Tamil girl in the north part of Sri Lanka, unaffected by the war until the LTTE take her two brothers as soldiers. Saraswathi aspires to become a teacher when she grows up, but her childhood dream is disrupted when she is raped by soldiers of the Sri Lankan army. After such barbarism, Saraswathi too is taken away from her family by the LTTE. Later she joins the "Black Tigers," a special squad, and becomes a suicide bomber. She is sent to Colombo after being trained to murder a moderate Tamil leader. In the process of murdering the politician, Saraswathi and Lanka (who is on the same bus) also die. Lanka's life tragically intersects with Saraswathi's, as Lanka is on her way home to meet Yasodhara who is returning to American the same day. (2)

10 Munaweera, *Island of a Thousand Mirrors*, 6.
11 Munaweera, 7.
12 Dictionary.com, s.v. "spoil," accessed August 2021, https://www.dictionary.com/browse/spoil.
13 Munaweera, *Island of a Thousand Mirrors*, 57.
14 Munaweera, 143.
15 Munaweera, 161.
16 Munaweera, 130.
17 Munaweera, 151–153.
18 Munaweera, 156.
19 Munaweera, 158.
20 Payel Chattopadhyay Mukherjee, "Unhomely Home, Unhomely Women: The Precariousness of Being, Belonging, and Becoming in the Sri Lankan Diasporic Fiction of Nayomi Munaweera," *South Asian Review* 42, no. 3 (2020): 7, https://doi.org/10.1080/02759527.2020.1827928.
21 Munaweera, *Island of a Thousand Mirrors*, 159–160.
22 Munaweera, 160.
23 Munaweera, 181.
24 Munaweera, 182.
25 Munaweera, 184.
26 Munaweera, 185.
27 Munaweera, 186.
28 Shamara Ransirini, "Excessive Becomings: Rethinking Women and Militancy," *Hecate* 43, nos. 1/2 (2017): 27.
29 Munaweera, *Island of a Thousand Mirrors*, 187.
30 Munaweera, 188.
31 Daya Somasundaram, "Suicide Bombers of Sri Lanka," *Asian Journal of Social Science* 38 (2010): 433.

32 Bhatia and Knight, "Female Suicide Terrorism," 20.

33 Munaweera, *Island of a Thousand Mirrors*, 215.

34 Munaweera, 211.

35 Munaweera, 8.

36 Munaweera, 215.

37 Munaweera, 121.

38 Bandarage, "Women, Armed Conflict," 658. See also Andrew Greenland, Damon
Proulx, and David A. Savage, "Dying for the Cause: The Rationality of Martyrs, Suicide Bombers and Self-Immolators," *Rationality and Society* 32, no. 1 (2020): 93–115,
in which the authors remind readers that research on terrorists has found that the
vast majority do not display personal pathologies or psychological disorders and
were relatively ordinary before being recruited and indoctrinated by terrorist organizations. However, there "may be fundamental psychological differences between the
thousands of terrorists (freedom fighters) who risk their lives for a cause, but fight
to survive, and the tiny percentage who intentionally blow themselves up" (99–100).
In Andrea Michelle Morris, "Who Wants to Be a Suicide Bomber? Evidence from
Islamic State Recruits," *International Studies Quarterly* 64 (2020): 306–315, Morris
observes that "terrorist organizations strategically choose their attackers" (307). As
Greenland, Proulx, and Savage remark, the act of killing others by killing oneself is
what sets these bombers apart from other warriors: "The suicide bomber makes an
active choice, from a position of relative safety to intentionally end their own life
and to kill as many others as possible. The last part of this choice is what sets suicide
bombers apart from others, that is, the intention to take the lives of others as part
of their own end of life choice" ("Dying for the Cause," 110). "The most effective
soldiers," Laurence Iannoccone says in "The Market for Martyrs," *Interdisciplinary
Journal of Research on Religion* 2, no. 4 (2006): 1–30, "are not those with nothing to
live for, but rather those with something they are willing to die for" (14).

     The important study by Bhatia and Knight, "Female Suicide Terrorism," posits
that the ultimate goal of suicide bombing is to instill fear or, better yet, hysteria (8). I
find this wording to be interesting, as *hysteria* derives from the Greek ὑστέρα (*hystera*;
uterus), gendering the outcome as well as the source of the terror. Bhatia and Knight
conclude that female suicide terrorism in Sri Lanka is "a product of several inter-related
factors that feed into each other: (i) tormented society, (ii) individual grievances, and
(iii) a terrorist organization with an effective indoctrination structure" (7)—in other
words, situated within specific socio-political contexts. Bhatia and Knight detail the
growth of the Liberation Tigers of Tamil Ealam (LTTE), from an uprising led by Vil-
lupillai Prabhkaran, to an ethno-nationalist struggle, to a separatist struggle marked by
brutal acts of terrorism (10). In 1987, the LTTE unleashed the new tactic of suicide terrorism, assembling a specialized squad named the Black Tigers, whose members were
willing to swallow cyanide capsules to escape capture by enemy forces (10). This is the
force that Saraswathi is recruited into. The LTTE also created an exclusive women's
group called Suthanthirap Paravaikal (Birds of Freedom; 11).

39 Munaweera, *Island of a Thousand Mirrors*, 216.

40 Munaweera, 216 (italic in the original).

41 Munaweera evokes the imagery of the hypersexualized goddess (such as Artemis
Ephesia) when she writes, "But there are also nightmares. . . . Over and over I [Yasod-
hara] dream of a . . . young girl. She stands before me and her large bruised eyes do not
leave mine. When she unpins the sari fold at her shoulder and pulls it away from her, I
see sunset-colored bruises on her delicate clavicles. When she undoes her sari blouse,
I see the grenades tucked like extra breasts under her own. It is grotesque" (125).

42 Mia Bloom, "Female Suicide Bombers: A Global Trend," *Daedalus* 136, no. 1 (Winter 2007): 94.

43 Bloom, 95.

44 According to Bandarage, "Rape has been used as a weapon of war in Sri Lanka, though the number of incidents has been much fewer than in conflicts, such as those in Bosnia and Rwanda" ("Women, Armed Conflict," 654). In Sri Lanka, "most rapes by the Sri Lankan armed forces, the IPKE (Indian Peace Keeping Force), and the LTTE, the JVP, and men from other armed groups will never be known" (655).

45 Bloom, "Female Suicide Bombers," 96.

46 Edmar Salem, "Attitudes towards Female Suicide Bombers in Palestine and Tamil Sri Lanka," *Behavioral Sciences of Terrorism and Political Aggression* 7, no. 3 (2015): 201, https://doi.org/10.1080/19434472.2015.1009482.

47 Bhatia and Knight, "Female Suicide Terrorism," 11.

48 Elisabeth Jean Wood, "Armed Groups and Sexual Violence: When Is Wartime Rape Rare?," *Politics and Society* 37, no. 1 (2009): 163. For a comprehensive definition of rape as a war crime (as delineated by the Geneva Convention), see the United Nations Office on Genocide Prevention and the Responsibility to Protect website, http://www.un.org/en/genocideprevention/war-crimes.shtml.

49 Bloom, "Female Suicide Bombers," 102.

50 Neloufer de Mel, "Body Politics: (Re)cognising the Female Suicide Bomber in Sri Lanka," *Indian Journal of Gender Studies* 11, no. 1 (2004): 77.

51 Robert J. Brym and Bader Araj, "Are Suicide Bombers Suicidal?," *Studies in Conflict & Terrorism* 35 (2012): 432.

52 Brym and Araj, 443.

53 Brym and Araj, 434–435.

54 Brym and Araj, 443.

55 Marko Krstić, "Personality Profile of a Suicide Bomber," *Polemos* 21, no. 1 (2018): 66.

56 Krstić, 68–69.

57 Krstić, 70.

58 Krstić, 74.

59 Somasundaram, "Suicide Bombers," 418.

60 Somasundaram, 421.

61 Bandarage, "Women, Armed Conflict," 658.

62 Bandarage, 657–658.

63 Anne McClintock, "Family Feuds: Gender, Nationalism, and the Family," *Feminist Review* 44 (1993): 62.

64 Munaweera, *Island of a Thousand Mirrors*, 219.

65 Munaweera, 222.

66 Bandarage, "Women, Armed Conflict," 654.

67 Ransirini, "Excessive Becomings," 20.

68 Ransirini, 21.

69 Munaweera, *Island of a Thousand Mirrors*, 190–191.

70 Ransirini, "Excessive Becomings," 32.

71 Bloom, "Female Suicide Bombers," 95.

72 Bhatia and Knight, "Female Suicide Terrorism," 11.

73 Munaweera, *Island of a Thousand Mirrors*, 76.

74 Jayasuriya and Halpé, "Contestation, Marginality," 24.

75 By the time Birte Heidemann wrote on the Sri Lankan war in 2019, that number was one hundred thousand. Heidemann, "Symbolic Survival," 385.

76 Munaweera, *Island of a Thousand Mirrors*, 236.

77 Munaweera, 227.
78 Jeslyn Sharnita Amarasekera and Shanthini Pillai, "Bound by the Sea: Transnational Sri Lankan Writings and Reconciliation with the Homeland," *Southeast Asian Journal of English Language Studies* 22, no. 1 (2016): 24. Amarasekera and Pillai's analysis of Munaweera's novel is excellent, especially in their relaying of census information about ethnic makeup and their recounting of the history of Ceylon, from British rule from 1796 to 1948, to the Republic of Sri Lanka in 1972, and to the civil war with the rise of the LTTE (20). In their article, though, there is no mention at all of suicide bombing. This chapter seeks to redress that lacuna.
79 Females, though, were vital in protesting the war violence in Sri Lanka: "Mothers' Fronts organized by Tamil women in the north and the east and by Sinhala women in the south to protest arbitrary arrests, disappearances, abductions, and killings, of their sons by the Sri Lankan state forces, the LTTE, the IPKF, the JPV, and other armed groups." Bandarage, "Women, Armed Conflict," 659.
80 Homi Bhabha, in his "The World and the Home," *Social Text in Text* 31/32 (1992): 141–153, https://doi.org/10.2307/466222, introduces the notion of "unhomeliness" as "a paradigmatic post-colonial experience" (142) of the alienation of being both/ and but also neither/nor, especially for writers of the diaspora. Mukherjee frames this very condition as "the sense of inconsistency in conceiving home as a stable and homely" ("Unhomely Home," 2). She avers that "home is a precarious locus of discontent which reveals a systemic psychological lacuna in the critical sensibilities of postcolonial belonging" (1). Further, the "metaphorical and physical home opens as a site of transition, foregrounding displacement, discontent, and fraught belonging" (3).
81 Munaweera, *Island of a Thousand Mirrors*, 231.
82 Munaweera, 233.
83 Munaweera, 237.
84 Robin E. Field, *Writing the Survivor: The Rape Novel in Late Twentieth-Century American Fiction* (Greenville, S.C.: Clemson University Press), 19.
85 Field, 226.

Bibliography

Amarasekera, Jeslyn Sharnita, and Shanthini Pillai. "Bound by the Sea: Transnational Sri Lankan Writings and Reconciliation with the Homeland." *Southeast Asian Journal of English Language Studies* 22, no. 1 (2016): 19–27.

Babcock, Barbara A. *The Reversible World: Symbolic Inversion in Art and Society*. Ithaca, N.Y.: Cornell University Press, 1978.

Bandarage, Asoka. "Women, Armed Conflict, and Peacemaking in Sri Lanka: Toward a Political Economy Perspective." *Asian Politics & Policy* 2, no. 4 (2010): 653–667.

Bhabha, Homi. "The World and the Home." *Social Text in Text* 31/32 (1992): 141–153. https://doi.org/10.2307/466222.

Bhatia, Vandana, and W. Andy Knight. "Female Suicide Terrorism in South Asia: Comparing the Tamil Separatists and Kashmir Insurgents." *South Asian Survey* 18, no. 1 (2011): 7–26.

Bloom, Mia. "Female Suicide Bombers: A Global Trend." *Daedalus* 136, no. 1(Winter 2007): 94–102.

Brym, Robert J., and Bader Araj. "Are Suicide Bombers Suicidal?" *Studies in Conflict & Terrorism* 35 (2012): 432–443.

de Mel, Neloufer. "Body Politics: (Re)cognising the Female Suicide Bomber in Sri Lanka." *Indian Journal of Gender Studies* 11, no. 1 (2004): 76–92.

Field, Robin E. *Writing the Survivor: The Rape Novel in Late Twentieth-Century American Fiction*. Greenville, S.C.: Clemson University Press, 2020.

Greenland, Andrew, Damon Proulx, and David A. Savage. "Dying for the Cause: The Rationality of Martyrs, Suicide Bombers and Self-Immolators." *Rationality and Society* 32, no. 1 (2020): 93–115.

Guruge, Sepali, Marilyn Ford-Gilboe, Colleen Varcoe, Vathsala Jayasuriay-Illesinghe, Mahesan Ganesan, Sivagurunathan Sivayogan, Parvathy Kanthasamy, Pushparani Shanmugalingam, and Hemamala Vithanarachchi. "Intimate Partner Violence in the Post-war Context: Women's Experiences and Community Leaders' Perceptions in the Eastern Province of Sri Lanka." *PLOS One* 12, no. 3 (2017): 1–16.

Heidemann, Birte. "The Symbolic Survival of the 'Living Dead': Narrating the LTTE Female Fighter in Post War Sri Lankan Women's Writing." *Journal of Commonwealth Literature* 54, no. 3 (2019): 384–398.

Heller-Nicholas, Alexandra. *Rape-Revenge Films: A Critical Study*. 2nd ed. Jefferson, N.C.: McFarland, 2021.

Iannoccone, Laurence. "The Market for Martyrs." *Interdisciplinary Journal of Research on Religion* 2, no. 4 (2006): 1–30.

Jayasuriya, Maryse. "Exploding Myths: Representing the Female Suicide Bomber in the Sri Lankan Context in Literature and Film." *Journal of Postcolonial Cultures and Societies* 4, no. 1 (2013): 233–257.

Jayasuriya, Maryse, and Aparna Halpé. "Contestation, Marginality, and (Trans)nationalism: Considering Sri Lankan Anglophone Literature." *South Asian Review* 33, no. 3 (2017): 17–28.

Kachhap, Bibhuti Mary, and Aju Aravind. "Narration of the Displaced: A Study of Female Characters in the Novel *Island of a Thousand Mirrors*." *Forum of World Literature Studies* 9, no. 1 (2017): 1–9.

Krstić, Marko. "Personality Profile of a Suicide Bomber." *Polemos* 21, no. 1 (2018): 65–80.

McClintock, Anne. "Family Feuds: Gender, Nationalism, and the Family." *Feminist Review* 44 (1993): 61–80.

Morris, Andrea Michelle. "Who Wants to Be a Suicide Bomber? Evidence from Islamic State Recruits." *International Studies Quarterly* 64 (2020): 306–315.

Mukherjee, Payel Chattopadhyay. "Unhomely Home, Unhomely Women: The Precariousness of Being, Belonging, and Becoming in the Sri Lankan Diasporic Fiction of Nayomi Munaweera." *South Asian Review* 42, no. 3 (2020): 1–16. https://doi.org/10.1080/02759527.2020.1827928.

Munaweera, Nayomi. *Island of a Thousand Mirrors*. New York: St. Martin's Press, 2012.

Ransirini, Shamara. "Excessive Becomings: Rethinking Women and Militancy." *Hecate* 43, nos. 1/2 (2017): 20–42.

Salem, Edmar. "Attitudes towards Female Suicide Bombers in Palestine and Tamil Sri Lanka." *Behavioral Sciences of Terrorism and Political Aggression* 7, no. 3 (2015): 200–209. https://doi.org/10.1080/19434472.2015.1009482.

Somasundaram, Daya. "Suicide Bombers of Sri Lanka." *Asian Journal of Social Science* 38 (2010): 416–441.

Wood, Elisabeth Jean. "Armed Groups and Sexual Violence: When Is Wartime Rape Rare?" *Politics and Society* 37, no. 1 (2009): 131–162.

III

Advocacy/Activism

••••••••••••••••••••••

9

Kashmiri Women Activists in the Aftermath of the Partition of India

● ●

NYLA ALI KHAN

Through my previous and current work, I attempt to recount a peregrination, which still continues, through the agency, volatility, turmoil, conflict, politics, and history of becoming Kashmiri. I will not deny that I am also trying to make sense of a "personal intellectual trajectory."[1] An important part of this work, for me, is the imperative situating of the female subject. It would be remiss of me to posit a hegemonic, North American, white middle-class feminist agenda as the reference point to gauge the import of other feminist concerns. On the contrary, I emphasize a politics of identity that would allow for the recuperation of the heterogeneous Kashmiri subject, which would undermine any attempt at homogenization. Although I am wary of the construction of a monolithic "Kashmiri" female subject and well aware of the repressive politics of a homogenizing cultural nationalism, I do not wish to forestall the possibility of a unified subjectivity as the basis of nationalist politics. I acknowledge the political productivity of the construct of a unified subjectivity while cautioning the reader against eliding specific, varied, and unique forms of agency deployed by Kashmiri women in times of relative calm, conflict, political turbulence, resurgence of nationalism, and internal critique not just of state nationalism but of insurgent nationalism as well. Although every instance of the resurgence of nationalism in Kashmir has strategically employed the term *women* to further engender this category of subjects, I reiterate that there is no monolithic "Kashmiri woman."

I trace my origin to the hegemonically defined "Third and First Worlds." While I am filiated to the Kashmir Valley in the regions of Jammu and Kashmir, a unit in the Indian Union, I remain affiliated to the restoration of an autonomous Jammu and Kashmir. My move to the Midwest complicated my already multilayered identity by adding one more layer to it: my affiliation with the South Asian diaspora in the United States. This affiliation, however, empowers me with an agency to inhabit a space that "slides both geographically and linguistically."[2]

My maternal grandfather, Sheikh Mohammad Abdullah, was the prime minister of the state of Jammu and Kashmir from 1948 to 1953. When the pledge to hold a referendum was not kept by the government of India, his advocacy of autonomy for the state led to his imprisonment. He was shuttled from one jail to another until 1972 and remained out of power until 1975. My maternal grandmother, Begum Akbar Jehan, supported her husband's struggle and represented Srinagar and Anantnag constituencies in Jammu and Kashmir in the Indian parliament from 1977 to 1979 and 1984 to 1989, respectively. It is paradoxical that although she was a determined political and social activist, "according to biographical-genealogical conventions, that the (lives of the) fathers are known and largely accounted for, while the (lives of the) mothers are unknown, unrecorded, and, until relatively recently, little explored," Akbar Jehan was also the first president of the Jammu and Kashmir Red Cross Society from 1947 to 1951.[3] But during my grandfather's incarceration, she had been burdened with the arduous task of raising five children in a politically repressive environment that sought to undo her husband's mammoth political, cultural, and legalistic attempts to restore the faith of Kashmiri society in itself. After the rumblings and subsequent explosion of armed insurgency and counterinsurgency in Kashmir in 1989, a few of those organizations that advocated armed resistance to secure the right of self-determination for the people of Kashmir—in accordance with the United Nations Resolutions of April 21 and June 3, 1948; of March 14, 1950; and of March 30, 1951—blamed the leader who had given the clarion call for Kashmiri nationalism, Sheikh Mohammad Abdullah, for having (purportedly) succumbed to pressures brought on by the government of India in 1975: putative capitulation to its insistence to relinquish the struggle for autonomy or self-determination.

•

Kashmiri women from different walks of life have managed against all odds to express their agency during the plethora of political, social, and military transformations in the past nine decades. The perception and manifestation of women's political struggle during the nationalist awakening in the 1930s became "a wider part of the politics of democratization and empowerment."[4] The women whose lives and politics I have analyzed in this chapter lived a life that most women of their generation could not envision for themselves. Professor Carolyn G. Heilbrun reminds students of literature that "acting to confront society's expectations for oneself requires either the mad daring of youth, or the colder determination of middle age. Men tend to move on a fairly predictable path to achievement; women transform themselves only after an awakening."[5] In addition to ensconcing themselves within a classic patriarchal structure—that is, they married, bore children, and encouraged their husbands to succeed in the world—their imaginations were stimulated by "dreams of some other life: of personal accomplishment, of the understanding and control of hard facts and complex problems, of a place in a community where women were in sufficient numbers to render the accomplished woman neither lonely nor an anomaly."[6] During the growing sense of nationhood in the 1930s and during the political awakening in the 1940s, Kashmiri women forged broad coalitions and informal networks to challenge state-centered, feudal, and elitist notions of identity and security. Kashmiri women perceived and articulated cultural and political resistance, during the invasion by raiders from the North-West Frontier Province of Pakistan in 1947, in terms of clear nation-building programs, which involved reviving civil society, resuscitating the shattered economy, and building social and political structures. Subsequent to the accession of the former princely state of Jammu and Kashmir to the Indian dominion in 1947, while the Indian subcontinent was reeling from the mayhem of the country's partition, women's organizations attempted to contribute peace-building work at the local and regional levels.

While collecting historical records and individual testimonies to trace the historical lineage of Kashmiri women's sociopolitical activism, my curiosity was piqued by the feisty debates that were aroused by the tribal invasion of 1947. So I dug into the archival material available to me. In a dog-eared copy of *Life* magazine reporter Margaret Bourke-White's book, I found riveting details of her rich conversations with twentieth-century political stalwarts of the Indian subcontinent. Bourke-White, who was sent to India on assignment in the eventful late 1940s, writes enthusiastically about the former princely state of Jammu and Kashmir.[7] She writes that the giant leaps taken toward democracy in the former princely state could be a harbinger for progressive movements and positive change in the rest of India. She sardonically tells the reader that the move toward achieving democracy in the state was expedited by the despotic ruler, Maharaja Hari Singh, when he fled his principality, leaving his subjects in the lurch.

This occurred at the inception of the invasion of Kashmir in October 1947, "when hordes of fanatical Muslim tribesmen were pouring in from Pakistan, killing, looting, and burning villages."[8] This onslaught convulsed the entire Kashmir Valley, carrying "the raiders to the outskirts of Srinagar, the capital."[9] In a quick and efficient response to the incursion, "the People's Party—or National Conference, as it is also known"—put a representative government in place, "which administered food stores, organized a people's militia for defense against the invader, and started working on a new constitution."[10] Jammu and Kashmir were terrorized by the willful infliction of pain and suffering on civilians during the fateful period of the Partition of India. The communal violence in the Jammu province of the state was remorseless. The rapacity of the fanatical invaders seemed insatiable. Amid that pandemonium, Kashmir was the first state in the newly freed Indian subcontinent to have its own written constitutional plan. "Members of the People's Party had studied constitutions from all over the world, particularly America," says Bourke-White.[11] The constitution guaranteed enfranchisement of all adult citizens, men and women, and took particular care to protect the dignity and religious freedoms of minorities. The admirable egalitarian and democratic quality of their achievement was partially a result of the political dissidence and collective consciousness that grew in response to oppressive monarchical institutions, which had curbed their freedom for generations and "is in large part a result of clear vision of their State People's leader, Sheikh Mohammad Abdullah. The Sheikh is a legendary figure and is the first popular prime minister to emerge after the coming of Indian independence."[12] A people newly emancipated from the clutches of an oppressive and rigorous monarchy blossomed. In that euphoric atmosphere, no force seemed powerful enough to militate against the dream of a democratic and emancipated society.

The Partition of India legitimized the forces of masculinist nationalism and enabled virile hatred for the "other" to irreparably mutilate a shared anticolonial legacy and cultural heritage so systematically that the wounds inflicted by the Partition are yet to heal. Shortly before the tribal invasion, while the princely state of Jammu and Kashmir was still an independent entity and had not acceded to either dominion, India or Pakistan, Sheikh Mohammad Abdullah sent emissaries of the All Jammu and Kashmir State People's Conference to Pakistan to hash out the terms of accession with those at the helm of affairs. Mohammad Ali Jinnah, leader of the Muslim League and founder of Pakistan, was hesitant at the time to get involved in the internal affairs of princely states. Consequently, he did not meet with these representatives, "and many people have since said this was a great mistake. He might have had Kashmir with its three million Muslims if he had been willing to recognize popular rule." The people's government of Jammu and Kashmir made a last-ditch effort to negotiate with the government of Pakistan. The negotiations were still in the fetal stage when the truculent tribesmen of the North-West Frontier Province began infiltrating Kashmir. The ink of their official seals on the "instruments of accession," affirming their loyalty to the Pakistani dominion, had not yet dried when these tribesmen began surging into Kashmir under the rallying cry of Islam, "making off with all removable loot—including women—leaving a trail of sacked and burned villages, and fighting their way through the heart of the

Valley."[13] These tribesmen, with their sacks full of booty and whetted appetites, arrived in Rawalpindi, part of Pakistan, only to indulge, yet again, in plunder and pillage to satiate their gluttonous selves. The fractious rioting of the tribal invaders caused the newspapers of Lahore, in the newly created Dominion of Pakistan, to scream themselves hoarse in vociferously demanding an immediate withdrawal of the "crusaders," who had become a law unto themselves and Pakistan's proverbial Frankenstein.[14]

Apologists of the tribal invasion in Pakistan and present-day Jammu and Kashmir emphasize the rationale of the invasion, which, according to them, was to save the Muslim populace from the persecution perpetrated on them by the non-Muslims in Kashmir. If that, indeed, had been the reason, it would have been strategically advantageous and beneficial to their "cause" to have entered the state through Sucheet Garh into the Hindu-dominated part of the former princely state Jammu. The Maharaja and his cohort were still licking their wounds and inciting the monarch's Dogra army to inflict atrocities on the Muslim populace of the Jammu province of the state. Such a maneuver would have enabled the unruly lot to damage the Srinagar-Jammu route beyond repair, thereby ensuring the severance of Kashmir from the rest of India and attenuating the possibility of its accession to the Indian dominion. The Kashmir Valley, with its large Muslim populace and its resolute volunteer corps, did not require the services of the marauding and disgruntled tribals, whose prodigality on the Baramullah-Uri route created terrible misgivings among the people whom the marauders were purportedly saving. Even the patrons of the tribesmen couldn't turn a blind eye to the savagery and barbarity evinced by them on that "campaign."[15]

While a political consciousness was evolving in the former princely state of Jammu and Kashmir, Kashmiri women like Akbar Jehan, Mehmooda Ahmad Ali Shah, Sajjida Zameer, and Krishna Misri made a smooth transition from their conventional lives to people engaged in sociopolitical activism. Organizing as the Women's Self-Defense Corps (WSDC), they were oriented toward the goal of generating and strengthening a nationalist consciousness and selfhood. Sajjida Zameer played a pivotal role in the cultural movement, designed to articulate how Kashmiri women of different political, religious, and class orientations could become resource managers and advocates for other women in emergency and crisis situations. She recalls that the women's militia played an inimitable role in repulsing the raiders and thwarting their short-term and haphazard tactics to forcibly annex Jammu and Kashmir, while unleashing a reign of terror in which even their coreligionists were not spared. The women's movement was by no means elitist or exclusionary. In addition to upper- and middleclass women, even grassroots workers like Zoon Gujjari of Nawakadal, Srinagar; Jana Begum of Amrikadal, Srinagar; and Mohuan Kaur, a refugee from Baramullah, Kashmir, were active participants in the women's movement. The cultural front of the militia sought to unite a variety of religious and regional groups in a single, national movement.[16] Most of the members of the WSDC were wives and mothers who shared the nationalist hopes, anxieties, and ardent desires to be the architects of their future and inscribe their own destinies along with their male counterparts. But their participation in the fervent political awakening and cultural resurgence of that era did not, by any means, endorse the traditionally submissive and self-denying role of the wife and mother.

Kashmiri women played an unparalleled role in the WSDC, formed during the creation of geographical borders, political animosities, and religious hatreds dividing India and Pakistan in 1947. Unfortunately, there is a dearth of substantive scholarly work on this revolutionary organization, which addressed women's initiation of political and cultural action in resisting brutal annexation. In my zeal to contextualize and historicize the culturally regenerative, politically emancipatory, and socially redemptive work done by this organization, I interviewed two of the three surviving members of the WSDC in 2008 for my monograph *Islam, Women, and Violence in Kashmir*.[17] The third member, Mehmooda Ahmed Ali Shah, then in her eighties, candidly admitted that she did not remember much about that era.[18] Both my interviewees, Krishna Misri and Sajjida Zameer, spoke eloquently about the formation of the National Militia and WSDC—volunteer forces of men and women organized under the leadership of Sheikh Mohammad Abdullah—to rally their opposition to the legion of tribesmen from the North-West Frontier Province, backed by the Pakistani army, when they crossed the border of the princely state of Jammu and Kashmir on October 22, 1947, in order to coercively capture the state. It is ironic that those who were considered invaders in 1947 were portrayed as liberators in the late 1980s and the early 1990s.

This organization, I underline, is a compelling example of the formation of a coalition across religious and class divides to further the nationalist consciousness of a society in the process of self-determination. In order to facilitate the understanding of the reader of the sort of regenerative work carried out by this organization during the cataclysmic events of 1947–1948, I have reproduced the testimonies of Krishna Misri and Sajjida Zameer. In their testimonies, Misri and Zameer highlight the courage that Kashmiri women exhibited in that period of nationalist awakening to step out of ascribed gender roles to significantly impact sociopolitical developments in the state. My role as a biographer requires that I grasp the social and political assumptions that surrounded Akbar Jehan's involvement with the WSDC at that time and in that place.

Acknowledging Akbar Jehan's role in political and social activism during the turbulent Partition of India in 1947, Sheikh Mohammad Abdullah observes that in the midst of mass migrations, rapidly changing political configurations, and emotional upheaval, "swarms of refugees were moving from one country to the other and sick and wounded were everywhere."[19] He, at the time, poured his resources into alleviating the lot of both Muslims and Hindus. Being cognizant of the work that Akbar Jehan and her colleagues could undertake to mitigate the misery of uprooted, grief-stricken, and indigent refugees, the sheikh asked her to join him in his task: "When I asked my wife about it, she agreed at once to help me in relief work. She gave up the *purdah* and did commendable work in organizing relief camps. For her hard work and sincere efforts, she was named 'The Benevolent Mother' by the Kashmiris and was known by this name throughout the state."[20] At the time, the purdah reinforced a powerful cultural ideal and was a pivotal element in the reproduction of family status. Akbar Jehan's parents were part of the aristocratic and wealthy strata of society in which women's seclusion from the public realm and the donning of purdah were status markers. So her relinquishment of the security, privilege, and dependence that the institution of purdah bestowed on women was a courageous move.[21]

Her valiance inspired other members of the women's militia whose conscripted worlds were becoming a thing of the past. Prior to my attempt at reconstructing Akbar Jehan Abdullah through written sources and an account of her life based on my memory and other surviving sources, history had done a rather inadequate job at memorializing her contributions. Her work of sustaining the community, caring for the marginalized and disempowered at a turbulent time, wasn't captured by the avid historian. Alas, "for centuries," observes Laurel Thatcher Ulrich, the hands-on work of women in tending to the needs of the infirm, buoying up local communities, raising food for the impoverished, and rebuilding societies after ravaging wars has been peripheralized in official histories.[22]

Marveling at her intrepidity and endurance, the sheikh believed that Akbar Jehan had the backbone and grit to "turn her veil into a banner." Every serious student of the history of Kashmir knows that during the 1946 "Quit Kashmir" movement, Maharaja Hari Singh and his loyal prime minister, Ram Chand Kak, deployed all the resources at their command to annihilate the aspiration of the Kashmiri people for responsible government.[23] In the wake of that movement, Akbar Jehan voluntarily relinquished her domestic role. She invested herself in inspiring the desire for a dignified existence in the despondent, the fires of whose hearths had been cruelly quenched. She stepped into the stream of public consequence by choice, not through "divine intervention."[24] Her foray into the public realm was not due to circumstances beyond her control but was agential. Akbar Jehan's commitment to work shared with the sheikh may have become indistinguishable from her commitment to him, but collaboration did not make her work invisible. If anything, they showed ingenuity "in the combination of different kinds of commitments, including the work of homemaking and relationship building, the caring needed to nurture ideas and institutions."[25]

I posit that similar to nineteenth-century French feminist leaders, Akbar Jehan, along with other women members of the WSDC, "used the concept of motherhood figuratively to refer to women's spiritual qualities and social mission."[26] They relied on the cultural and moral authority of the mother, which is religiously sanctioned, and carved a niche for themselves in the public space. In doing so, they articulated a new sensibility linked by multilayered identities in which politics and selfhood are profoundly interrelated. Akbar Jehan was one of the harbingers of state feminism in Jammu and Kashmir. I borrow Gul Ozyegin's proficient definition of state feminism as "the inclusion of women in political citizenship and top-down reforms initiated by the State, without the notable participation of women, for the improvement of the legal, social, and economic status of women."[27]

Akbar Jehan's political and social activism for the empowerment of women vocalized the desire for freedom and liberation as "a historically situated desire whose motivational force cannot be assumed a priori, but needs to be reconsidered in light of other desires, aspirations, and capacities that inhere in a culturally and historically located subject."[28] She was a passionate advocate of women's education, which would place girls, including those of impoverished backgrounds, in the public realm of ambition, power, and material well-being "and scientific and intellectual life with a mission of modernizing the country and its people, side by side with their male peers."[29]

Although the members of the WSDC were harbingers of the political participation of women and fashioned educational opportunities for them, I take the liberty of reminding the reader to complicate the conceptualization and measurement of Kashmiri women's empowerment. The enfranchisement of both women and men and ensuring women equal opportunities in education are not empowering in themselves, but they cause a momentous shift in traditional gender relationships. The consequent opening up of new possibilities for the pursuit of democracy and regional peace creates "the vantage point of alternatives which allows a more transformatory consciousness to come into play."[30] The social activism of the WSDC created spheres of emancipation for Kashmiri women.

I observe that the interactive grassroots outreach and mobilization tactics of the WSDC initiated an advocacy "on behalf of women which builds on claimed synergies between feminist goals and official development priorities." This strategy made a more significant foray "into the mainstream development agenda than advocacy," which calls for the liberation of women "on intrinsic grounds."[31] As women's concern with family and society often manifests itself in social and social regeneration, this organization did not give either an essentialist Muslim identity or a Hindu one a privileged place in political discourse. The goals of this organization in a turbulent and chaotic time were much higher than simply propagating and whipping up "combat locked within action and reaction."[32] The WSDC did not espouse an identity politics that appealed only to that part of "individual identity that is shared in a collective identity." The question to ask about that kind of essentialist politics the WSDC disavowed is, "'Which collective identity?' It is a question that is never asked in the process of political mobilization on the basis of identity; indeed, the question is often actively suppressed, sometimes violently."[33]

One of the most formidable challenges facing the sheikh and the social activism of Akbar Jehan was the palpable hostility between Muslims and Hindus and each community's assertion of an essentialist identity, which was the insidious fallout of the Partition of India. About his tenure as prime minister of Jammu and Kashmir in 1948, the sheikh admits, "The biggest problem for me was to create mutual confidence between the two communities and to remove all fear from their minds."[34] It was in this climate of fear, paranoia, mutual suspicion, and vendetta that Akbar Jehan undertook the arduous task of attempting to bridge the nigh impassable gulf between the two communities in the state. It is necessary to recognize the determination and perseverance of other members of the WSDC as well in overcoming seemingly insurmountable challenges. The personal and political trajectory of Akbar Jehan's life affirms my belief that addressing wider political, socioeconomic, and democratic issues in Kashmir requires "rethinking the relationship between state and non-state actors, between state and society, and therefore between the structures of decision-making in these two arenas."[35] How did she do this?

Another example of women's agency in that era is the institute Markazi Behboodi Khwateen, established by Akbar Jehan. It exists yet today and continues to impart literacy, training in arts and crafts, health care, and social security as tools of empowerment. She invested her time and energy in the struggle for a vibrant Kashmir. She diligently garnered funds to build schools for indigent children and championed adult education in a state where a significant part of the population was illiterate. Building on the earlier gains, Akbar Jehan sought to ensure further economic, social, and educational gains for women and marginalized groups. The institute founded by Akbar Jehan, the Jammu and Kashmir Markazi Behboodi Khwateen, was registered under the Societies Registration Act of 1998. Its current vice chairperson and younger daughter of Akbar Jehan, Suraiya Ali Matto (née Abdullah), provided information about the aims and objectives of the Markazi Behboodi Khwateen.[36] This institute aims to impart intensive training to women in various arts and crafts, which would become a source of livelihood for them, enabling them to become better citizens and homemakers. Jammu and Kashmir Markazi Behboodi Khwateen also runs homes for destitute women and disenfranchised orphans and provides supplementary nutrition to preschool children in ghettoized areas. In addition to vocational training, they also provide lodging for working women from rural areas. This establishment effectively employs an instrumentalist form of advocacy that "combine[s] the argument for gender equality/women's empowerment with demonstrations of a broad set of desirable multiplier effects," offering "policy makers the possibility of achieving familiar and approved goals, albeit by unfamiliar means."[37]

Suraiya goes on to say that this institute was the first nongovernmental organization (NGO) in the valley to help destitute women, indigent Gujjar and Bakarwal tribes of Jammu and Kashmir who are officially regarded as socioeconomically disadvantaged, and orphaned boys belonging to those tribes: "This particular NGO was later named after her and has grown by leaps and bounds in its infrastructure and activities."[38] One of the great strides made is that a parcel of land that had been donated to her by the residents of Gulab Bagh, a locality on the outskirts of Srinagar city, now houses a school with a well-equipped dormitory for the students, most of whose parents struggle below the poverty line. The educational activities at the school are supplemented by the honing of students' creativity at the adjacent craft center. She is hopeful that students' health issues and hygiene will be well cared for at the school dispensary. She passionately observes, "Mummy was a role model for women's emancipation and empowerment, which is her lasting legacy not just to the Kashmiri nation, but to other South Asian Muslim women as well."[39]

In order to correct the more simplistic generalizations that characterize formulations of Muslim women's identity, it is important to highlight the groundbreaking work accomplished by local agencies, cadres, and social networks in Kashmir. As I have said elsewhere, the distinction between traditional praxes and progressive roles prescribed for women within Islamic jurisprudence needs to be underscored by responsible scholarship and social work. It is in the arena of domestic politics and social activism that changes in gender composition "to favour women can have significant effects on policies and practices, and here that such rearrangements of personnel can themselves be seen as responses to the presence of real and growing social processes of a pro-democratic . . . kind."[40] There is still a questionable unwillingness, which I see in several forums in both India and Pakistan, to recognize progressive women's narratives in the larger political context of Kashmir.

Akbar Jehan's organization worked within the material reality and multi-layered sociopolitical contexts of different groups of women in Kashmir. The institute founded by her endeavored to further the project of women's empowerment by deploying "collective solidarity in the public arena as well as individual assertiveness in the private."[41] Akbar Jehan, by virtue of her positioning within the institutional domains that make up Kashmiri society, had a decision-making authority, which formed the vantage point from which she could conceive alternatives that would shape the processes of empowerment in a particular context.

Women's empowerment in the state entailed the participation of women activists in establishing a more inclusive democracy and new forums for citizen cooperation. Women active in politics in that era aimed not just to improve the position of their particular organizations but also to forge connections between the group's agendas for the progress of society and the agendas of other groups in the population who had also suffered from the ongoing conflict. The assiduous work of Kashmiri women in civic associations and in government to lead the way toward a peaceful, pluralistic democracy was further bolstered in 1950, when the government of Jammu and Kashmir developed educational institutions for women on a large scale, including the first university and a college for women, as I outline in my monograph on Kashmir as well as in my article in the *Oxford Encyclopedia of Islam and Women*.[42]

The idea behind establishing these institutions was to develop the ability to organize and mobilize for social change, which requires the creation of awareness not just at the individual level but at the collective level as well. These institutions sought to develop self-esteem in Kashmiri women, for which some form of financial autonomy is a basis. The goal was to provide women with the wherewithal to make strategic life choices that are critical for people to establish a more inclusive democracy and new forums for citizen cooperation. The educational methods employed in these institutions, back then, departed from established authority and doctrine but were not, by any means, revolutionary.[43]

In my interactions with women from Kashmir, I have realized that there is a serious lack of a feminist discourse in political/activist roles taken on by women in Kashmir, where the dominant perception still is that politics and policy making are the jobs of the pragmatic, powerful male, not the archetypal maternal, accommodating woman. As in other nations in South Asia, women politicians are relegated to the "soft areas" of social welfare and family affairs. Political parties in Kashmir, either mainstream or separatist, have not relinquished paternalistic attitudes toward women, and women's rights and gender issues remain secondary to political power. Today in Jammu and Kashmir, women politicians and activists constitute a minority, increasing the pressures of high visibility, unease, stereotyping, inability to make substantial change, and overaccommodation to the dominant male culture in order to avoid condemnation as "overly soft." I am not sure how effective sloganeering and street protests by women in the recent past have been. This kind of activism will not produce any results unless it is integrated with institutional mechanisms.

Notes

1   Susan Pederson, "Comparative History and Women's History: Explaining Convergence and Divergence," in *Comparative Women's History: New Approaches*, ed. Anne Cova (New York: Columbia University Press, 2006), 125.

2   Linda Warley, "Assembling Ingredients: Subjectivity in Meatless Days," *A–B Autobiography Studies* 7, no. 1 (1992), 113.

3   Janet Beizer, *Thinking through the Mothers: Reimagining Women's Biographies* (Ithaca, N.Y.: Cornell University Press, 2009), 3.

4   Anuradha Mitra Chenoy and Achin Vanaik, "Promoting Peace, Security and Conflict Resolution: Gender Balance in Decision Making," in *Gender, Peace and Conflict*, ed. Inger Skjelsbæk and Dan Smith (London: Sage, 2001), 123.

5   Carolyn Heilbrun, *Writing a Woman's Life* (New York: Norton, 1988), 118.

6   Heilbrun, 119.

7   Margaret Bourke-White, *Halfway to Freedom: A Report on the New India in the Words and Photographs of Margaret Bourke-White* (New York: Simon & Schuster, 1949).

8   Bourke-White, 13.

 9 Bourke-White, 28.
10 Bourke-White, 105.
11 Bourke-White, 130.
12 Mohammad Abdullah and Y. D. Gundevia, *The Testament of Sheikh Abdullah* (New Delhi: Abhinav, 1968), 193–194.
13 Abdullah and Gundevia, 202–203.
14 Abdullah and Gundevia, 204.
15 See Sardar Muhammad Ibrahim Khan, *The Kashmir Saga* (Lahore, Pakistan: Ripon Printing Press, 1965), for details of the ruthlessness exhibited by the tribals during the invasion, which the author characterizes as an inevitability of war, but cannot ignore.
16 Sajjida Zameer, email communication with the author, April 1, 2008. Zameer is a member of the 1947 Women's Militia organized by the National Conference and a former director of the Education Department, Jammu and Kashmir.
17 Nyla Ali Khan, *Islam, Women, and Violence in Kashmir* (New York: Palgrave Macmillan, 2010).
18 Mehmooda Ahmed Ali Shah passed away in March 2014.
19 Abdullah and Gundevia, *Testament of Sheikh Abdullah*, 35.
20 Abdullah and Gundevia, 35.
21 While reminiscing about Akbar Jehan's significant role in 1947, Krishna Misri writes about the formation of the national militia and WSDC—volunteer forces of men and women organized under the leadership of Sheikh Mohammad Abdullah—to ward off the onslaught that occurred on October 22, 1947, when hordes of tribesmen from the North-West Frontier Province, under the patronage of the Pakistani army, crossed the border of the princely state of Jammu and Kashmir in order to coercively annex the region. In an email to the author on April 5, 2008, Misri says,

> In the absence of a competent civil authority, volunteers of the National Militia filled the void. They patrolled the city day and night with arms, kept vigil, guarded strategic bridges, approaches to the city, banks, offices, etc. With preliminary training in weapons, some of them were deployed with army detachments to fight the enemy at the war front. With its multi-faceted and radical activities, Women's Self Defense Corps (WSDC) was a harbinger of social change. It provided a forum where women steeped in centuries-old traditions, abysmal ignorance, poverty and superstition could discuss their issues. Attired in traditional Kashmiri clothes and carrying a gun around her shoulders, Zoon Gujjari symbolized the WSDC. A milk vendor's charismatic daughter, hailing from a conservative Muslim family that lived in downtown Srinagar, she received well-deserved media coverage. My elder brother, Pushkar Zadoo, joined the National Militia, while I along with my sisters, Kamla and Indu, became volunteers of WSDC. We were first initiated into physical fitness and then divided into smaller groups where weapons' training was imparted. It was essential to follow the instructions given by our instructor, an ex-army serviceman to a tee. Soon we understood the operational details of loading and unloading a gun, taking aim, and finally pressing the trigger. To get acclimatized to shooting the 303 rifle, sten-gun, bren gun and pistol, practice drills were organized in an open area, known as "Chandmari." The initial nervousness soon gave way to confidence and we would hit the target when ordered. For all parades including "ceremonial guards" and "guard of honor," the practice was that men's contingents were followed by women's contingents.

During that invasion of 1947, Begum Akbar Jehan undertook exhaustive relief work to rehabilitate displaced and dispossessed villagers. She addressed the volunteers on political issues to raise their political consciousness. Miss Mahmuda Ahmad Shah, a pioneering educationist and champion of women's empowerment, along with other women, was in the forefront of WSDC. Begum Zainab was a grass-root level leader. She took charge of the political dimension of WSDC. Shouldering a gun, she was in the forefront, leading women's contingents. Sajjada Zameer Ahmad, Taj Begum Renzu, Shanta Kaul, and Khurshid Jala-u-Din joined the "cultural front" and worked with Radio Kashmir as anchors, announcers, and actors. The mobilization of women from various socioeconomic classes meant that they could avail themselves of educational opportunities, enhance their professional skills, and attempt to reform existing structures so as to accommodate more women.

22 Laurel Thatcher Ulrich, *Well-Behaved Women Seldom Make History* (New York: Alfred A. Knopf, 2007), 227.

23 The Quit Kashmir movement was launched to oust the Dogra monarchy and to establish responsible government.

24 Ulrich, *Well-Behaved Women*, xxi.

25 Mary Catherine Bateson, *Composing a Life* (New York: Grove Press, 1989), 78.

26 Ann Taylor Allen, "Lost in Translation? Women's History in Transnational and Comparative Perspective," in *Comparative Women's History: New Approaches*, ed. Anne Cova (New York: Columbia University Press, 2006), 104.

27 Gul Ozyegin, "My Father, an Agent of State Feminism and Other Unrelatable Conversations," in *Transatlantic Conversations: Feminism as Travelling Theory*, ed. Kathy Davis and Mary Evans (London: Routledge, 2011), 33.

28 Saba Mahmood, "Feminist Theory, Embodiment, and the Docile Agent: Some Reflections on the Egyptian Islamic Revival," *Cultural Anthropology* 16, no. 2 (2001): 223.

29 Ozyegin, "My Father," 33.

30 Naila Kabeer, "Resources, Agency, Achievements: Reflections on the Measurement of Women's Empowerment," *Development and Change* 30, no. 3 (1999): 462.

31 Kabeer, 435.

32 Inderpal Grewal, "Autobiographic Subjects and Diasporic Locations: *Meatless Days* and *Borderlands*," in *Scattered Hegemonies: Postmodernity and Transnational Feminist Practices*, ed. Inderpal Grewal and Caren Kaplan (Minneapolis: University of Minnesota Press, 1997), 249.

33 Dan Smith, "The Problem of Essentialism," in *Gender, Peace, and Conflict*, ed. Inger Skjelsbæk and Dan Smith (London: Sage, 2001), 36.

34 Abdullah and Gundevia, *Testament of Sheikh Abdullah*, 41.

35 Chenoy and Vanaik, "Promoting Peace," 124.

36 Suraiya Ali Matto, email communication with the author, April 10, 2008. Matto is a professor emeritus; vice chairperson of Behboodi Khawateen, an organization dedicated to uplifting downtrodden women and children; and younger daughter of Akbar Jehan and Sheikh Mohammad Abdullah.

37 Kabeer, "Resources, Agency, Achievements," 436.

38 Matto, email, April 10, 2008.

39 Matto, email communication with the author, February 14, 2012.

40 Chenoy and Vanaik, "Promoting Peace," 128.

41 Kabeer, "Resources, Agency, Achievements," 462.

42 Nyla Ali Khan, "Kashmir," in *The Oxford Encyclopedia of Islam and Women*, ed. Natana J. Delong-Bas (New York: Oxford University Press, 2013), 113–144, 563–565.

43 Krishna Misri, "Kashmiri Women down the Ages: A Gender Perspective," *Himalayan and Central Asian Studies* 6, nos. 3/4 (2002): 25–26.

Bibliography

Abdullah, Mohammad, and Y. D. Gundevia. *The Testament of Sheikh Abdullah*. New Delhi: Abhinav, 1968.

Allen, Ann Taylor. "Lost in Translation? Women's History in Transnational and Comparative Perspective." In *Comparative Women's History: New Approaches*, edited by Anne Cova, 87–115. New York: Columbia University Press, 2006.

Bateson, Mary Catherine. *Composing a Life*. New York: Grove Press, 1989.

Beizer, Janet. *Thinking through the Mothers: Reimagining Women's Biographies*. Ithaca, N.Y.: Cornell University Press, 2009.

Bourke-White, Margaret. *Halfway to Freedom: A Report on the New India in the Words and Photographs of Margaret Bourke-White*. New York: Simon & Schuster, 1949.

Chenoy, Anuradha Mitra, and Achin Vanaik. "Promoting Peace, Security and Conflict Resolution: Gender Balance in Decision Making." In *Gender, Peace and Conflict*, edited by Inger Skjelsbæk and Dan Smith, 122–138. London: Sage, 2001.

Grewal, Inderpal. "Autobiographic Subjects and Diasporic Locations: *Meatless Days* and *Borderlands*." In *Scattered Hegemonies: Postmodernity and Transnational Feminist Practices*, edited by Inderpal Grewal and Caren Kaplan, 231–254. Minneapolis: University of Minnesota Press, 1997.

Heilbrun, Carolyn. *Writing a Woman's Life*. New York: Norton, 1988.

Kabeer, Naila. "Resources, Agency, Achievements: Reflections on the Measurement of Women's Empowerment." *Development and Change* 30, no. 3 (1999): 435–464.

Khan, Nyla Ali. *Islam, Women, and Violence in Kashmir*. New York: Palgrave Macmillan, 2010.

———. "Kashmir." In *The Oxford Encyclopedia of Islam and Women*, edited by Natana J. Delong-Bas, 563–565. New York: Oxford University Press, 2013.

Khan, Sardar Muhammad Ibrahim. *The Kashmir Saga*. Lahore, Pakistan: Ripon Printing Press, 1965.

Mahmood, Saba. "Feminist Theory, Embodiment, and the Docile Agent: Some Reflections on the Egyptian Islamic Revival." *Cultural Anthropology* 16, no. 2 (2001): 202–235.

Misri, Krishna. "Kashmiri Women down the Ages: A Gender Perspective." *Himalayan and Central Asian Studies* 6, nos. 3/4 (2002): 3–27.

Ozyegin, Gul. "My Father, an Agent of State Feminism and Other Unrelatable Conversations." In *Transatlantic Conversations: Feminism as Travelling Theory*, edited by Kathy Davis and Mary Evans, 31–39. London: Routledge, 2011.

Pederson, Susan. "Comparative History and Women's History: Explaining Convergence and Divergence." In *Comparative Women's History: New Approaches*, edited by Anne Cova, 117–142. New York: Columbia University Press, 2006.

Smith, Dan. "The Problem of Essentialism." In *Gender, Peace, and Conflict*, edited by Inger Skjelsbæk and Dan Smith, 32–46. London: Sage, 2001.

Ulrich, Laurel Thatcher. *Well-Behaved Women Seldom Make History*. New York: Alfred A. Knopf, 2007.

Warley, Linda. "Assembling Ingredients: Subjectivity in Meatless Days." *A–B Autobiography Studies* 7, no. 1 (1992): 107–123.

10

Teaching Narratives of Rape Survivors of the Bangladesh War in a Classroom

• •

A Survey

SHAFINUR NAHAR

In one of our class discussions at a university in Bangladesh, I brought up the issue of wartime rapes of women in 1971 and found the students embarrassed by the topic. Upon my insistence, some of them came forward with their opinions. Some of the female students found the topic of rape to be a private matter; some considered the discussion of sexual violence to be traumatic and therefore did not want to participate in the discussion at all. But the majority of students chose not to respond. The discussion drew my attention, and I was interested to know how the millennial generation of students deals with the stories of wartime sexual violence and also what their opinions are about reading memoirs and stories about women who were raped during the Liberation War of 1971. I conducted a survey, offering the respondents a questionnaire and asking them to share their views on the topic. While doing the survey, I found that the respondents hold a suppressed fear and a misconstrued notion about raped women. I realized that even though Bangladesh witnessed hundreds of thousands of women raped during the war, most of the students still are not ready to acknowledge them as respectable women, let alone brave war heroes. This chapter resulted from that classroom survey. In the survey, more than a thousand students from twenty different universities shared their views on the reading of the texts concerning war rapes in a university classroom. For my research purpose, I did a background reading of the texts, which are included as essential readings for the students from primary to secondary levels in Bangladesh. Unfortunately, there is not a single memoir or story included in those texts provided by the national curriculum textbook board. Even at the tertiary level of education, there is a tendency to exclude texts concerning narratives of sexual violence that happened during the war of 1971. In the teaching of the texts on the war history, we often avoid the details of sexual violence of that time when instructing a particular age group of students. This sort of avoidance is partly accounted for by the strict religious and patriarchal culture that hardly approves of any public discussions on rape and sexual violence, especially in schools and college classrooms here. As a result, the teachers face difficulty in addressing the issue of rape and sexual violence and tend to avoid discussing the issue in question in their classrooms altogether. However, I attempted to conduct the survey with the intention to make a point to the students that in order to understand traumatic texts, it is necessary to delve deep into the traumatic details. My intent was to illustrate how trauma is manifested in the texts and how it can be understood. More importantly, the survey objective was to make the students aware of the history, politics, and significance of the rape survivors.

Tracing the History of Rape in the Liberation War of Bangladesh

In *Against Our Will: Men, Women and Rape* (2000), Susan Brownmiller explains how throughout history, rape has been used as a tactical strategy during wars, such as during World War I and the Vietnam War. German soldiers raped women when they invaded Belgium in World War I, and women were raped not because they were "the enemy" but because they were "women." For the same reason, women were raped by several military groups—including German, Japanese, American, Russian, and Moroccan soldiers, among others—during World War II. War rape occurred in Vietnam, Yugoslavia, Bangladesh, Rwanda, and Bosnia as part of *ethnic cleansing*.[1] However, what made the difference for Bangladesh during 1971 is that sexual violence against women was justified in the name of religion. A fatwa (religious verdict) was publicly announced by the Pakistani Islamic religious leaders that the Bengali freedom fighters were Hindus and their women were to be taken as *gonimoter maal* (war booty).[2] The religious leaders propagated their belief that a "pure" Muslim will never stand against their biological father, so they encouraged the Pakistani army and local supporters of Islamist political parties to rape Bengali "Hindus" and "impure" and "half Muslims" to produce a new, obedient generation.[3] As the majority of the population of then East Pakistan (now Bangladesh) was Muslim, 80 percent of the rape victims, as a consequence, were Muslim women. However, Hindus, Buddhists, and Christians were not exempt either.[4] Pakistani major general Khadim Hussain Raja reported that Pakistani commander-in-chief General Niazi, in the presence of Bengali officers, used to say that he would "change the race of the Bengalis."[5] This was the statement that was later testified by a Pakistani soldier in the Hamoodur Rahman Commission.[6] The Pakistani soldier relayed to the commission how the soldiers were encouraged to rape fearlessly: "The troops used to say that when the Commander [Lt. Gen. Niazi] was himself a rapist, how could they be stopped?"[7]

Bangladesh got its independence from Pakistan after a nine-month-long war in which three million people died and hundreds of thousands of women were raped.[8] The exact figure of the raped women during 1971 is still not apparent. However, in an interview with Bina D'Costa, Dr. Geoffrey Davis, who worked for the International Planned Parenthood Federation (IPPF) and the United Nations in Dhaka in 1972, states,

> They'd keep the infantry back and put artillery ahead and they would shell the hospitals and schools. And that caused absolute chaos in the town. And then the infantry would go in and begin to segregate the women. Apart from little children, all those who were sexually matured would be segregated. And then the women would be put in the compound under guard and made available to the troops.... Some of the stories they told were appalling. Being raped again and again and again. A lot of them died in those [rape] camps. There was an air of disbelief about the whole thing. Nobody could credit that it really happened! But the evidence clearly showed that it did happen.[9]

The rapes mainly took place in army concentration camps, causing pregnancies, abortions, births of war children, deaths, and suicides. Those rapes, therefore, were of a genocidal nature, stemming not only from ethnic enmity but also from communal violence in the name of religion.[10] Yasmin Saikia states that Bangladeshi men who participated in the war became "*mukti judha*, a war hero,"[11] and Bina D'Costa and Sara Hossain indicate in their research that rape victims were named *birangonas*, or "war heroines," to recognize their contributions to and sufferings in the liberation war.[12] But even after such recognition, they remained silent because if they spoke out, they would face more difficulties in the strict patriarchal society in Bangladesh.[13] This silence has continued for years in Bangladesh except for some interviews, reports, and most importantly, very few memoirs written by the war heroines who decided to open up about their experience during 1971.[14]

The U.S.-based Women Under Siege Project of the Women's Media Center, founded by Gloria Steinem, did an investigation on rape and sexual violence and found that they were used as tools by the Pakistani army in 1971 war and reported that there were eight- to seventy-five-year-old rape victims imprisoned in the Pakistani military barracks.[15] The brutal and nightmarish experiences of the rape victims have been documented in literature and films and were published as reports and interviews as well. Neelima Ibrahim published her account in 1994 in a book form, titled *Ami birangona bolchi* (*A War Heroine, I Speak*).[16] Wartime rape survivors like Ferdousi Priyabhashini and Rama Chowdhury wrote autobiographies and memoirs in which they bravely utter their traumatic experiences.[17] None of these books had much attention for years, and the issue of the *birangonas* thus remained dormant for years as well.

Manifestation of Trauma in Texts

While most of the raped women chose to remain silent, there were a few of them who decided to speak out. After the end of the Liberation War of 1971, Neelima Ibrahim, a professor of the Bengali Department at the University of Dhaka, along with other activists worked as volunteers in the new government's project of registering and rehabilitating the raped women of 1971. Ibrahim had conversations with many raped women and compiled stories of seven women in her book. All of them were from different socioeconomic classes and family backgrounds. However, their rape stories and traumatic experiences shared common denominators. These women described their rapists as "animals"; for example, Tara Neilson says, "I watched the transformation of a human being into an animal. I only saw animals after that day, animals, all around and over me; I did not see one human being around me until December 16."[18] Each *birangona* in Ibrahim's book shares her feelings of humiliation, hatred, grief, anger, and sorrow. For example, Rina, who was one of those war heroines who decided to go to Pakistan with the Pakistani army, described her traumatizing life in the rape camp in the following way:

> The Animals in this camp were more desperate than the ones in my previous cell. At least I had the luxury of being raped in a private room. Here, they would just enter and pull a girl out from the flock and jump over her right in front of the rest. They would make us watch the whole gangrape and let us wait for our turn. As I watched their brutality and watched others watching me being gangraped, I saw many of the women laughing and screaming, or sitting there with a face devoid of any expression. The horror of war had already desensitized them.[19]

Rama Chowdhury, a war heroine, wrote in her memoir, *Ekattorer jononi* (Mother of seventy-one; 2010), about how she was raped by a Pakistani soldier even after saying she just had a child. Another important text on the true story of war rape in 1971 is *Rising from the Ashes: Women's Narratives of 1971*,[20] which is a collection of different experiences of violence faced by twenty-two women during the war. Their personal narratives speak of their agony and suffering caused by the Pakistani army and their native allies during the 1971 war, but sadly, their plight was not eased in the independent Bangladeshi society afterward.

The stories of the rape survivors were kept under a shadow of shame for three decades so that there would be no evidence of how many rape camps were there and how rape was used as a war strategy.[21] Some human rights activists criticized the international war crime tribunals in Bangladesh for leaving war rape issues aside.[22] They also questioned the role of the state in dealing with this matter, while the state, as always, has denied their accountability. In fact, Bangladesh has never tried to form a tribunal for war rape incidents. Ferdousi Priyabhashini, a war heroine and a renowned sculptor of Bangladesh, said in a documentary film directed by Tareq Masud and Catherine Masud that "when Bangladesh got its independence, I, who suffered from all kinds of extreme torture in camp, found myself not much welcome to the society. I was accused severely. I was tormented extremely. What I haven't gone through? Then I decided I don't need any human being!"[23] This explains how the people actually reacted to the war rape survivors and how unwelcomed the victims had been in the society. All personal narratives reflect how the rape victims continue to remain in a state of "permanent rape" and how the *birangonas* have been treated as prostitutes in the society. The postwar life was a lot more horrible for those rape victims who dwelled in the villages than the victims who lived in cities such as Dhaka. The participation of city women in war was represented in a heroic way; those women fought in the liberation war and sacrificed their honor through surviving rape. Nayanika Mookherjee illustrates in her research how it was common to have these women compared to Prophet's wives as long as their identities were unknown.[24]

Teaching about Rape Survivors in Classrooms

Bangladesh has shown less interest in dealing with the sufferings of *birangonas* in its historiography.[25] Since the independence of Bangladesh, the role and contributions of *birangonas*, or war heroines, have been ignored in mainstream media or, at best, have been mentioned briefly for sacrificing "their supreme honor"[26] to free the country. It even took forty-four years to recognize their contribution as freedom fighters. In 2014, the high court ordered the government of Bangladesh to "upgrade the social status"[27] of the war heroines and to provide them with the "state honor and facilities" their male counterparts enjoy. Following that court order, the process of recognizing *birangonas* began, and four hundred *birangonas* gained the status of freedom fighters and a monthly stipend from the government. Visual representations of *birangonas* in the media also portray them as social stigmas, suffering from the unspeakable, shameful experience that befell them. Moreover, there is a collective sense of embarrassment for the victims' families. Therefore, the *birangonas* realized that they need to hide their faces or commit suicide to save their families' honor. These malignant representations affect the direction of how young students in colleges and universities, who have no access to credible sources concerning war rape victims and have hardly any social enthusiasm to read them, formulate their mindset and attitude toward war heroines of their parents' generation. When students were asked about what images appear in their heads when they hear the word *birangona*, almost every one said that they picture some broken, wounded, and ashamed woman with a hidden face covered by her hair. Some respondents further said they could not imagine anything but a "dead body." The respondents admit that TV shows and movies influence the way they think about these aspects of the *birangonas*. The state's media can be, in that sense, blamed for perpetuating such negative views. Moreover, the recognition of the sacrifices made by the *birangonas* in national or higher educational curricula has remained a deferred project. Stories, memoirs, or journals of freedom fighters or martyrs are included in textbooks in the curricula from primary to higher education to let the students know the history of the birth of the nation. In contrast, memoirs, autobiographies, and stories of the *birangonas* have not been given a place in the same curricula.

Research Methodology

This study is an attempt to explore how the current generation's students feel about wartime rape survivors of 1971 and what are the opinions of the teachers concerning discussing the stories of war heroines in the classroom. As part of taking their opinions and thoughts regarding wartime rape in 1971, I sent out a set of questions of two categories—multiple choices and some open-ended questions—to the graduate and undergraduate students of different universities. Students who participated in the survey are all from social sciences and humanities departments. The questionnaire was shared through various student groups on social media. One thousand and seventy students participated in the survey. Around 80 percent of the respondents were between twenty and twenty-six years of age. Female students' responses were slightly 1 percent more than the male students. The study is a narrative and qualitative study, as it analyzes and assesses a data source from primary and secondary sources. Memoirs, journals, research articles, reports, interviews, features, and news broadcasts have been used as secondary data sources for the study. This study exploited a questionnaire survey and key informant interviews (KIIs) for its data collection methods.

A semistructured online questionnaire was developed for collecting field data from the students of three different departments of twenty institutions from different parts of the country during the academic years of 2020 and 2021. The questionnaire was sent to a targeted number of participants, which was around 2,000; however, only 1,070 participants responded spontaneously, while the rest considered not taking part in the survey. Seventy of the responding students did not answer all the questions, so I removed those seventy to keep the data authentic. A minimum of ten in-depth interviews were conducted among the relevant faculty members of the said institutions. The respondents of the study covered mainly two types of population groups: (1) bachelor- and master-level students from twenty different universities, both male and female, aged between eighteen and forty-five, and (2) respective teachers from the universities. This study entirely followed the protocol of research ethics that involves human participants who gave the data for the study. The participants were informed about the purpose of the study, and they all were assured that their information would be kept confidential and used only for research purposes. The respondents' consent to participate in the study was taken before the interviews. They were also informed that they were free to refuse to give interviews, could terminate interviews any time, refuse to answer any question that they did not want to answer or made them uncomfortable, and withdraw any answer without any fear or prejudice. All data were analyzed without disclosing their identity.

Findings

Almost 83 percent of the students are in their bachelor's programs, while 17 percent of them are from master's programs. Most of the students (96 percent) know about the *birangonas* and war rape. After books, social media is the main source of their knowledge about wartime rape and war heroines. Those who said that they learned about the *birangonas* from books read only Ibrahim's *Ami birangona bolchi* either in the original or in Hasanat's translation (*A War Heroine, I Speak*). They do not know about the majority of the other memoirs or autobiographies written by other war heroines.

An open-ended question asked if the respondents were comfortable in discussing sexual violence that took place in 1971. About 58 percent of students responded positively, while others either did not know or were uncomfortable answering it. Surprisingly, a good number of students (29 percent) considered wartime rape or sexual violence during 1971 a matter of shame for the nation, although they agreed that those women sacrificed their honor for the nation. From their perspective, it is elaborated that rape brings dishonor to a nation. This perspective is mainly based on the sociocultural stigma that narrowly defines women's sexual chastity to be more important than anything else in their life. The same perspective considers a girl or woman impure or bereft of the most valued thing of her life once she gets raped, irrespective of a war or nonwar situation. Moreover, in classrooms, most of the students find it uncomfortable, embarrassing, and even painful to read the particular part of the story where sexual violence occurs or have those sections read aloud by their teachers in class. At the same time, the respondents admit that it is important and relevant to bring this issue up in classrooms to increase awareness of sexual violence and to acknowledge its importance in the real history of Bangladesh.

Of the participating students, 50 percent said they have "no feeling" when they hear any rape narrative, whether it is about 1971 war rape or non-wartime ones. Most of the female students prefer female teachers to discuss rape in the classes. Some male students said male teachers should discuss rape or sexual violence with male students and female teachers with female students. Of the male students, 45 percent said that they are uncomfortable hearing female teachers discuss the sexual violence of wartime. Thus, this research found that students' and teachers' gender match is also important when it comes to classroom discussions on wartime rape stories. Of the students, 23.8 percent preferred not to say which gender of teacher they prefer mostly to discuss such issues in the classroom, and among them, three-fourths are male students. Out of the female students, 28.7 percent said they prefer female teachers, but the teachers' gender does not matter to a large number of students (28.1 percent). Some of them added that even though the teachers themselves are respectful and comfortable with discussing this issue, female teachers are more comfortable, and they can describe it in an emphatic way more than their male counterparts.

In an open-ended question, most students (94 percent) showed their interest to include the memoirs of *birangonas* in their syllabi, and in fact, they are interested mostly to hear war heroines' stories from their teachers in the classrooms. The reason behind their interest is that they are quite familiar with the contributions and sacrifices of the *muktishena*, or the male freedom fighters, but they are less informed about *birangonas*, the female counterparts of the *muktishena*. They agree that reading more stories about *birangonas* will increase their respect for them. Apart from this, 6 percent of students feel there is no need to include stories of *birangonas* in curricula or syllabi because it is a waste of their time and will hinder their academic studies.

When the students were asked if religion is a sensitive issue or if they would like to bring the issue of religious propaganda triggering the 1971 wartime rapes while reading the texts, around 49 percent of students said they would like to discuss fatwas by Muslim scholars, which actually justified the rape by Pakistani armed forces back then; 20.6 percent of students were not sure; and nearly 30 percent of students preferred not to bring up such sensitive issues at all. Apart from this, they all agreed that new generations will only know half of the history of their nation if the stories of *birangonas* are not referred to or, even worse, if the society continues to be in complete denial of their stories.

Five male and five female educators from ten different institutes took part in this online survey and shared their views with me. The faculty members were asked if they have ever talked to students about sexual violence or rape in 1971. Most of them said they had not talked specifically about that, but they have discussed incidents of sexual violence against women or rape during 1971 in several issues. Only one teacher said that he often brings up the rape issue during wartime occasionally while lecturing to undergraduate students. Most of the time, the reactions of students in his class have varied. Female teachers said they often find the students showing no interest in participating in discussions of wartime rape but that they listened to the issue attentively. The faculty members said that students are sympathetic to the rape survivors, but a female teacher is skeptical as to whether they were "empathetic" enough. On the contrary, male teachers find that if they start the conversation, students come forward to talk openly about rape or sexual violence against women with a feeling of long-deepened disgust and distress and "with a look of strong disapproval." Most of the teachers agreed that they do not find it awkward to discuss this issue, but a male teacher said that "in times of the discussion of sexual violence, to be specific, my own gender sometimes makes me feel awkward. It restricts and thereby censors my discussion." All the teachers agreed on not avoiding or skipping sexual violence or rape during war as a classroom subject matter because they all believe such discussions may help them raise awareness of gendered violence. It may eventually help them break the taboos regarding women's bodies or women's issues including rape and sexual violence against them. While reading such texts, particularly the ones with rape stories, teachers prefer not to avoid the detailed descriptions, as they feel assured and confident of the adult students' strength and maturity to stomach the sensitive issues like rape. A male teacher considered not to avoid but to make spontaneous class discussions on the issue so that both the groups (students and teachers) do not feel awkward. A female teacher also added that "avoidance [of] such topics in [the] classroom may allow some students to possess supportive attitudes toward sexual violence because we live in a society where rape victims are often accused by a good number of people instead of the criminal. Thus, these groups of people view this crime as an accepted incident, which plays a crucial role in its recurring occurrences. A teacher acts like a role model to many young adults, and it is their duty to morally guide the youth through classroom discussions." Female teachers pointed out that some conservative students may not like reading such texts in class. These types of students need some preparation for reading or discussing such texts. Other educators also approved that such discussions may increase awareness for sexual violence against women, and it "will eventually make them aware and a well-informed nation." A female faculty member explained in addition that such discussions should be normalized to let students realize how pathetic and despicable these rapist soldiers were. According to her, "Students will learn also how to stand against such brutalities." The educators also admitted that such memoirs or autobiographies by the *birangonas* should be included in the syllabus so that students become more familiar with the nation's whole history of independence. A male teacher declared, "Such a discussion is important not only for knowing the history of Bangladesh but also for increasing social, cultural, and moral awareness."

Conclusion

The primary purpose of this survey was to find out how much the college students in Bangladesh know about the history of the war heroines. In so doing, the survey revealed that the stories of the heroines were never included along with the stories of the male freedom fighters in any state curricula or textbooks. Even at the university level, the stories and memoirs of the heroines are not included in the curricula. It is not that discussions on freedom fighters are absent in classroom talks and lectures, but these are not inclusive or comprehensive enough. Discussions remain limited to the stories of the male freedom fighters and the glory of their sacrifices. Very sadly, the female counterparts of the freedom fighters, especially wartime rape victims, do not come up in class discussions. And it is often not an accidental avoidance but an intentional one. Searching for the reason behind this, two teachers said that reading or discussing wartime rape in 1971 is not necessary, as their overall learning objectives do not require them to.

It is unfortunate that it took Bangladesh more than twenty years to publish a book on wartime rape survivors of 1971, and more sadly, it took the state more than forty-two years to give only a fraction of the rape survivors the status of freedom fighters. Now Bangladesh will be celebrating its silver jubilee of independence in 2021, at a time when the stories of war heroines have not gained much attention yet. Without war heroines' sacrifices and contributions, the nation's independence would not have been achieved. While brave stories of freedom fighters are included in primary and secondary education, the stories of the *birangonas* are still intentionally excluded from school curricula. This research found that students are vaguely aware of war heroines' contributions to the 1971 war effort. Their sacrifices are mentioned only in passing. Their sacrifices, in other words, have been trivialized. The narrative testimonies of their trauma are essential to read and should be included in university classes in order to provide a holistic approach to the history of Bangladesh as an independent nation. Teaching the *birangonas'* traumatic texts in classrooms is necessary for the new generation to understand that the history of the nation's independence is partly built on the history of women raped during the war. Likewise, including such texts in classrooms can be a step toward helping students change the stigmatized beliefs about raped women. Furthermore, teaching narratives of war heroines may finally help resurface these "forgotten" injustices against Bangladeshi women who have been long silenced by history.

Notes

1 Leslie Alan Horvitz and Christopher Catherwood, *Encyclopedia of War Crimes and Genocide*, vol. 1, *A–L* (New York: Facts on File, 2011).
2 Bina D'Costa, *Nationbuilding, Gender and War Crimes in South Asia* (London: Routledge, 2013), 108.

3 Anthony Mascarenhas, *The Rape of Bangla Desh* (Delhi: Vikas, 1972), 18.

4 Susan Brownmiller, *Against Our Will: Men, Women and Rape* (New York: Fawcett, 2000), 80.

5 Veenu Sandhu, "1971: A War Story," *Business Standard*, January 13, 2014, http://www .business-standard.com/article/beyond-business/1971-a-war-story-114011000691_1 .html.eenu.

6 The Hamoodur Rahman Commission was formed by Z. A. Bhutto in December 1971 to determine the reasons behind the failures of the war of 1971. The commission's head was Chief Justice Hamoodur Rahman. The commission's report was first submitted in 1972, but the government decided not to publish the report publicly due to political and military issues. The report got leaked in 2000 and some parts were published in Indian and Pakistani newspapers. See "The Hamood-ur-Rahman Commission Report," Story of Pakistan, last modified June 1, 2003, http://storyofpakistan .com/the-hamood-ur-rahman-commission-report/.

7 Sumit Walia, "1971 War: What Happened before Pakistan's Public Surrender to India," Sify, December 15, 2017, http://www.sify.com/news/1971-war-what-happened -before-pakistans-public-surrender-to-india-news-columns-rmpqGydddeajd.html.

8 Rounaq Jahan, "Genocide in Bangladesh," in *Century of Genocide: Eyewitness Accounts and Critical Views*, ed. Samuel Totten, William S. Parsons, and Israel W. Charny (New York: Routledge, 1997), 291.

9 Bina D'Costa, "1971: Rape and Its Consequences," bdnews24.com, December 15, 2010, https://opinion.bdnews24.com/2010/12/15/1971-rape-and-its-consequences/.

10 Lisa Sharlach, "Rape as Genocide: Bangladesh, the Former Yugoslavia, and Rwanda," *New Political Science* 22, no. 1 (2000): 89–102.

11 Yasmin Saikia, "Beyond the Archive of Silence: Narratives of Violence of the 1971 Liberation War of Bangladesh," *History Workshop Journal*, no. 58 (2004): 277, http:// www.jstor.org/stable/25472765.277.

12 Bina D'Costa and Sara Hossain, "Redress for Sexual Violence before the International Criminal Tribunal in Bangladesh: Lessons from History, and Hopes for the Future," *Criminal Law Forum* 21, no. 2 (2010): 333, http://doi.org/10.1007/s10609 -010-9120-2.

13 Nayanika Mookherjee, "'Remembering to Forget': Public Secrecy and Memory of Sexual Violence in the Bangladesh War of 1971," *Journal of the Royal Anthropological Institute* 12, no. 2 (2006): 444, https://doi.org/10.1111/j.1467-9655.2006.00299.x.

14 Annika Wolke, "Silent Birangonas: Sexual Violence, Women's Voices and Male Conflict Narratives," E-International Relations, September 19, 2017, http://www.e-ir.info/ 2017/09/19/silent-birangonas-sexual-violence-womens-voices-and-male-conflict -narratives/.

15 Lauren Wolfe, "The Index: Justice for Rape in War," Women's Media Center, 2014, https://womensmediacenter.com/women-under-siege/the-index-justice-for-crimes -of-rape-in-war.

16 Neelima Ibrahim worked as an educator, writer, and social worker in Bangladesh. Her *Ami birangona bolchi* (Dhaka, Bangladesh: Jagriti Prokashoni, 1994) is the first book or collection of testimonials of wartime rape survivors of the Liberation War of Bangladesh. For the English translation, see Fayeza Hasanat, trans., *A War Heroine, I Speak* (Dhaka, Bangladesh: Bangla Academy, 2017).

17 Ferdousi Priyabhashini, *Nindito nandan* (Dhaka, Bangladesh: Shobdoshoilee, 2014); Rama Chowdhury, *Ekattorer jononi* (Chattogram, Bangladesh: Madhukari, 2010).

18 Hasanat, *War Heroine*, 10.

19 Hasanat, 63.

20 Shaheen Akhtar et al., eds., *Rising from the Ashes: Women's Narratives of 1971* (Dhaka, Bangladesh: University Press, 2012).
21 D'Costa, *Nationbuilding*, 99.
22 Bina D'Costa, "War Crimes, Justice and the Politics of Memory," *Economic and Political Weekly* 48, no. 12 (2013): 39, http://www.jstor.org/stable/23527147.
23 Tareq Masud and Catherine Masud, "Narir Kotha (Women and War)," Tareque Masud Memorial Trust, August 7, 2016, http://www.youtube.com/watch?v=BsazbwBGSoM.
24 Nayanika Mookherjee, *The Spectral Wound: Sexual Violence, Public Memories, and the Bangladesh War of 1971* (Durham, N.C.: Duke University Press, 2015), 40–41.
25 Mookherjee, 39–43.
26 Tuhin Shubhra Adhikary, "30 Lakh Martyrs a Settled History," *Daily Star*, February 3, 2016, http://www.thedailystar.net/frontpage/30-lakh-martyrs-settled-history-211537.
27 "Sixty-One More Recognised as Birangonas," *Daily Star*, December 16, 2020, https://www.thedailystar.net/frontpage/news/sixty-one-more-recognised-biranganas-2011961.

Bibliography

Adhikary, Tuhin Shubhra. "30 Lakh Martyrs a Settled History." *Daily Star*, February 3, 2016. http://www.thedailystar.net/frontpage/30-lakh-martyrs-settled-history-211537.
Akhtar, Shaheen, Suraiya Begum, Meghna Guhathakurta, Hameeda Hossain, and Sultana Kamal, eds. *Rising from the Ashes: Women's Narratives of 1971*. Dhaka, Bangladesh: University Press, 2012.
Brownmiller, Susan. *Against Our Will: Men, Women and Rape*. New York: Fawcett, 2000.
Chowdhury, Rama. *Ekattorer jononi*. Chattogram, Bangladesh: Madhukari, 2010.
Daily Star. "Sixty-One More Recognised as Birangonas." December 16, 2020. https://www.thedailystar.net/frontpage/news/sixty-one-more-recognised-biranganas-2011961.
D'Costa, Bina. *Nationbuilding, Gender and War Crimes in South Asia*. London: Routledge, 2013.
———. "1971: Rape and Its Consequences." bdnews24.com, December 15, 2010. https://opinion.bdnews24.com/2010/12/15/1971-rape-and-its-consequences/.
———. "War Crimes, Justice and the Politics of Memory." *Economic and Political Weekly* 48, no. 12 (2013): 39–43. http://www.jstor.org/stable/23527147.
D'Costa, Bina, and Sara Hossain. "Redress for Sexual Violence before the International Criminal Tribunal in Bangladesh: Lessons from History, and Hopes for the Future." *Criminal Law Forum* 21, no. 2 (2010): 331–359. http://doi.org/10.1007/s10609-010-9120-2.
Hasanat, Fayeza, trans. *A War Heroine, I Speak*. Dhaka, Bangladesh: Bangla Academy, 2017.
Horvitz, Leslie Alan, and Christopher Catherwood. *Encyclopedia of War Crimes and Genocide*. Vol. 1, *A–L*. New York: Facts on File, 2011.
Ibrahim, Neelima. *Ami birangona bolchi*. Dhaka, Bangladesh: Jagriti Prokashoni, 1994.
Jahan, Rounaq. "Genocide in Bangladesh." In *Century of Genocide: Eyewitness Accounts and Critical Views*, edited by Samuel Totten, William S. Parsons, and Israel W. Charny, 291–316. New York: Routledge, 1997.
Mascarenhas, Anthony. *The Rape of Bangla Desh*. Delhi: Vikas, 1972.
Masud, Tareq, and Catherine Masud. "*Narir kotha* (Women's words)." Tareque Masud Memorial Trust, August 7, 2016. http://www.youtube.com/watch?v=BsazbwBGSoM.
Mookherjee, Nayanika. "'Remembering to Forget': Public Secrecy and Memory of Sexual Violence in the Bangladesh War of 1971." *Journal of the Royal Anthropological Institute* 12, no. 2 (2006): 433–450.

————. *The Spectral Wound: Sexual Violence, Public Memories, and the Bangladesh War of 1971*. Durham, N.C.: Duke University Press, 2015.

Priyabhashini, Ferdousi. *Nindito nandan*. Dhaka, Bangladesh: Shobdoshoilee, 2014.

Saikia, Yasmin. "Beyond the Archive of Silence: Narratives of Violence of the 1971 Liberation War of Bangladesh." *History Workshop Journal*, no. 58 (2004): 275–287. http://www.jstor.org/stable/25472765.

Sandhu, Veenu. "1971: A War Story." *Business Standard*, January 13, 2014. http://www.business-standard.com/article/beyond-business/1971-a-war-story-114011000691_1.html.

Sharlach, Lisa. "Rape as Genocide: Bangladesh, the Former Yugoslavia, and Rwanda." *New Political Science* 22, no. 1 (2000): 89–102.

Walia, Sumit. "1971 War: What Happened before Pakistan's Public Surrender to India." Sify, December 15, 2017. http://www.sify.com/news/1971-war-what-happened-before-pakistans-public-surrender-to-india-news-columns-rmpqGydddeajd.html.

Wolfe, Lauren. "The Index: Justice for Rape in War." Women's Media Center, 2014. https://womensmediacenter.com/women-under-siege/the-index-justice-for-crimes-of-rape-in-war.

Wolke, Annika. "Silent Birangonas: Sexual Violence, Women's Voices and Male Conflict Narratives." E-International Relations, September 19, 2017. http://www.e-ir.info/2017/09/19/silent-birangonas-sexual-violence-womens-voices-and-male-conflict-narratives/.

11

They Fear Us Because We Are Fearless

● ●

Women-Led Global
Environmental Advocacy and Its
Enemies

MATTHEW SPENCER

On March 2, 2016, Honduran environmentalist, indigenous rights activist, and Goldman Environmental Prize winner Berta Cáceres was murdered in her home by unidentified intruders. Two years before, a total of twelve environmental activists had been murdered in Honduras. How and why did a small Central American nation become a global epicenter of violence against environmental activism? To answer this question, it is first necessary to confront the steadily growing number of such deaths in Central America, South America, and indeed, worldwide. The intertwining of worldwide extractive capitalism with oppressive governmental regimes has created a global apparatus that views any form of direct environmental activism and protection as a threat to the bottom line. This phenomenon ranges from direct actions and tree sit-ins in the United States to "martyr squads" opposing dam construction in India to Greta Thunberg and the youth climate strike movement to the work of indigenous groups in the Americas and beyond. In each of these struggles, women take an active or leading role and are, therefore, often those most directly targeted by violence. This chapter combines readings of such movements in literary texts with real-world instances to form a picture of how and why these brave women do the work of protecting the earth in the face of terrible opposition and the constant threat of harm or death. In doing so, a narrative unique to the Anthropocene emerges, that of an international antideforestation, anti–environmental degradation front of activists led or inspired by women that seeks to halt the rampant exploitation of land by capital and reaffirm the interconnectedness of humanity and the natural world in ways that suggest alternative futures in the face of impending climate catastrophe.

While this chapter takes as its central axis the looming threat of global climate change, the theoretical means by which it radiates outward is ecofeminist political ecology. While definitions of ecofeminism abound in the ongoing academic debates on the topic, this examination will rely on an understanding synthesized from the foundational work of Val Plumwood and Ariel Salleh. Central to these conceptions is a dismantling of essentialist dualisms at the heart of hierarchical relations, including man/woman, man/nature, reason/emotion, and numerous others. These dualisms create a bipolar worldview in which domination over women's bodies *and* the planet takes place, a worldview in which men and the culture they are said to have created are the arbiters of reason and power while women and nature are subordinate and subject to exploitation at will. In the grips of a dualistic culture, it is difficult or even impossible to imagine alternatives, or, as Plumwood posits, dualisms create "central cultural concepts and identities so as to make equality and mutuality literally unthinkable."[1] When alternatives to alienated individual existence, resource and human exploitation, and capital-dominated environmental destruction are unthinkable, we become trapped in the funhouse of the Anthropocene, what Andreas Malm names "the warming condition," a state in which "our daily life, our psychic experience, our cultural responses, even our politics show signs of being sucked back by planetary forces into the hole of time, the present dissolving into past and future alike,"[2] a sinister turn in the "postmodern condition" that "has sunk more deeply than ever into the mind *in step with* the warming."[3] Such a state—one in which major governments and the nongovernmental organizations (NGOs) that often supersede their power ignore the clear signs of climate change in favor of profits and maintaining the status quo and the average citizen has no recourse to being made complicit in environmental devastation—must necessarily subdue movements that pose a threat to business as usual, even when they do so by calling for more equitable relations with the planet. To escape these hierarchies and the state they leave us is to "develop an alternative culture which fully recognises *human* identity as continuous with, not alien from, nature"[4] in the vein of deep ecology and indigenous ways of being in the world that, attributed or not, are its foundation. With this in mind, a working definition of ecofeminism is an intersectional, transnational, and intraspecies theoretical and activist stance that recognizes the links between the oppression of women and environmental exploitation and degradation. Additionally, once the organizing hierarchies of man/woman, man/nature, and so on begin to fall like dominoes, it becomes immediately evident that minorities of multiple definitions benefit from their demise. In this way, ecofeminism can serve as an organizational framework for building solidarity across peoples and organizing collective action against the forces that plunder the earth and rob us of our collective human inheritance of a livable planet.

As this intersectional approach hopefully makes clear, to abandon difference altogether is to miss the point of ecofeminist discourse and risk asserting the hegemony of homogeneity regarding environmentalist discourse. While all humanity will suffer the effects of global climate change, and therefore shares a common existential threat, not all regions or peoples will suffer it at the same time, in the same way, or to the same degree. For instance, those living in the Sundarbans near the India/Bangladesh border watching their home islands and their characteristic mangrove forests disappear are more keenly aware of changing sea levels than those living in the midwestern United States, but the Americans know something about extreme weather like flooding even if they fail to make the connection to a global change. By affirming difference but refusing dualistic, hierarchical thinking, a more collective front can be put up against such massive shifts in the Earth's biosphere to endorse a "non-instrumentalising relationship with nature, where both connection and otherness are the basis of interaction." Not doing so is akin to the colonizing mindset of the preceding centuries, in which the colonial self "denies the other through the attempt to incorporate it into the empire of the self, and which is unable to experience sameness without erasing difference."[5] Along these lines, the relationship of the Lenca people of Honduras, of which Berta Cáceres was a representative, with their ancestral home along the Gualcarque River is a spiritual and conceptual other of similar relationships between peoples and the lands they inhabit, but the core concepts of respect, care, and stewardship of the land are ones around which to build a global consensus. In building this consensus, sameness would be emphasized while also maintaining cultural differences that now exist in a freer state due to the destructive human/nature dualism being abandoned. In this way, the "colonial self" that exists in a world of overlapping relationships of domination is replaced with a "relational self" more attuned to the connectedness of human to human and human to nature. Ariel Salleh lays out the political goals of such a self:

> An ecofeminist analysis suggests that the way to survive is not by constructing ever-further political hierarchies, with more grey-suited mullahs or more electronic decrees enshrining ostensibly universal rights. Rather, by acknowledging our libidinal grounding in the cycles of nature, we begin to talk sense about security and sustainability. Through connectedness, relational selves already exercise communal integration with sensitivity to the needs of future generations

and other species. Being responsive to other selves, only the relational self has the reflexivity to examine its contingent identities and actions. If ecology is the matter and internal relations its theory, then a relational psychology and politics are the practice.[6]

An ecofeminist reevaluation of individual cultural values is therefore necessary to create cross-cultural, multinational mass movements to break global inertia around adapting to a changing climate. If it seems as if "Western values" or the cultural values of the Global North are the ones that fall most heavily under attack in this view, that is by design. As the long-standing stewards of colonialism, resource exploitation, and a deeply unequal world economy, the "developed" nations of the Global North are those most in need of a shift in their relationality to the planet, and so the bulk of any ecofeminist critique must fall at their feet. Only by attacking the core of these issues can a true change be made. This may be the only way to create a more equitable future or any future at all.

What ecofeminism brings to the critical lens of this chapter is a real-world extension of political ecology that reaches the lives of those who struggle against hegemonic forces. An ecofeminist spin on political ecology is necessary to maintain a balance between the local and the global so as not to privilege certain struggles over others and instead field a united front against extractivism worldwide. Richard Peet and Michael Watts cite such balance as a strength of political ecology's originality, which "resided in its efforts to integrate human and physical approaches to land degradation, through an explicitly theoretical approach to the ecological crisis capable of addressing diverse circumstances . . . and [is] capable of accommodating both detailed local study and general principles."[7] Synthesizing this view with ecofeminism allows for a globe-trotting theoretical lens that is also supple enough to have material application within the lived experience of individuals. Such a view is crucial when so many diverse peoples globally are struggling not just for political agency and autonomy but for survival. The intersection of identity, place, and survival instinct creates collectivity and mass movement, especially when survival is threatened. This includes not only personal safety and survival but the survival of a way of being in the world. The reliance of the Honduran Lenca people on the Gualcarque River and the surrounding area for both a contemporary livelihood and an ancestral link to identity means that a threat to the river and the surrounding area threatens to destroy both their ability to earn a living and their culture. In this way, a multi-faceted approach to understanding such issues as well as creating change within them can be deployed both in academic studies such as this one and in the material world in which we all live under the threat of environmental disaster.

The rise and murder of Honduran activist Berta Cáceres is an unfortunate encapsulation of how ecofeminist political action can be effective in fostering mass movements and creating material change and is therefore consistently in the sights of hegemonic extractivist forces. Honduras served as a perfect setting for this tragedy as a nexus of exploitative conservative capitalism: "Standing on a conservative extreme, Honduras's praise of the military, support of the criollo elites (ladinos), and neocolonial alliance with the US situates this Central American country on the edge of a human rights crisis paralleled to the ecological crisis that pervades the tiny nation."[8] Cáceres stood at the intersection of these forces and posed a challenge to all of them through her work on the ground with the people of Honduras and in the halls of power. As a radical, indigenous woman who fostered equity within an international mass movement of exploited people, she was a force for change that could not be allowed to grow in strength.

Cáceres was a founder of the Consejo Cívico de Organizaciones Populares e Indígenas de Honduras (Council of Popular and Indigenous Organizations of Honduras; COPINH) in 1993 to defend the environment of Honduras and the interests of the Lenca people in the country. It was the success of this organization in opposing proposed dam construction on the Gualcarque River that directly contributed to her assassination. What made the organization's success so intimidating for forces within Honduras was its collective nature and the support it fostered among the people:

> COPINH, founded as a grassroots organization, managed to stay true to its roots partly because Berta was never power-hungry. Whenever possible, everywhere she went, busloads of COPINH members went with her, meaning she and the organization evolved together. At one anti-FTAA meeting in Cuba, Gustavo and Berta were invited as speakers and put up in a fancy Havana hotel. Berta preferred the cheaper digs with the rest of the COPINH faction. "COPINH was never a closed shop," recalls Alba Marconi, who worked alongside Berta for over a decade. "For Berta, sharing ideas and experiences was fundamental to ensure COPINH was a true grass-roots organization where the power and energy came from its base."[9]

Cáceres and her allies also sought to tear down boundaries between worldwide struggles and bring them together under the banner of strong general resistance. Those around her noted, "Her ability to cite community struggles in Kurdistan, Brazil, Guatemala or Canada to explain big issues like capitalism, militarization and patriarchy was impressive."[10] So although COPINH was formed to defend the enviro-cultural interests of the Lenca people, Cáceres sought international solidarity within networks of diverse groups. Cáceres pursued a similar outcome through her involvement with the Convergence of Movements of the Peoples of the Americas (COMPA), a multinational association taking on a similar role as COPINH but on a larger scale. COMPA's six agreed-upon objectives, which Cáceres had a hand in developing, show an ecofeminist understanding of international struggles against extractive capital as well as cultural norms that undermine such efforts, such as Latin American machismo. The objectives were "struggle *for* gender equality, indigenous rights and sustainable rural development, and *against* the FTAA [Free Trade Area of the Americas], militarization, and external debt and structural adjustment policies imposed by international banks under the Washington Consensus."[11] In helping establish such objectives for COMPA, Cáceres expanded from the more specialized goals of COPINH to more expansive and, to the ruling class of Honduras and elsewhere, dangerous plans, such as resistance to the influence of international financial institutions and unfair trade agreements between nations. While direct opposition to dam construction on the Gualcarque was probably the most immediate cause of her assassination, her shift to a global stance likely contributed to the decision to silence her.

Before her murder, Cáceres was awarded the Goldman Environmental Prize for her work organizing within the Honduran Lenca community, with the awarding committee citing her work organizing a blockade of a supposed dam site that lasted well over a year and led to Desarrollos Energeticos SA (DESA), the company that would be building the dam and was ultimately responsible for directing Cáceres's killers, to withdraw from the project.[12] Despite this international recognition, she was added to the growing list of environmentally minded activists killed. Global Witness has noted that in 2014, 116 environmental activists were murdered worldwide, nearly doubling the number of journalists killed during the same time. Honduras has been especially treacherous, with 101 activist deaths recorded between 2010 and 2014.[13] These staggering figures have led to Global Witness declaring Honduras "the deadliest country in the world for environmental activists."[14] The brazenness of the killings is especially telling. Prominent voices like Cáceres and Jeannette Kawas were targets despite their public profiles. However, their profiles helped these women, alongside the numerous unknown others, reach the status of environmental martyrs. This lofty title makes clear that their deaths are not seen as having been in vain. Their work is not over; rather, it continues through their influence and the networks they forged in life. Irune del Rio Gabiola reflects on Cáceres's legacy: "Although the night of March 2nd, 2016 marks an unsurmountable tragedy, it represents a moment of global disruption and the rebirth of Berta, an activist committed to social and environmental justice and equality. Her assassination was condemned unprecedentedly all over the world, and her indefatigable work has since been commemorated and carried on by hundreds of social movements that demand justice, human and territorial rights, and a protected environment."[15]

Beyond Honduras, Congressman Hank Johnson (D-GA-4) introduced the Berta Cáceres Human Rights in Honduras Act in 2016. The act sought to suspend funding to the government of Honduras until an investigation into its violation of citizens' human rights was complete.[16] While this legislation is a step in the right direction in terms of denying the corrupt extractivist powers in Honduras the U.S. aid that they need to silence activists, it leaves a bitter taste, since investigations in Cáceres's murder have revealed that at least two of the men involved received training at the former School of the Americas—now the Western Hemisphere Institute for Security Cooperation—training camp at Fort Benning in Georgia, Congressman Johnson's home state.[17] Like Cáceres, Jeannette Kawas's efforts in life continue in the form of Jeannette Kawas National Park, which was renamed in her honor for her work in keeping the palm industry out of the park's lands. The renaming of the park, the law inspired by Cáceres's death, and other similar actions may signal coming victories for Earth protectors worldwide as networks of resistance grow and destructive hierarchies are challenged.

An encouraging albeit ideologically marred mass movement emerged two years after Cáceres's murder and signaled a new addition to the solidarity networks of global environmental activists: the young. Greta Thunberg shot to international prominence as a founder of the School Strike for Climate (alternatively known as Youth Strike for Climate, Fridays for Future, and a handful of other unofficial names) in 2018. Her frankness about climate change–related issues, as well as her Asperger's syndrome and the depression and anxiety from which she suffers, brought her to the center of global attention. She quickly became a figurehead for a loose international youth movement against climate change, specifically in the Global North, has repeatedly been placed on lists of most influential people, and has twice been nominated for the Nobel Peace Prize. However, this sudden fame has been double-sided, and she has faced myriad abuse focusing primarily on her age and neuroatypicality and the political nature of her message. These attacks escalated following the intensification of Thunberg's rhetoric, which included telling the World Economic Forum "I want you to panic" while visibly physically upset in 2019, as well as similar speeches delivered around the world. Sky News Australia host Andrew Bolt openly referred to Thunberg and those around her as liars and claimed that educating Thunberg and other children about climate change is tantamount to child abuse, describing Thunberg herself as "a kid from a rich country, pampered by elites, who still thinks her life has been destroyed—and she can't handle that fear."[18] Bolt also targeted Thunberg's Asperger's, although Thunberg has referred to the syndrome as a personal "superpower" that allows her to focus on the seriousness of climate change: "To me that [climate change] is black or white. There are no grey areas when it comes to survival."[19] Bolt posited that "Asperger's is very rarely an advantage" and that "[Thunberg] seems chronically attracted to apocalyptic visions chronically attracted to fear."[20] Thunberg also faced criticism from former president Donald Trump before the controversial deactivation of his infamous Twitter account. After seeing Thunberg's passionate public speaking, he responded, "So Ridiculous. Greta must work on her Anger Management problem, then go to a good old-fashioned movie with a friend! Chill Greta, Chill!"[21] Earlier he had sarcastically referred to Thunberg as "a very happy young girl looking forward to a bright and wonderful future. So nice to see!"[22] Such attacks from the news media and politicians were of course joined by more serious and aggressive threats against Thunberg's safety and various other forms of online bullying. But how effective can such movements be when they are so easily absorbed into mainstream culture while national governments and international corporations do little to change the policies that are directly contributing to global climate change? Thunberg's passionate speeches before the likes of the United Nations are rhetorically effective and translate into compelling sound bites, video clips, and even books, but they have had little effect on emissions.

Amitav Ghosh attempts to address this phenomenon in his *The Great Derangement: Climate Change and the Unthinkable*, observing that "this vision of politics as moral journey has also had the consequence of creating an ever-growing divergence between a public sphere of political performance and the realm of actual governance."[23] As the inability of the general public to affect actual, meaningful change becomes obvious, their outpourings become more performative rather than instrumental, and whatever change they might create is attenuated to the desires of hegemonic forces. Greta Thunberg can become a figurehead for youth climate movements, berate the United Nations for not doing enough, and be showered with plaudits for her efforts, but global emissions keep ticking away, and when governments do make "promises" to curb them, they come with heavy caveats or deadlines too far in the future to be effective. This is the warped logic of "the warming condition" that leaves peaceful mass movements to perform rage while creating little change. One can find a stark parallel in Ghosh's analysis of the global protests following the United States' invasion of Iraq in 2003. These were enormous demonstrations in which millions of people around the globe took part, perhaps even the "largest single manifestation of public dissent in history," yet they did little to stop the invasion, and "even at that time there was a feeling of hopelessness."[24] He expands upon this idea: "In other words, the public sphere, where politics is performed, has been largely emptied of content in terms of the exercise of power: as with fiction, it has become a forum for secular testimony, a baring-of-the-soul in the world-as-church. Politics as thus practiced is primarily an exercise in personal expressiveness."[25] He further elaborates that many countries of the Global North have become "post-political spaces" managed by diverse forces such as news media, popular culture, and social media, and "for many, this creates a haunting sense of loss that manifests itself in an ever-more-desperate yearning to recoup a genuinely participatory politics."[26] In a world of content, of floating signifiers that can find no real purchase in material needs and desires, an ambitious and relentless climate activist pleading to the most powerful political forces on Earth for change becomes just "a very happy young girl looking forward to a bright and wonderful future," despite her efforts.

Such an admittedly harsh critique of Thunberg's work is born not of any malice or lack of appreciation but of the need to emphasize the ways in which even the sincerest climate action can be swept aside or ignored through its absorption into a larger cultural framework that creates no real-world change. In January 2021, a Forbes article was published that detailed how Thunberg had "trolled" the departing President Trump one last time. Referencing his tweet about her years earlier, she posted a picture of Trump boarding *Marine 1* for the last time with the text, "He seems like a very happy old man looking forward to a bright and wonderful future. So nice to see!"[27] The article goes on to include more details from the feud and denigrate Trump's nonexistent environmental policy before a stark conclusion: "With the willfully ignorant Trump finally out of office, Thunberg can drop her long-running Twitter feud and turn her attention to Joe 'I am not banning fracking' Biden."[28] While there is a certain level of cultural schadenfreude attached to seeing a president with a vocal antipathy to environmental causes be defeated and leave office, the reality is that the Biden administration is unlikely to make the necessary changes that humanity needs now, and the ones they do make will likely be too little and too late. What matters for Thunberg's influence and future legacy are the solidarity networks that can be formed in this moment and how those movements can force change on the ground, like Cáceres's Lenca blockade.

Visible movements are valuable, especially among world youth, but they must translate their energy into material outcomes. Rather than relying primarily on stark, emotional rhetoric, which is admittedly good for drawing attention, that rhetoric must be paired with movement building and direct resistance to destructive forces. Without such force in material space, movements are doomed to be performative and ineffectual. In writing about environmental martyrs, Rob Nixon borrows from Ta-Nehisi Coates's writing on the Black Lives Matter movement in the United States to posit that it must never be forgotten that those who suffer from environmental degradation—here he is referring to martyrs but the same can be said of those suffering from the inequities of global climate change—are human, that they exist in fragile bodies that can be shattered by violence, and so they must be recognized: "The fate of such communities is twinned to the fate of the great rain forests in our age of climate breakdown, twinned to the future of forests where the economics, the graphs, the charts, the regressions all land, with great violence, upon the soon-to-be martyred body."[29] Without intersectional, ecofeminist movements that grow from loss and incorporate past lessons into future action, rather through a recognizable figurehead or mass of members, the only option left will be violent opposition. Malm is one of only a few writers pondering the question of violent confrontation at the moment: "At what point do we escalate? When do we conclude that the time has come to also try something different? When do we start physically attacking the things that consume our planet and destroy them with our own hands? Is there a good reason we have waited this long?"[30] Or, to put it bluntly, "all has already been said; now is the time for confrontation."[31] If women climate activists cannot make the change humanity needs today, then they will surely be on the front lines of climate conflicts in the future, whether fighting or fleeing from untenable living conditions. If the strength of Cáceres's COPINH and COMPA movements can meet the social virality and youthful vigor of Thunberg's School Strike for Climate and create a supple yet strong global mass movement for climate, then there is no reason we cannot create more equitable futures in the face of unavoidable climate change.

Notes

1   Val Plumwood, *Feminism and the Mastery of Nature* (New York: Routledge, 1993), 47.
2   Andreas Malm, *The Progress of This Storm: Nature and Society in a War Time World* (New York: Verso, 2017), 11.
3   Malm, 13.
4   Malm, 36.
5   Malm, 174.
6   Ariel Salleh, *Ecofeminism as Politics* (London: Zed Books, 1997), 275–276.
7   Richard Peet and Michael Watts, *Liberation Ecologies: Environment, Development, Social Movements*, 2nd ed. (New York: Routledge, 1997), 6.
8   Irune del Rio Gabiola, *Affect, Ecofeminism, and Intersectional Struggles in Latin America: A Tribute to Berta Cáceres* (New York: Peter Lang, 2020), 79.
9   Nina Lakhani, *Who Killed Berta Cáceres? The Murder of an Indigenous Defender and the Race to Save the Planet* (New York: Verso, 2020), 55.
10 Lakhani, 55.
11 Lakhani, 56. Known as ALCA in Spanish, this "free trade" agreement sought to smooth the nature of trade between North American countries, excluding Cuba, and was generally seen as a neoliberal policy of further exploitation by several leaders. It was abandoned in 2005 when the involved nations were unable to come to an agreement. In 2004, Venezuelan president Hugo Chávez and Cuban president Fidel Castro established the Bolivarian Alliance for the Americas (ALBA) as an alternative, with a focus on social welfare and regional cooperation.
12 "Berta Cáceres," Goldman Environmental Prize, accessed March 15, 2021, https://www.goldmanprize.org/recipient/berta-caceres/.
13 "How Many More?," Global Witness, April 20, 2015, https://www.globalwitness.org/en/campaigns/environmental-activists/how-many-more/. It should be noted that these numbers may be underreported and could be higher.
14 "Honduras: The Deadliest Country in the World for Environmental Activists," Global Witness, January 31, 2017, https://www.globalwitness.org/en/campaigns/environmental-activists/honduras-deadliest-country-world-environmental-activism/.
15 Gabiola, *Affect, Ecofeminism*, 2.
16 "Rep. Johnson Introduces 'The Berta Caceres Human Rights in Honduras Act,'" HankJohnson, June 15, 2016, https://hankjohnson.house.gov/media-center/press-releases/rep-johnson-introduces-berta-c-ceres-human-rights-honduras-act.
17 Nina Lakhani, "Berta Cáceres Court Papers Show Murder Suspects' Links to US-Trained Elite Troops," *Guardian*, February 28, 2017, https://www.theguardian.com/world/2017/feb/28/berta-caceres-honduras-military-intelligence-us-trained-special-forces. The School of the Americas was notorious for training anti-leftist forces for repressive governments in the Global South, most notably during Operation Condor in the 1970s and 1980s.
18 Climate Realists (@Climate Realists), "Andrew Bolt," Twitter, September 30, 2019, 6:55 p.m., https://twitter.com/ClimateRealists/status/1178820673768185856.

19   Greta Thunberg, *No One Is Too Small to Make a Difference* (New York: Penguin, 2019), 6.
20   Joel Day, "Great Thunberg a Victim of 'Child Abuse' Claims Aussie Conservative in TV Tirade," Express, accessed March 15, 2021, https://www.express.co.uk/news/world/1182818/greta-thunberg-latest-news-climate-change-activism-un-summit-2019-global-warming.
21   Donald Trump (@realDonaldTrump), "So ridiculous," Twitter, December 12, 2019, 7:22 a.m.
22   Donald Trump (@realDonaldTrump), "A very happy young girl," Twitter, September 23, 2019, 11:36 p.m.
23   Amitav Ghosh, *The Great Derangement: Climate Change and the Unthinkable* (Chicago: University of Chicago Press, 2017), 129.
24   Ghosh, 129–130.
25   Ghosh, 131.
26   Ghosh, 132.
27   Greta Thunberg (@GretaThunberg), "He seems like a very happy old man," Twitter, January 20, 2021, 7:54 a.m., https://twitter.com/GretaThunberg/status/1351890941087522820.
28   Dani Di Placido, "Greta Thunberg Trolls Trump on Twitter, for the Last Time," Forbes, January 20, 2021, https://www.forbes.com/sites/danidiplacido/2021/01/20/greta-thunberg-trolls-trump-on-twitter-for-the-last-time/?sh=5fe456d4a31b.
29   Rob Nixon, "Indigenous Forest Defenders around the World Are Dying Anonymous Deaths," Literary Hub, January 16, 2020, https://lithub.com/indigenous-forest-defenders-around-the-world-are-dying-anonymous-deaths/.
30   Andreas Malm, *How to Blow Up a Pipeline* (New York: Verso, 2021), 8–9.
31   Malm, *Progress of This Storm*, 16.

Bibliography

Day, Joel. "Great Thunberg a Victim of 'Child Abuse' Claims Aussie Conservative in TV Tirade." Express. Accessed March 15, 2021. https://www.express.co.uk/news/world/1182818/greta-thunberg-latest-news-climate-change-activism-un-summit-2019-global-warming.

Di Placido, Dani. "Greta Thunberg Trolls Trump on Twitter, for the Last Time." Forbes, January 20, 2021. https://www.forbes.com/sites/danidiplacido/2021/01/20/greta-thunberg-trolls-trump-on-twitter-for-the-last-time/?sh=5fe456d4a31b.

Gabiola, Irune del Rio. *Affect, Ecofeminism, and Intersectional Struggles in Latin America: A Tribute to Berta Cáceres*. New York: Peter Lang, 2020.

Ghosh, Amitav. *The Great Derangement: Climate Change and the Unthinkable*. Chicago: University of Chicago Press, 2017.

Global Witness. "Honduras: The Deadliest Country in the World for Environmental Activists." January 31, 2017. https://www.globalwitness.org/en/campaigns/environmental-activists/honduras-deadliest-country-world-environmental-activism/.

———. "How Many More?" April 20, 2015. https://www.globalwitness.org/en/campaigns/environmental-activists/how-many-more/.

Goldman Environmental Prize. "Berta Cáceres." Accessed March 15, 2021. https://www.goldmanprize.org/recipient/berta-caceres/.

HankJohnson. "Rep. Johnson Introduces 'The Berta Cáceres Human Rights in Honduras Act.'" June 15, 2016. https://hankjohnson.house.gov/media-center/press-releases/rep-johnson-introduces-berta-c-ceres-human-rights-honduras-act.

Lakhani, Nina. "Berta Cáceres Court Papers Show Murder Suspects' Links to US-Trained Elite Troops." *Guardian*, February 28, 2017. https://www.theguardian.com/world/2017/feb/28/berta-caceres-honduras-military-intelligence-us-trained-special-forces.

———. *Who Killed Berta Cáceres? The Murder of an Indigenous Defender and the Race to Save the Planet*. New York: Verso, 2020.

Malm, Andreas. *How to Blow Up a Pipeline*. New York: Verso, 2021.

———. *The Progress of This Storm: Nature and Society in a War Time World*. New York: Verso, 2017.

Nixon, Rob. "Indigenous Forest Defenders around the World Are Dying Anonymous Deaths." Literary Hub, January 16, 2020. https://lithub.com/indigenous-forest-defenders-around-the-world-are-dying-anonymous-deaths/.

Peet, Richard, and Michael Watts. *Liberation Ecologies: Environment, Development, Social Movements*. New York: Routledge, 1997.

Plumwood, Val. *Feminism and the Mastery of Nature*. New York: Routledge, 1993.

Salleh, Ariel. *Ecofeminism as Politics*. London: Zed Books, 1997.

Thunberg, Greta. *No One Is Too Small to Make a Difference*. New York: Penguin, 2019.

Conclusion

● ●

Detangling Resistance

FAYEZA HASANAT

While narrating her horrendous experiences during the Liberation War of Bangladesh in her memoir, *Nindito nandan* (The blighted garden; 2015), Ferdousi Priyabhashini (1948–2018), a Bangladeshi feminist activist, sculptor, and a wartime rape survivor, evaluates her identity in the postwar society in the following way:

> During the war of 1971, I could not leave my job and hide somewhere to ensure my safety. I had to work in an office where I was basically imprisoned and was constantly sexually violated. For the nine whole months, while the nation fought for freedom, I kept fighting for survival, and after the war was over, I realized that my war was nowhere near its finish line. I had to gain strength to face a hostile world filled with hatred and prejudice against me. And at the same, I realized the crucial truth: that the war has toughened me so much that I felt I was larger than the world that I lived in; that my war in this world will never end; that people will never cease to stain my name and blame me for what happened to me. But I am not afraid to face them and outlive their hostility. No matter how much they try to ruin me, I will not give up. I am ready and I will always be ready to fight back for my existence and to keep my sense of dignity intact.[1]

Priyabhashini waged a personal war against the patriarchal suppression and socioreligious prejudice that tried to define her body as a sexual victim of war.[2] She expressed her resistance through her writing and her sculptures by portraying the raped woman's body as a figure of strength. Farzana Akhter in chapter 2 and Shafinur Nahar in chapter 10 have elaborated on the issue of the raped women of the Bangladesh war and discussed how the visual media and literary culture framed the bodies of the *birangonas* (war heroines), or the wartime raped women, as objects of pity, shame, and romanticized passivity. Using contemporary Bangladeshi movies as her point of reference, Akhter explores the changing attitude of the new generation of filmmakers who re-presents the raped body of war as that of resilience and agency. On the other hand, Nahar's analysis of the reluctance to include wartime rape narratives in college classrooms indicates the ongoing ideological violence against the raped body, an issue that Priyabhashini has pointed out in the previously quoted lines. Through her art, Priyabhashini wanted to detangle the raped female body from the webs of such neglect and negation by locating her at the center as a plain and simple truth: the raped woman of war is a fighter too because she fought with her body. Take the image in figure C.1, for example. Titled *Birangona*, the sculpture is made with two pieces of driftwood, portraying the body of a woman sitting by the hollow bend of a tree. The woman, however, does not lean on the tree; instead, she sits aloof, keeping the arch of her spine straight and distanced from the body of the tree. Her folded arms and closed legs denote a physical composure of resistance.

The ecofeminist aspect that Matthew Spencer so poignantly explores in chapter 11 resonates with Priyabhashini's philosophy of art as a tool against deforestation and the destruction of nature. Priyabhashini uses body posture as a signifier of resistance in her sculptures. The same framework of strength is visible in figure C.2, in the image of the robust body carved out of the trunk of a dead tree. Holding a weapon in her right arm and her left leg placed forward in a walking posture, the woman warrior in figure C.2 emerges out of death (signified by the dead tree) and stands in a gait of defiance that emphasizes her active subject position and individual agency as a woman of war.[3]

Stefanie Sevcik's chapter 1 portrays similar images of imprisoned Syrian women's bodies as a canvas of resistance, linking the body to art and activism. Similarly, Lucía García-Santana's chapter 5 defines Argentinian female prisoners' bodies as the location of political agency and resistance. Nyla Ali Khan's chapter 9 echoes the same concern as she historically contextualizes the grassroots insurgencies of Kashmiri women against religious, economic, and political divides. Moumin Quazi's chapter 8 also articulates the female body as a space of and at war in Sri Lanka. Doaa Omran's chapter 5 examines autobiographical fiction of Palestinian women writers as works of resistance. All these chapters examine the issues of victimization, empowerment, and resistance in the context of women's bodies being "trapped in war zones," agreeing on the fact that idealizing female resistance and romanticizing female empowerment are not solutions. If anything, these methods further entangle the woman's body in the myths and mystification of her agency.

FIG. C.1 "The *Birangona*." Credit: Ferdousi Priyabhashini, courtesy of Fuleshwary
Priyanandini

FIG. C.2 "The *Birangona*." Credit: Ferdousi Priyabhashini, courtesy of Fuleshwary Priyanandini

Margaret Hageman and Carolyn Ownbey in their chapters 6 and 7, respectively, focus on the similar issues of border women and sexual violence as represented in the Partition literature, pointing at the complexities of displacement and trauma in the war-inflicted countries of South Asia. Lava Asaad's chapter 3 on Kurdish women furthers the argument as it reiterates the strength presented through Priyabhashini's art by refusing to fall into the trap of feminization of empowerment.

Ferdousi Priyabhashini fought all her life against the classification of a woman warrior's body as that of a victim. Eventually, she earned back her dignity only two years before her death in 2016, when the government of Bangladesh finally recognized her as a freedom fighter. In 2021, Priyabhashini's daughter Fuleshwary Priyanandini visited an old and abandoned guard's room in a jute mill in a town named Khalispur in Khulna, where her mother was held captive in 1971. She painted a picture of the doors of that room in which her mother was raped for months (figure C.3).[4]

In Priyanandini's painting, the room is viewed from the outside, with its wooden door panels closed, but not locked. The locked padlock is hanging on one of the doorknobs, keeping the other doorknob free, as if unable to force the doors to stay closed. The padlock is locked in itself and thus useless as a tool of oppression. The two panels of the doors, even though closed, stand erect, like Priyabhashini's sculpture of the woman warrior in figure C.2, demanding to close all doors of negation and romanticization of woman's resistance.

•

Romanticization debilitates the impact of resistance and deviates it from its goal. The concept of empowerment loses its weight when it is "offered" to women as a reward for their resistance. It earns a new meaning in a gendered connotation, making empowerment (in women's case) an obligation of privilege, an earned responsibility to take on more burdens of life or to face extra challenges. Empowerment is futile if it does not give a woman the power to be strategic about her choice of options and instead dumps on her a (socially/culturally/ideologically) regulated list of options to choose from. A woman's choice of her desired agency is what defines her empowerment in its true sense. Otherwise, what she enjoys as empowerment is only a controlled choice—offered to her in a form of freedom, which results from her struggles being romanticized by society, culture, and power as an embodiment of resistance. Such notions of empowerment and agency are nothing but revamped forms of abuse and oppression and do not allow women to be actively involved in the power structure according to their own terms.[5] Solava Ibrahim and Sabina Alkire define empowerment "as the expansion of agency, where agency is the ability to pursue whatever a person regards as important."[6] In "Passive Empowerment: How Women's Agency Became Women Doing It All," Serene Khader addresses the issue of passive

FIG. C.3 "Khalishpur '71." Credit: Fuleshwary Priyanandini

agency and power and explains how a woman's agency gets restricted as she is deprived of her ability to make her own choices (regarding her involvement in the domestic or public work force, for example). Khader says that women are disempowered "by being forced to choose among unacceptable options" that "incentivize, and influence" them to "accept and perpetuate gender inequality."[7] Women's empowerment should not be feminized as virtuous activity. "Because we think that empowerment is choice, and that the ability to choose consists in being freed from external constraints to pursuing our goals," writes Khader, "it is unsurprising that development interventions keep asking women to do more."[8] A marginalized woman finds herself trapped in the hamster wheel of empowerment and has to put her two fragile feet in too many shoes at the same time. Social norms, political structures, and the religious culture of her nation challenge her to surrender and be submissive while at the same time expecting her to act as an empowered and emancipated (saved) woman. But her empowerment is constantly contested, as she has to outshine the man in order to be his equal, and she will stay both a subject and an object of disempowerment until she proves to be better than the man. She is "being pushed to choose (among unacceptable options), being expected to do, and especially being expected to do more."[9] And in order to break that chain, a woman has to defy the notion of resistance as a trope of the feminine ideal and redefine it in accordance with the structure of equal division of power and labor. In a war-stricken society and for a woman who is violated by the war in all possible forms, the demystification of her image as a victim is necessary, as is detangling resistance from romanticization and empowerment from feminization.

In *Wartime Sexual Violence* (2017), Kerry Crawford records the haunting list of sexual violence committed against women and children all over the world. According to Crawford, several hundred thousand women and girls were raped in Berlin in 1945. Between 20,000 and 80,000 women and girls were raped, and an unknown number of their male relatives were forced to witness or commit sexual violence during the Japanese invasion of Nanjing in 1937. Several hundred thousand women were raped and forced into sexual slavery by the Japanese military during World War II. In the 1990s, the international media and various human rights groups condemned the systematic use of rape and forced pregnancy and other forms of sexual violence in the former Yugoslavia and Rwanda. According to Catherine Niarchos's report published in 1995 in *Human Rights Quarterly*, more than 60,000 women and girls were raped and impregnated in Bosnia, and about 250,000 to 500,000 women and girls were raped and tortured in Rwanda.[10] Hundreds of thousands of women and girls were raped in Latin America, Africa, the Middle East, and South Asia. "The seeming ubiquity of sexual violence in war," Crawford writes, "cemented its perception as an inevitable aspect of armed conflict and cast sexual violence both as a taboo and as commonplace, stifling effective political and legal discussion and action. Wartime sexual violence failed to evoke international condemnation, regardless of the knowledge of atrocities committed on a massive scale."[11] While analyzing the conflict regarding women's role in a war-affected area, Tsjeard Bouta and Georg Freaks identify seven specific roles played by women. They are victims of sexual violence, combatants, peace activists, participants in political frameworks, coping-skills strategists, homemakers, and wage earners.[12] No matter how categorically ordained and ideologically harmonized they may look, the fact cannot be denied that in a war-inflicted country, the policies and issues regarding women's roles during and after war are always a reflection of gendered power relations. The religious and social dynamics of the conflicted zone have an impact too complicated to ignore and, at times, too controversial to address. In a Muslim country, wartime rape is one such contentious issue. The political turmoil in the Middle East, South Asia, and various parts of Africa, where women and underage girls and boys are raped or kidnapped and then forced into "sex slavery," constantly challenges the political hypocrisies of religion. The world has gone through many phases of development; civilization has boomed and was enlightened; and yet, when the time of war comes, men—the "lighthouse" of civilization—disembark into darkness and choose sexual violence as a tool to wage war and attain peace, leaving the battered and violated bodies to be saved (by other men), allowing them to be resilient and "empowered" yet again—until the next war.

In January 2011, the release of a Bengali film titled *Meherjaan* caused public backlash in Bangladesh because of its apparently insensitive treatment of the issue of war and rape.[13] Its director, Rubaiyat Hossain, was criticized for demasculinizing the freedom fighters of the war and for belittling the role of raped women by presenting them as somewhat aggressive and unwomanly per the cultural custom of Bangladesh. In her article "Love in the Time of 1971: The Furore over *Meherjaan*" (2011), Nayanika Mookherjee quotes from the film's press release, in which the director introduces it as an attempt "to offer an aesthetic solution to war and violence by seeking refuge in love and spiritual submission." Mookherjee comments that the director of the film was "attempting to address the various unresolved accounts of the war of 1971 through aesthetics accounts which are not acceptable within the mainstream nationalist and feminist narratives of 1971" and therefore was confronted with public rage.[14] The plot of the film presents itself in the framework of the protagonist Meherjaan's diary and expands into multiple stories of love, rape, and trauma of war, among others. The intertwined stories of four women in the movie narrate the life of Neela (a woman raped during the Liberation War of Bangladesh), her daughter Sarah (a war child of rape), Salma (another war child born during the Partition of 1947), and Meherjaan (Neela's cousin who fell in love with a soldier of the enemy army). In "When Love and Violence Meet: Women's Agency and Transformative Politics in Rubaiyat Hossain's *Meherjaan*" (2015), Elora Halim Chowdhury argues that in its gendered telling of the war of 1971, Hossain's movie refuses "to objectify trauma," opening up a "dialogue between the past and present" and positing "a shift in perspective, from a focus on the lived and imagined liberatory potential of identities resulting from trauma and wounding, to one that embraces a principle of shared humanity, vulnerability, and universal love."[15] In the movie, the woman named Meherjaan uses love and romance as her powers of passive agency.

Meherjaan's cinematic expression of embodied resistance and its characters' refusal to be objectified as victims of traumatic memory bear a close resemblance to the story of another woman named Meher Jan, a rape survivor of 1971, whose survival was documented by Neelima Ibrahim in 1994 in her reportage

Ami birangona bolchi (*A War Heroine, I Speak*).[16] The resemblance between the two women is not only in their names but also in their life stories. The Meher Jan in Ibrahim's reportage also married a soldier of the Pakistan army. But unlike the Meherjaan of the movie, the second Meher Jan was raped for months by that soldier and many others in that army camp. She later informed Ibrahim that her decision to marry her perpetrator was not a romantic one; it was a conscious and cautious bargain. The fourteen-year-old Meher Jan took matters into her own hands when, after being pregnant in the rape camp, she singled out the possible father of her unborn child—a middle-aged Pathan soldier—and proposed to save him from being arrested as a prisoner of war by marrying him and offering to go to his country with him, a proposal that the soldier willingly accepted.[17] Neelima Ibrahim first met Meher Jan in 1972 in Dhaka Cantonment, where she was waiting with hundreds of other women to willingly depart the country with their perpetrators. Ibrahim tried to dissuade Meher Jan from leaving the country. In Meher Jan's narrative, the conversation between Neelima Ibrahim and Meher Jan goes as follows:

> Neelima kept coaxing me to stay.
> "Don't go with them," she said, "stay here."
> I exploded in anger, "Stay, where? Who is going to give me shelter?"
> "I will give you shelter; you will stay with me." She looked at me with her compassionate eyes.
> "Why? You want to display me as part of a freak show and feel proud for being my saviour? I don't want your pity!"
> "Okay, fine. Then go!" Neelima said. "Go live the life of an unwanted woman in a country that is not yours. You know what they will do to you? They will sell you to a brothel or something. What good will that do?"
> "At least I will have some mental peace, and feel that I am not being slighted by my own countrymen, and know that my father and brothers are not being humiliated for me!"[18]

When Ibrahim met Meher Jan again in the early 1990s, during her visit to Pakistan as a delegate of the Bangladesh Women's Organization, Meher Jan had established herself as a successful entrepreneur. While interviewing Meher Jan for the second time, Ibrahim shared her frustration regarding the mistreatment of the wartime rape survivors of Bangladesh: "Even though I had thought I could have done so much for you back then, I can admit now that making you stay might have been a bad idea. At least you are living here as an independent woman."[19]

Upon Ibrahim's invitation, Meher Jan later visited Bangladesh as a delegate of the Pakistan Women's Organization and spoke at a women's conference, where she shared her stories—not of shame but of strength: "My exit from my country was on the back of a truck through the Benapole border of India. When

I deserted the country that had abandoned me, I had not imagined in my wild-est dream that I would be received back with so much love . . . I didn't know how to bear the pain of self-loathing. I couldn't forget the fact that the story of my present accomplishment is built on the ruins of my tainted past—my life as a war heroine."[20]

The Meherjaan in Hossain's movie represents the anxiety of wartime rape in terms of a romanticized, cinematic version of a damsel saved from the enemy by an enemy soldier. Her story of suppressed fear was hidden in her diary—a diary that she later unfolds in order for Sarah (the war child of Neela) to retrace her footsteps back to the womb of history, where she was conceived out of a rape of her mother/land. Neelima Ibrahim's Meher Jan, on the other hand, re-presents her life through her lived experiences as a raped woman of war, as a voice of refusal (to be saved or victimized and later branded as a by-product of war), and as an example of agency and strength who, without romanticizing the notion of resistance, is able to choose her options by dismantling the protected image of a wartime raped body as an ineffective subject of suppressed trauma. Social structures, writes Serene Khader, "constrain the behavior of individuals by making certain courses of action more readily available and more appealing than others, and by funneling them into a place within the overall structure."[21] The true meaning of empowerment is dependent on a woman's freedom to choose and on her ability to take a stand and regulate her life from that stand-point, without being constantly pushed to do more than men.

In "War and Rape: A Preliminary Analysis," Ruth Seifert identifies the main three functions of wartime rape in terms of power, communication, and disrup-tion. Wartime rape has been interpreted as a reward and practice (of power), a trope of communication (of power), and a tool to disrupt and destroy social cohesion.[22] In 2008, the United Nations Security Council's Resolution 1820 did address these issues and recognized wartime rape as a destructive function and called to end all acts of wartime sexual violence against civilians. The crit-ics, such as Elvan Isikozlu and Ananda S. Millard, have deemed the resolution as a faulty one, since it does not focus on rape perpetrated by peacekeepers against civilians, men, and women or rape perpetrated within armies and armed groups.[23] In the Global South, gender relations are still nothing but power rela-tions, a binary in which a woman is always deemed an auxiliary praxis. To eradi-cate the binary of power, the feminist activists from the Global South in the 1990s initiated an approach demanding women's empowerment and the inclu-sion of women's contribution to the economic and political discourse. This empowerment, according to Srilatha Batliwala, was "a foundational process" that "enables marginalized women to construct their own political agendas and form movements and struggles for achieving fundamental and lasting transform in gender and social power structures."[24] Women from the war-affected areas of the Global South should generate the discourse of women's human rights from this standpoint of empowerment. Exploring knowledge from the standpoint of marginalized people on a platform that includes all races, sexes, genders, and classes, women from the war-stricken countries offer multiple ways to address epistemic decentering and violence by interrogating the construction, production, and justification of knowledge/power, thus resisting being branded as having a passive agency. In her article "Feminist Standpoint" (2015), Kristen Intemann says that "feminist standpoint requires a commitment to a particular social and political aim of inquiry—namely, a commitment to understand and challenge systems of oppression" and involves "revealing the ways in which gender, race, class, sexuality, ability, and colonization have shaped and influenced objects of investigation."[25] Feminist standpoint theories aim at producing knowledge for the marginalized groups with the intent to challenge and counteract the oppressive ways that limit the well-being of the marginalized and restrict their ability to participate in the production of knowledge.[26] In the preface to *Sexes and Genealogies* (1993), Luce Irigaray writes that "it is all too clear that there is no equality of wealth, and claims of equal rights to culture have blown up in our faces." She later says that any woman "who is seeking equality (with whom? With what?) needs to give this problem serious consideration. It is understandable that women should wish for equal pay, equal career opportunities. But what is the real goal?" The real goal, according to Irigaray, is identity: "Salaries and social recognition have to be negotiated on the basis of identity, not equality. Women have to proclaim this message loud and clear and demand a justice that fits their identity instead of some temporary rights befitting justice for men."[27] It is not equal rights that women ought to fight for; it is the right to think, to be, and to express themselves. By inserting themselves into the androcentric center as thinkers and knowers of equal level and thus by becoming pseudo-men with equal rights, women can only become a replica, a reflection, and not a corporeal and ontological entity of their own accord. Their lived experience is not a thing to romanticize or a trauma to suppress. On the contrary, the lived experience of trauma and sexual violence can be used as a motivating force of collective resistance, which Gayatri Chakravorty Spivak coins as "strategic essentialism."[28] In certain geopolitical locations (the Global South, for example), strategic essentialism as a force of collective resistance has a greater impact on addressing issues of discrimination and violence against women and minorities. Spivak's notion of "strategic essentialism" in the context of marginalized women delivers an ontology of a collective identity of resistance. This should not be misunderstood as a universal "sisterhood"; rather, it should be seen as a conjuncture in which all the elements of passive agency, romanticized resistance, and provisional empowerment dissolve, and in the process, there emerges a sense of collective political identity that may help them secure their rights. "Strategic essentialism" can be a means of resistance, but not a goal. By questioning the privileging identity and by "constantly looking into how truths are produced,"[29] they can question and challenge the normative framework of identity.[30] As Veena Das notes in her *Life and Words: Violence and the Descent into the Ordinary*, these women can express their trauma and address their injuries "through complex transactions between body and language"[31] and thus assert their subjectivity and agency. Because androcentric epistemic privilege is an oppressive authorial power in the Global South, feminist standpoint theories can provide effective methods to address the issues of gender(ed) oppressions and counteract or limit such oppressions. We have to keep in mind that passivity is not an option; neither is subjectivity. Subjectivity is a requirement because language does not speak without subjectivity. Subjectivity is a prerequisite for active agency. In the same light, victimization is also not an option because it does not do any justice; it only reinforces the body as an object—of desire, gaze, shame, and violence. There should not be any fight for equal rights anymore because such demand reinforces phallocentric power. The demand for equal rights presupposes inequality as an abstract truth. In this millennial, postpoststructuralist, postmodernist world, no gender should be avowed as better or greater than the rest. Every gender and every sexed body must be deemed as already equal.

Until the 1990s, international institutions interpreted sexual violence on the model of freedom and human rights as depicted by the liberal viewpoints of the United States. Unlike many other countries of the world, the representations of rape have a crucial place in constructing America's gender, racial, ethnic, and class categories in relation to ideals of freedom. World War I showed governmental efforts to document rape as a political atrocity. It also invoked the debate on how women should be accommodated and adjusted in wars. Both American and British governments wanted to mobilize women in support of the war and protect the younger ones from the dangers of the war.[32] After World War II, the politicized concept of rape was later medicalized and advocated as a public health issue. With the anti-rape movement of the 1970s, the discourse of rape included in its agenda the psychological aspects of the traumatized experience. After the fall of the Soviet Union, U.S. international leagues created a field of sexual and gender-based violence (U.N. acronym SGBV) policy to discuss sexual violence as a legal issue for countries involved in war. With its broader program at sites of international intervention, it aimed to rehabilitate the traumatized population. However, as the world progressed and nations began to engage more and more in wars, rape remained a popular weapon of war in various nations and tribes of Africa, in Bosnia and Herzegovina, in the Middle East, and in South Asia, while sexual violence and national/international legal policies became complicated issues and the legal recognition of rape as a war crime became difficult to attain.[33] In her "Policy Violence against Women in War" (2016), Gill Hague quotes from the U.N. Commission's report that concludes the following way: "On every continent, in refugee camps, bars, brothels, prisons, women survivors . . . told us about their struggles to heal from the violence and the enduring psychological pain. It is impossible to capture the magnitude of the anguish that permeated their lives. . . . And yet, we saw something else as well. Time and again, we met women who had survived trauma and found cour-age and the will to recommit to life . . . to rebuild community."[34]

The fixation on the raped subject and the identification of the raped body as a victim simply marginalize the subjects and bring them back into the power hierarchy of an active/passive, savior/saved binary—a hierarchy prevalent in the literature and political culture of the Global South.[35] Since rape is both a pre-ferred weapon of political violence against women and an execution of power, the resistance to such violence invokes a call for policy change regarding gen-dered notions of power and economy and a demand for "greater gender equality as well as high levels of women's participation in decision making and in the public sphere."[36] The time has come to challenge the stereotypical identification and generalization of the elements of trauma and explore the discourse on geno-cidal sexual violence and its socio-politico-cultural impact on women as active subjects with agency. We present this collection of chapters as a testimonial of resilient women who recommitted to rebuilding not only their communi-ties but also their own identities. Calling gender a socially imposed division of the sexes, Gayle Rubin once asked us to "liberate human personality from the straight jacket of gender."[37] In the discourse of war and gender, we side with those who urge us to liberate women's resistance from the straitjacket of roman-ticization and objectification.

Notes

1 Ferdousi Priyabhashini, *Nindito nandan* [The blighted garden] (Dhaka, Bangladesh: Shobdoshoilee, 2015), 180 (my translation). Priyabhashini was the first Bangladeshi woman to publicly declare herself as a wartime rape survivor (*birangona*) of the Ban-gladesh Liberation War of 1971. She was held captive and was raped and tortured for nine months. A renowned sculptor, she later used art as her medium of resistance by creating sculptures on the theme of women's strength and endurance. Using drift-wood, she created a series of sculptures on the theme of the *birangonas*, or war hero-ines, of Bangladesh, some of which are preserved at the Liberation War Museum. The government of Bangladesh later recognized her as a freedom fighter for her bravery in 2016 and honored her with the nation's most prestigious award, the Independence Day Award, in 2010.

2 Nayanika Mookherjee (*The Spectral Wound: Sexual Violence, Public Memories, and the Bangladesh War of 1971* [Durham, N.C.: Duke University Press, 2015]), Yasmin Saikia (*Women, War, and the Making of Bangladesh: Remembering 1971* [Durham, N.C.: Duke University Press, 2011]), and Chaity Das (*In the Land of Buried Tongues: Testimonials and Literary Narratives of the War of Liberation of Bangladesh* [London: Oxford University Press, 2017]) have written on Priyabhashini in their discussions of wartime sexual violence in Bangladesh in 1971.

3 This sculpture is now at the Liberation War Museum in Bangladesh.

4 I am indebted to the artist, Fuleshwary Priyanandini, for giving me permission to include her painting here.

5 Since Foucault is always present in any discourse on power, I have willfully deviated from a direct reference to him. I have instead focused on the empowerment theories

of Naila Kabeer, Serene Khader, Andrea Cornwall, Solava Ibrahim, and Sabina Alkire in this regard. Kabeer argues that real choices should have the ability to contravene social norms, and a woman needs to have access to social capital in order to convert/transform agency to achievement. See Kabeer, "Resources, Agency, Achievements: Reflections on the Measurement of Women's Empowerment," *Development and Change* 30, no. 3 (1999): 435–464. Serene Khader's discussion focuses on how women's empowerment is associated with more activity than real agency—a tendency that burdens women with more work and deprives them of the agency to choose their options. See Khader, "Identifying Adaptive Preferences in Practice: Lessons from Postcolonial Feminisms," *Journal of Global Ethics* 9, no. 3 (2013): 311–327. See also Andrea Cornwall, "Women's Empowerment: What Works," *Journal of International Development* 28, no. 3 (2016): 342–359; and Solava Ibrahim and Sabina Alkire, "Agency and Empowerment," *Oxford Development Studies* 35, no. 4 (2007): 370–403.

6   Ibrahim and Alkire, "Agency and Empowerment," 384.
7   See Khader, "Passive Empowerment: How Women's Agency Became Women Doing It All," *Philosophical Topics* 46, no. 2 (Fall 2018): 154.
8   Khader, 142.
9   Khader, 159.
10 See Catherine Niarchos, "Women, War, and Rape: Challenges Facing the International Tribunal for the Former Yugoslavia," *Human Rights Quarterly* 17, no. 4 (1995): 649–690.
11 See Kerry Crawford, *Wartime Sexual Violence: From Silence to Condemnation of a Weapon of War* (Washington, D.C.: Georgetown University Press, 2017), 33–34.
12 See the introduction in Kathleen Kuehnast, Chantal de Jonge Oudraat, and Helga Hernes, eds., *Women and War: Power and Protection in the 21st Century* (Washington, D.C.: United State Institute of Peace Press, 2011), 4–5, where the editors have analyzed Tsjeard Bouta and Georg Freaks's contribution to that volume, "Women's Role in Conflict Prevention, Conflict Resolution, and Post-conflict Reconstruction: Literature Review and Institutional Analysis." Also see Fayeza Hasanat, *The Voices of War Heroines: Sexual Violence, Testimony, and the Bangladesh Liberation War* (Leiden: E. J. Brill, 2022), 3–17.
13 Rubaiyat Hossain, dir., *Meherjaan* (Dhaka, Bangladesh: Era Motion Picture, 2011).
14 Mookherjee, *Spectral Wound*, 25. See also Mookherjee, "Love in the Time of 1971: The Furore over 'Meherjaan,'" *Economic and Political Weekly* 46, no. 12 (March 2011): 25–27.
15 See Elora Halim Chowdhury, "When Love and Violence Meet: Women's Agency and Transformative Politics in Rubaiyat Hossain's *Meherjaan*," in *Hypatia* 30, no. 4 (2015): 768–769.
16 In Bengali, the name is spelled as both *Meherjaan* and *Meher Jan*. Neelima Ibrahim's book was first published in 1994 in Bangladesh by Jagriti Prokashoni. A second unabridged edition came out in 1998 from the same publisher. The book was translated into English by Fayeza Hasanat and was published in Bangladesh in 2017.
17 According to an article by Jalal Alamgir and Bina D'Costa, after the liberation war ended in 1971, India had custody of more than ninety-two thousand Pakistani prisoners of war. See Alamgir and D'Costa, "The 1971 Genocide: War Crimes and Political Crimes," *Economic and Political Weekly* 46, no. 13 (2011): 38–41.
18 See Fayeza Hasanat's translation in *A War Heroine, I Speak* (Dhaka: Bangla Academy, 2017), 39.
19 Hasanat, 49.
20 Hasanat, 52.

21 Khader, "Identifying Adaptive Preferences," 152.

22 See Ruth Seifert, "War and Rape: A Preliminary Analysis," in *Mass Rape: The War against Women in Bosnia-Herzegovina*, ed. Alexandra Stiglmayer (Lincoln: University of Nebraska Press, 1994), 54–55.

23 See Elvan Isikozlu and Ananda S. Millard, "Wartime Rape: Identifying Knowledge Gaps and Their Implications," *Sicherheit und Frieden (S+F) / Security and Peace* 28, no. 1 (2010): 39.

24 See Srilatha Batliwala, "Taking the Power Out of Empowerment," *Development in Practice* 17, nos. 4/5 (2007): 558.

25 See Kristen Intemann, "Feminist Standpoint," in *The Oxford Handbook of Feminist Theory*, ed. Lisa Disch and Mary Hawkesworth (Oxford University Press, 2015), 288.

26 For a detailed discussion on various aspects of standpoint feminism, see Intemann, 267–284. Also see Sandra Harding, "Rethinking Feminist Epistemology: What Is Strong Objectivity?," in *Feminist Epistemologies*, ed. Linda Alcoff and Elizabeth Potter (London: Routledge, 1992), 49–82; Harding, "A Socially Relevant Philosophy of Science? Resources from Standpoint Theory's Controversiality," *Hypatia* 19, no. 1 (2004): 25–47; Helen Longino, *Science as Social Knowledge* (Princeton, N.J.: Princeton University Press, 1990); Longino, *The Fate of Knowledge* (Princeton, N.J.: Princeton University Press, 2004); and Alison Wylie, "Why Standpoint Matters," in *Science and Other Cultures: Issues in Philosophies of Science and Technology*, ed. Robert Figueroa and Sandra Harding (New York: Routledge, 2003), 26–48.

27 See Luce Irigaray's preface to *Sexes and Genealogies* (New York: Columbia University Press, 1993), vi–vii.

28 See Gayatri Chakravorty Spivak, "Bonding in Difference: Interview with Alfred Artega," in *The Spivak Reader*, ed. Donna Landry and Gerald MacLean (London: Routledge, 1996), 15–28.

29 Spivak, 16.

30 Spivak, 15–28.

31 See Veena Das, *Life and Words: Violence and the Descent into the Ordinary* (Berkeley: University of California Press, 2007), 59.

32 See Christa Hämmerle, Oswald Überegger, and Birgitta Bader Zaar, eds., *Gender and the First World War* (New York: Palgrave Macmillan, 2014). Also, for an in-depth critical discussion on the issues of sexual violence in the context of the two World Wars in particular, see Carol Harrington, *Politicization of Sexual Violence: From Abolitionism to Peacekeeping* (London: Routledge, 2016); Ayse Gul Altina and Andrea Peto, eds., *Gendered Wars, Gendered Memories: Feminist Conversations on War, Genocide and Political Violence* (London: Routledge, 2016); and Sara Sharratt, *Gender, Shame and Sexual Violence: The Voices of Witnesses and Court Members at War Crimes Tribunals* (London: Routledge, 2016).

33 For a comparative survey on World War II and other wars in the twentieth century, see Amy E. Randall, ed., *Genocide and Gender in the Twentieth Century* (London: Bloomsbury, 2015).

34 See Gill Hague, "Violence against Women in War and Conflict," *Middle East Research Institute* 3, no. 1 (2016), http://www.meri-k.org/publication/violence-against-women-in-war-and-conflict/.

35 For a detailed discussion, see Nicola Henry, "Theorizing Wartime Rape: Deconstructing Gender, Sexuality, and Violence," *Gender and Society* 30, no. 1 (February 2016): 44–56.

36 See Pratiksha Baxi, "Sexual Violence and Its Discontents," *Annual Review of Anthropology* 43 (2014): 142.
37 See Gayle Ruben, "The Traffic in Women: Notes on the Political Economy of Sex," in *Towards an Anthropology of Women*, ed. Rayna Rap (New York: Monthly Review Press, 1975), 179.

Bibliography

Alamgir, Jalal, and Bina D'Costa. "The 1971 Genocide: War Crimes and Political Crimes." *Economic and Political Weekly* 46, no. 13 (2011): 38–41.

Altina, Ayse Gul, and Andrea Peto, eds. *Gendered Wars, Gendered Memories: Feminist Conversations on War, Genocide and Political Violence*. London: Routledge, 2016.

Batliwala, Srilatha. "Taking the Power Out of Empowerment." *Development in Practice* 17, nos. 4/5 (2007): 557–565.

Baxi, Pratiksha. "Sexual Violence and Its Discontents." *Annual Review of Anthropology* 43 (2014): 139–154.

Bouta, Tsjeard, and Georg Freaks. "Women's Role in Conflict Prevention, Conflict Resolution, and Post-conflict Reconstruction: Literature Review and Institutional Analysis." In *Women and War: Power and Protection in the 21st Century*, edited by Kathleen Kuehnast, Chantal de Jonge Oudraat, and Helga Hernes, 1–18. Washington, D.C.: United State Institute of Peace Press, 2011.

Chowdhury, Elora Halim. "When Love and Violence Meet: Women's Agency and Transformative Politics in Rubaiyat Hossain's *Meherjaan*." *Hypatia* 30, no. 4 (2015): 760–777.

Cornwall, Andrea. "Women's Empowerment: What Works." *Journal of International Development* 28, no. 3 (2016): 342–359.

Crawford, Kerry. *Wartime Sexual Violence: From Silence to Condemnation of a Weapon of War*. Washington, D.C.: Georgetown University Press, 2017.

Das, Chaity. *In the Land of Buried Tongues: Testimonials and Literary Narratives of the War of Liberation of Bangladesh*. London: Oxford University Press, 2017.

Das, Veena. *Life and Words: Violence and the Descent into the Ordinary*. Berkeley: University of California Press, 2007.

Hague, Gill. "Violence against Women in War and Conflict." *Middle East Research Institute* 3, no. 1 (2016), http://www.meri-k.org/publication/violence-against-women-in-war-and -conflict/.

Hämmerle, Christa, Oswald Überegger, and Birgitta Bader Zaar, eds. *Gender and the First World War*. New York: Palgrave Macmillan, 2014.

Harding, Sandra. "Rethinking Feminist Epistemology: What Is Strong Objectivity?" In *Feminist Epistemologies*, edited by Linda Alcoff and Elizabeth Potter, 49–82. London: Routledge, 1992.

———. "A Socially Relevant Philosophy of Science? Resources from Standpoint Theory's Controversiality." *Hypatia* 19, no. 1 (2004): 25–47.

Harrington, Carol. *Politicization of Sexual Violence: From Abolitionism to Peacekeeping*. London: Routledge, 2016.

Hasanat, Fayeza. *The Voices of War Heroines: Sexual Violence, Testimony, and the Bangladesh Liberation War*. Leiden: E. J. Brill, 2022.

———, trans. *A War Heroine, I Speak*. Dhaka, Bangladesh: Bangla Academy, 2017.

Henry, Nicola. "Theorizing Wartime Rape: Deconstructing Gender, Sexuality, and Violence." *Gender and Society* 30, no. 1 (February 2016): 44–56.

Hossain, Rubaiyat, dir. *Meherjaan*. Dhaka, Bangladesh: Era Motion Picture, 2011.

Ibrahim, Neelima. *Aami birangona bolchi*. 2nd unabridged ed. Dhaka, Bangladesh: Jagriti Prokashoni, 1998.

Ibrahim, Solava, and Sabina Alkire. "Agency and Empowerment." *Oxford Development Studies* 35, no. 4 (2007): 370–403.

Intemann, Kristen. "Feminist Standpoint." In *The Oxford Handbook of Feminist Theory*, edited by Lisa Disch and Mary Hawkesworth, 267–284. London: Oxford University Press, 2015.

Irigaray, Luce. *Sexes and Genealogies*. New York: Columbia University Press, 1993.

Isikozlu, Elvan, and Ananda S. Millard. "Wartime Rape: Identifying Knowledge Gaps and Their Implications." *Sicherheit und Frieden (S+F) / Security and Peace* 28, no. 1 (2010): 35–41.

Kabeer, Naila. "Resources, Agency, Achievements: Reflections on the Measurement of Women's Empowerment." *Development and Change* 30, no. 3 (1999): 435–464.

Khader, Serene. "Identifying Adaptive Preferences in Practice: Lessons from Postcolonial Feminisms." *Journal of Global Ethics* 9, no. 3 (2013): 311–327.

———. "Passive Empowerment: How Women's Agency Became Women Doing It All." *Philosophical Topics* 46, no. 2 (Fall 2018): 141–164.

Longino, Helen. *The Fate of Knowledge*. Princeton, N.J.: Princeton University Press, 2004.

———. *Science as Social Knowledge*. Princeton, N.J.: Princeton University Press, 1990.

Mookherjee, Nayanika. "Love in the Time of 1971: The Furore over 'Meherjaan.'" *Economic and Political Weekly* 46, no. 12 (March 2011): 25–27.

———. *The Spectral Wound: Sexual Violence, Public Memories, and the Bangladesh War of 1971*. Durham, N.C.: Duke University Press, 2015.

Niarchos, Catherine. "Women, War, and Rape: Challenges Facing the International Tribunal for the Former Yugoslavia." *Human Rights Quarterly* 17, no. 4 (1995): 649–690.

Priyabhashini, Ferdousi. *Nindito nandan* [The blighted garden]. Dhaka, Bangladesh: Shobdoshoilee, 2015.

Randall, Amy E., ed. *Genocide and Gender in the Twentieth Century*. London: Bloomsbury, 2015.

Ruben, Gayle. "The Traffic in Women: Notes on the Political Economy of Sex." In *Towards an Anthropology of Women*, edited by Rayna Rap, 157–210. New York: Monthly Review Press, 1975.

Saikia, Yasmin. *Women, War, and the Making of Bangladesh: Remembering 1971*. Durham, N.C.: Duke University Press, 2011.

Seifert, Ruth. "War and Rape: A Preliminary Analysis." In *Mass Rape: The War against Women in Bosnia-Herzegovina*, edited by Alexandra Stiglmayer, 54–65. Lincoln: University of Nebraska Press, 1994.

Sharratt, Sara. *Gender, Shame and Sexual Violence: The Voices of Witnesses and Court Members at War Crimes Tribunals*. London: Routledge, 2016.

Spivak, Gayatri Chakravorty. "Bonding in Difference: Interview with Alfred Artega." In *The Spivak Reader*, edited by Donna Landry and Gerald MacLean, 15–28. London: Routledge, 1996.

Wylie, Alison. "Why Standpoint Matters." In *Science and Other Cultures: Issues in Philosophies of Science and Technology*, edited by Robert Figueroa and Sandra Harding, 26–48. New York: Routledge, 2003.

Notes on Contributors

FARZANA AKHTER is an associate professor and chair of English at East West University in Dhaka, Bangladesh. She holds a PhD in English from the University of Arkansas. Her areas of interest include contemporary American ethnic and immigrant literature, immigrant nostalgia, and women of the Bangladesh Liberation War. She is also the assistant editor of *East West Journal of Humanities*. Her major works have appeared in *Asiatic: IIUM Journal of English Language and Literature*, the *Brecht Yearbook*, *South Asian Review*, and the *Journal of the Midwest Modern Language Association*.

LAVA ASAAD is a postdoctoral teaching fellow at Auburn University. Her research areas include but are not limited to Anglophone literatures, modern British literature, women and gender studies, and Middle Eastern literature. She received her doctoral degree from Middle Tennessee State University. She is particularly interested in depictions of immigrants and refugees in literature. She is the author of *Literature with a White Helmet: The Textual-Corporeality of Being, Becoming and Representing Refugees*.

MARGARET HAGEMAN is currently a PhD candidate in English literature at the University of Southern Mississippi in Hattiesburg, Mississippi, and teaches English composition. Her research area involves examining representations of the uncanny and the other in American and British Gothic literature, as shown in her thesis, "Black Cats and Puma Women: Marginalized Bodies and Violence in Gothic Literature." Margaret plans to pursue her research interest in Gothic portrayals of animal archetypes in literature and further examine representations of violence against marginalized bodies in Gothic literature.

FAYEZA HASANAT completed her MA and PhD in English from the University of Florida. She is the author of *Nawab Faizunnesa's Rupjalal: Translation and Commentary* and *The Voices of War Heroines: Sexual Violence, Testimony, and the Bangladesh Liberation War*. Her debut short story collection, *The Bird Catcher and Other Stories*, was simultaneously published in the United States and Bangladesh. Hasanat teaches at the English Department of the University of Central Florida.

NYLA ALI KHAN is a faculty member at Rose State College, former associate professor at the University of Nebraska at Kearney, and visiting professor at the University of Oklahoma. Dr. Khan is the author of multiple critically acclaimed books, including *Educational Strategies for Youth Empowerment in Conflict Zones: Transforming, Not Transmitting, Trauma, The Fiction of Nationality in an Era of Transnationalism, The Life of a Kashmiri Woman: Dialectic of Resistance and Accommodation*, and *Sheikh Mohammad Abdullah's Reflections on Kashmir*, and many others published articles.

SHAFINUR NAHAR is a PhD candidate in English literature at the University of Brunei Darussalam. She is an adjunct faculty at the Asian University for Women in Chittagong, Bangladesh. She completed her MA in English from the University of Chittagong, Bangladesh. She also earned a second MA degree in gender studies from the University of Kashmir, India. Her main research interests are in women writing, creative writing, gender studies, cultural studies, and minority studies. Her research articles and papers on women writing, gender violence, and minority studies have been published in renowned international and national books and journals.

DOAA OMRAN is a research fellow and adjunct faculty in the English Department at the University of New Mexico. Her research interests include comparative literature, medieval literature, feminism, and postcolonial theory. Doaa completed her master's and PhD at the University of New Mexico. She wrote her dissertation, titled "Female Hero Mega-archetypes in the Medieval European Romances," in which she explores Koranic and biblical female characters as mega-archetypes in medieval literature (2019). She coedited *Memory, Voice, Identity: Muslim Women Writers from across the Middle East* (2021) and contributed her essay, "Muslim Face, White Mask: Out al-Kouloub al-Dimerdashiyyah's *Ramza* as a Mimic (Wo)man" to it as well. Her essay "Ambivalence in the Poems of the Slave-Knight 'Antarah Ibn Shaddād: An Engagement with Historicism(s)" is appearing in *Incarceration and Slavery in the Middle Ages and the Early Modern Age* edited by Albrecht Classen. Her "Anachronism and Anatopism in the French *Vulgate Cycle* and the Forging of English Identity through Othering Muslims/Saracens" was included in Albrecht Classen's edited volume *Travel, Time, and Space in the Middle Ages and Early Modern*

Time: Explorations of World Perceptions and Processes of Identity Formation (2018). Currently, she is working on the second part of her coedited volume on Muslim women writers.

CAROLYN OWNBEY (PhD McGill University) is an assistant professor and chair of English, communications, and literature at Golden Gate University in San Francisco. Her work focuses on anticolonial literature and performance, new media and protest, and theories of democracy and citizenship. She has essays published in *Law & Literature, Textual Practice, Critique: Studies in Contemporary Fiction*, and *Safundi: The Journal of South African and American Studies*, among others. Her research and teaching interests include postcolonial and global Anglophone literature, contemporary performance and new media storytelling, political theory and theories of state, human rights and citizenship, and social media and protest.

LUCÍA GARCÍA-SANTANA is an assistant professor of Spanish and Latin American studies at the University of the South. Her current research focuses on displacement in the Americas, in particular the relationship between mobility and social exclusion and the dynamics of social and gender stereotyping. Her published work focuses on Argentina's cultural production of dictatorship, displacement in the Hispanic World, and the place of women's production in mainstream cultural and social movements. She is currently working on a monograph with the tentative title *Within and Without Spanishness: Narratives of Displacement and Exclusion in the Contemporary Hispanic World*. Her research and teaching interests also relate to ecocriticism, gender studies, the Global South, memory and transitional justice, and Hispanic theater.

STEFANIE SEVCIK is a lecturer in the department of English at Georgia College and State University. Her research engages with questions of gender and resistance in twentieth- and twenty-first-century conflicts across the Global South, including the Algerian War of Independence, the Liberian civil war, and the Arab Spring uprisings in Tunisia, Egypt, and Syria. Most recently, she published an essay on representations of women during the Algerian war with France titled "Veiling and Unveiling Nedjma: Political Consciousness and Domesticity in Kateb Yacine's Nedjma Cycle" in *Research in African Literatures*. She is currently working on a manuscript titled *Bloggers, Bombers, and Babies: Women's Resistance across the Global South*.

MATTHEW SPENCER is a faculty member at Auburn University. His research interests include ecocriticism, global Anglophone literature, American environmental and nature writing, climate fiction, and the intersection between race, gender, and environment. His current projects include a genealogy of the radical tradition in American environmentalism and an examination of racialized landscapes of the American south in neoslave narratives. His work has appeared in *Mississippi Quarterly*, *Transnational Literature*, *Medical Humanities*, and the forthcoming volume *Teaching South Asian Diasporic Literature* in the Modern Language Association's Options for Teaching series.

MOUMIN QUAZI is a professor of English at Tarleton State University, past president of the South Asian Literary Association, founder of Scheherazade Press, fourteen-year coeditor of *Langdon Review*, member of the College English Association Board of Directors, and widely published author. He authored the mixed-genre *Migratory Words* (2016).

Index

Available titles in the War Culture series: